Atlas of the World

GEDDES & GROSSET

CONTENTS

4-5 THE WORLD

6-27 NORTH & CENTRAL AMERICA

28-41 SOUTH AMERICA

42-95 EUROPE

96-133 ASIA

134-151 AFRICA

152-165 AUSTRALIA & OCEANIA

166-171 THE POLAR REGIONS

172 INDEX TO MAPS

LEGEND

oads

Motorway/Highway

Other Main Road

at scales smaller than 1 : 3 million

Principal Road: Motorway/Highway

Other Main Road

Main Railway

owns & Cities - Population

> 5,000,000

1-5,000,000

500,000-1,000,000

< 500,000

Paris National Capital

Airport

International Boundary

International Boundary
- not defined or in dispute

Internal Boundary

River

Canal

Marsh or Swamp

Relief

Note -

The 0-100 contour layer appears only at scales larger than 1 : 3 million

1510 Peak (in meters)

5000 meters

4000

3000

2000

1000

500

200

100

0

Land below sea level

THE WORLD

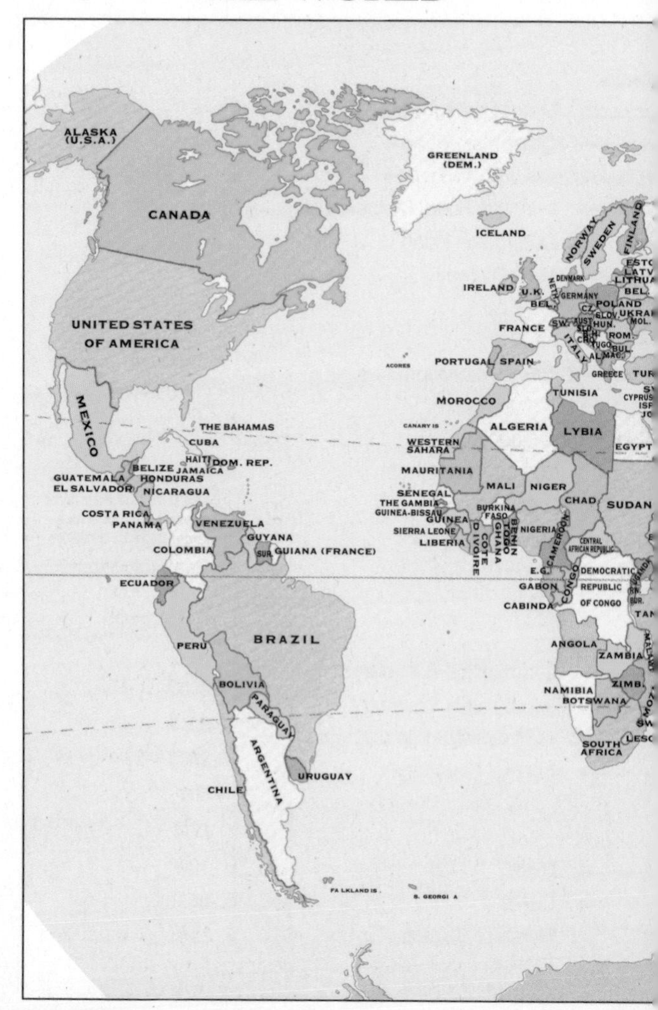

ALASKA (U.S.A.)
CANADA
GREENLAND (DEM.)
ICELAND
NORWAY
SWEDEN
FINLAND
IRELAND
U.K.
DENMARK
GERMANY
POLAND
FRANCE
PORTUGAL
SPAIN
ITALY
GREECE
UNITED STATES OF AMERICA
MEXICO
ACORES
MOROCCO
TUNISIA
ALGERIA
LYBIA
EGYPT
CANARY IS
WESTERN SAHARA
MAURITANIA
MALI
NIGER
CHAD
SUDAN
SENEGAL
THE GAMBIA
GUINEA-BISSAU
GUINEA
SIERRA LEONE
LIBERIA
COTE D'IVOIRE
BURKINA FASO
GHANA
TOGO
BENIN
NIGERIA
CAMEROON
CENTRAL AFRICAN REPUBLIC
E.G.
GABON
CONGO
CABINDA
DEMOCRATIC REPUBLIC OF CONGO
ANGOLA
ZAMBIA
ZIMB.
NAMIBIA
BOTSWANA
SOUTH AFRICA
THE BAHAMAS
CUBA
HAITI
DOM. REP.
JAMAICA
BELIZE
HONDURAS
GUATEMALA
EL SALVADOR
NICARAGUA
COSTA RICA
PANAMA
VENEZUELA
GUYANA
SUR.
GUIANA (FRANCE)
COLOMBIA
ECUADOR
PERU
BRAZIL
BOLIVIA
PARAGUAY
ARGENTINA
CHILE
URUGUAY
FALKLAND IS.
S. GEORGIA

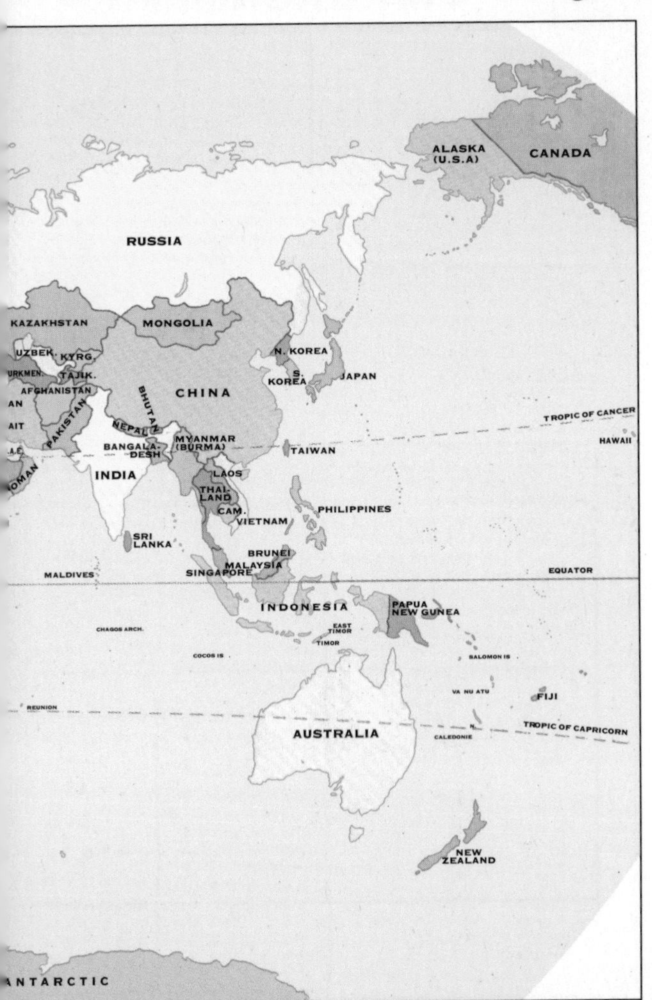
ALASKA (U.S.A)
CANADA
RUSSIA
KAZAKHSTAN
MONGOLIA
UZBEK.
KYRG.
URKMEN.
TAJIK.
AFGHANISTAN
AN
AIT
N. KOREA
S. KOREA
JAPAN
CHINA
BHUTAN
NEPAL
PAKISTAN
TROPIC OF CANCER
HAWAII
MYANMAR (BURMA)
BANGALA-DESH
TAIWAN
OMAN
INDIA
LAOS
THAI-LAND
CAM.
VIETNAM
PHILIPPINES
SRI LANKA
BRUNEI
MALAYSIA
MALDIVES
SINGAPORE
EQUATOR
INDONESIA
PAPUA NEW GUNEA
CHAGOS ARCH.
EAST TIMOR
TIMOR
COCOS IS
SALOMON IS
VA NU ATU
FIJI
REUNION
TROPIC OF CAPRICORN
AUSTRALIA
N. CALEDONIE
NEW ZEALAND
ANTARCTIC

NORTH & CENTRAL AMERICA

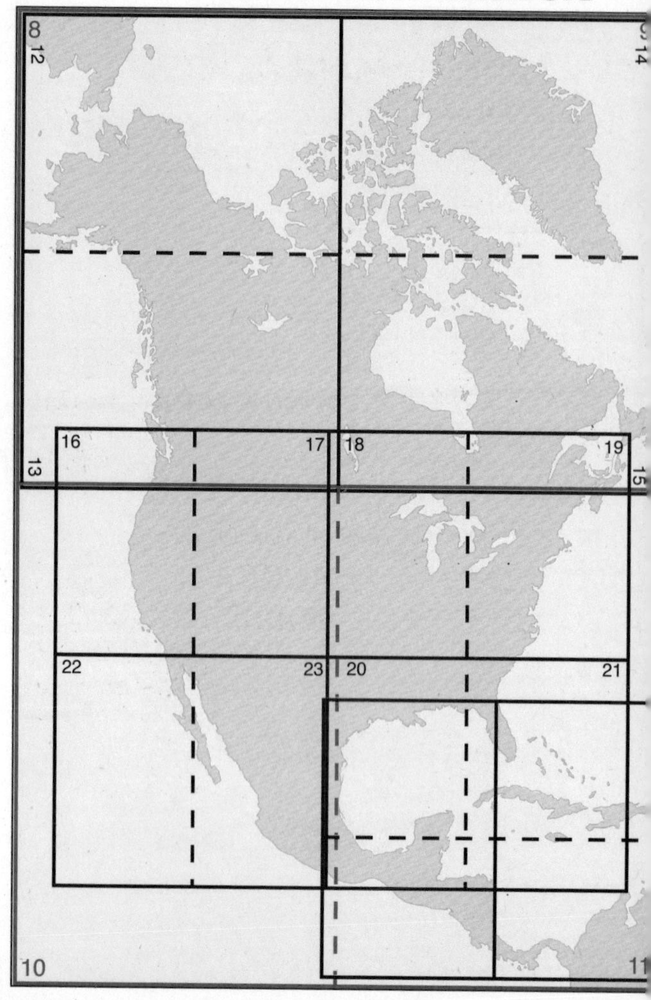

INDEX TO PAGES

8-9 NORTH AMERICA POLITICAL (N)
10-11 NORTH AMERICA POLITICAL (S)
12-13 CANADA (W)
14-15 CANADA (E)
16-17 U.S.A. (N.W.)
18-19 U.S.A. (N.E.)
20-21 U.S.A. (S.E.) & WESTERN CARIBBEAN
22-23 U.S.A. (S.W.), MEXICO, ALASKA & HAWAIIAN ISLANDS
24-25 CENTRAL AMERICA
26-27 EASTERN CARIBBEAN

NORTH AMERICA POLITICAL (N)

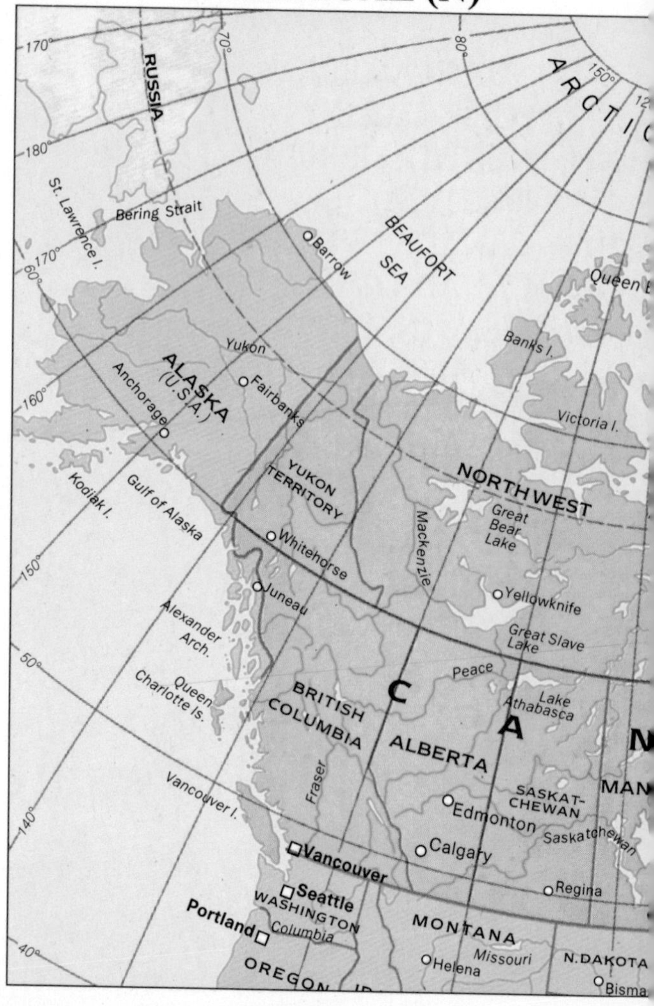

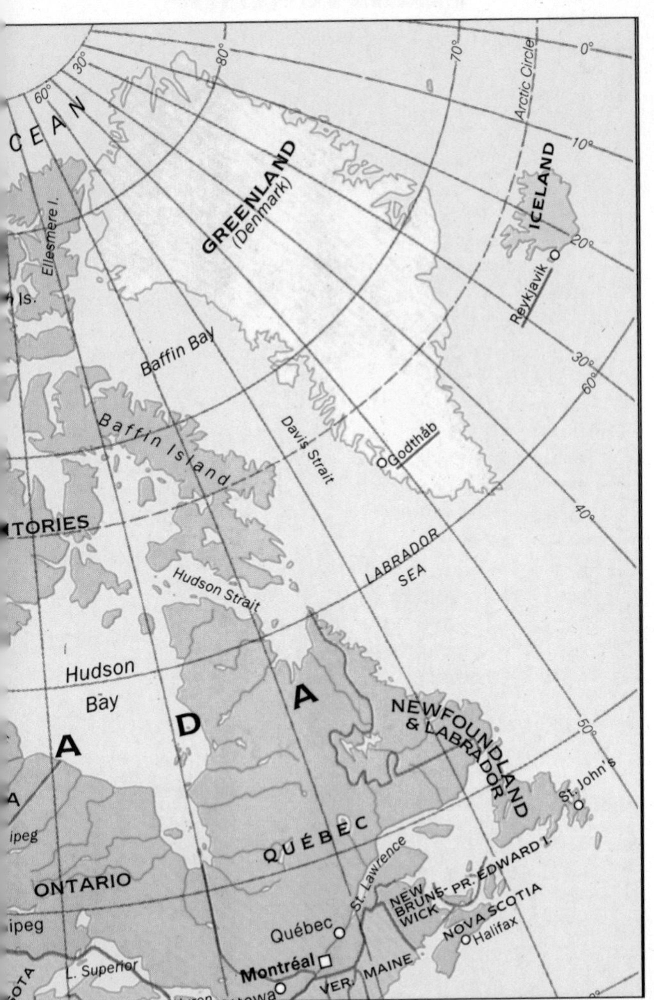

CEAN
GREENLAND
(Denmark)
ICELAND
Reykjavik
Ellesmere I.
Baffin Bay
Baffin Island
Davis Strait
Godthåb
TORIES
LABRADOR
SEA
Hudson Strait
Hudson
Bay
A
D
A
NEWFOUNDLAND
& LABRADOR
St. John's
QUÉBEC
ONTARIO
St. Lawrence
NEW
BRUNS-
WICK
PR. EDWARD I.
NOVA SCOTIA
Halifax
Québec
Montréal
L. Superior
VER.
MAINE
Arctic Circle
0°
10°
20°
30°
40°
50°
60°
70°
80°

NORTH AMERICA POLITICAL (S)

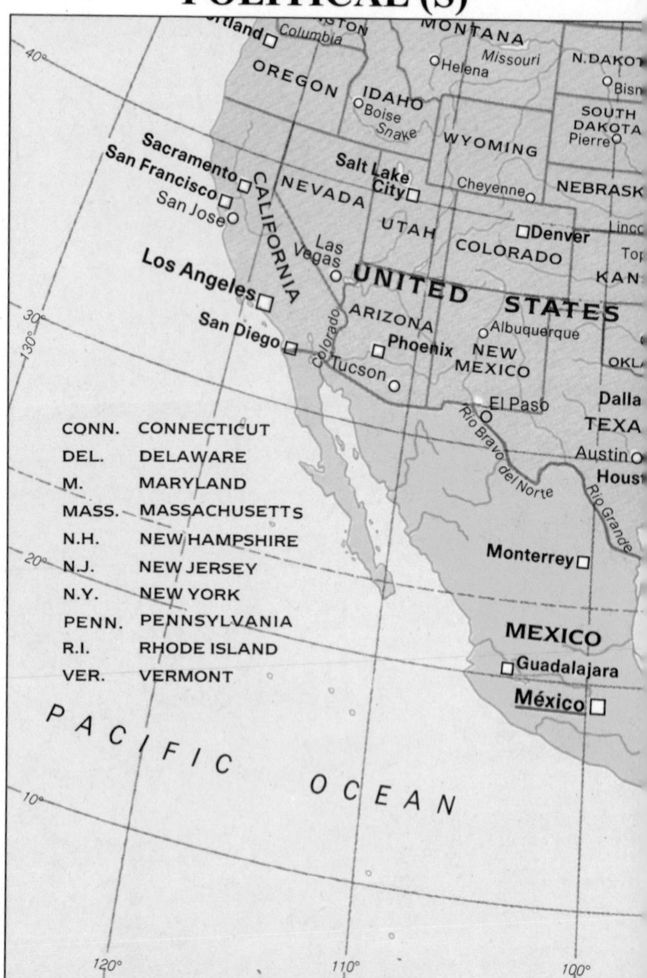

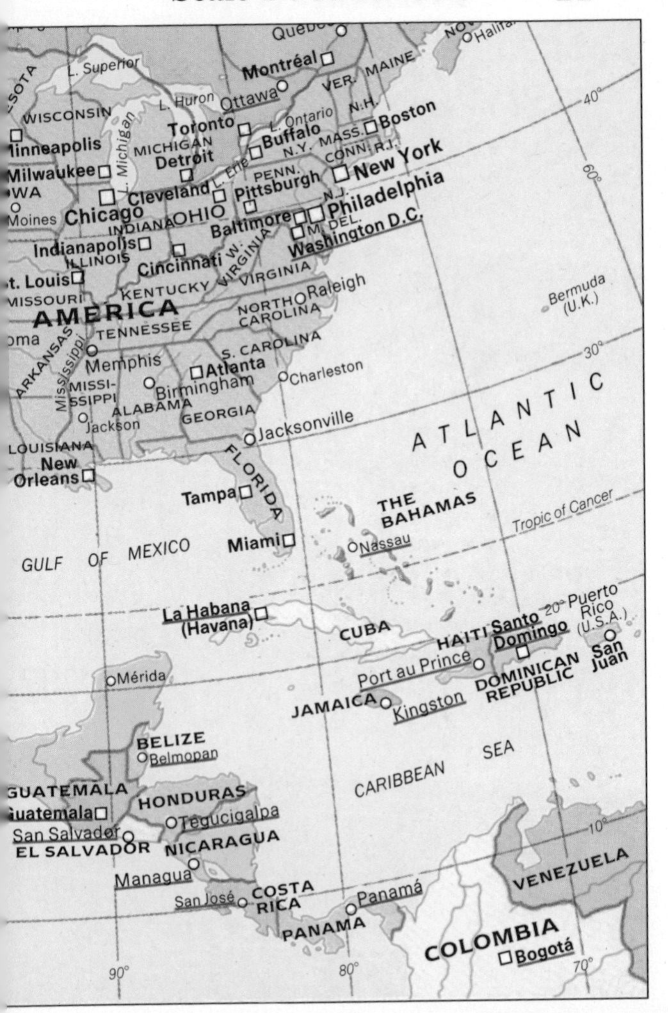

L. Superior
WISCONSIN
Minneapolis
Milwaukee
Moines
Chicago
INDIANA
OHIO
Indianapolis
ILLINOIS
St. Louis
MISSOURI
AMERICA
ARKANSAS
Mississippi
TENNESSEE
Memphis
MISSISSIPPI
Jackson
ALABAMA
Birmingham
LOUISIANA
New Orleans
L. Michigan
MICHIGAN
Detroit
L. Huron
Toronto
Ottawa
Montréal
Quebec
Halifax
MAINE
VER.
N.H.
L. Ontario
Buffalo
N.Y.
MASS.
Boston
CONN.
R.I.
New York
L. Erie
Cleveland
PENN.
Pittsburgh
N.J.
Philadelphia
Baltimore
DEL.
Washington D.C.
Cincinnati
W. VIRGINIA
KENTUCKY
VIRGINIA
NORTH CAROLINA
Raleigh
S. CAROLINA
Atlanta
GEORGIA
Charleston
Jacksonville
FLORIDA
Tampa
Miami
Bermuda (U.K.)
40°
30°
60°
ATLANTIC OCEAN
THE BAHAMAS
Nassau
Tropic of Cancer
GULF OF MEXICO
La Habana (Havana)
CUBA
20°
Puerto Rico (U.S.A.)
San Juan
HAITI
Santo Domingo
Port au Prince
DOMINICAN REPUBLIC
JAMAICA
Kingston
Mérida
BELIZE
Belmopan
GUATEMALA
Guatemala
HONDURAS
Tegucigalpa
San Salvador
EL SALVADOR
NICARAGUA
Managua
San José
COSTA RICA
Panamá
PANAMA
CARIBBEAN SEA
10°
VENEZUELA
COLOMBIA
Bogotá
90°
80°
70°

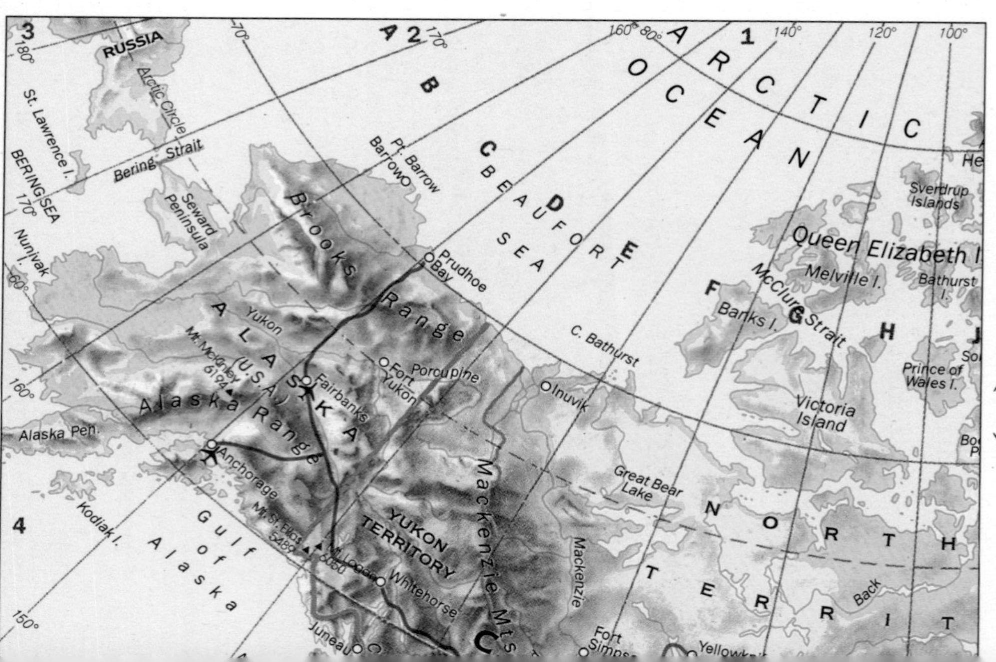
ARCTIC OCEAN
RUSSIA
Arctic Circle
Bering Strait
St. Lawrence I.
BERING SEA
Nunivak I.
Seward Peninsula
Pt. Barrow
Barrow
BEAUFORT SEA
Prudhoe Bay
Brooks Range
ALASKA (U.S.A.)
Yukon
Mt. McKinley 6194
Alaska Range
Fairbanks
Fort Yukon
Porcupine
Alaska Pen.
Anchorage
Kodiak I.
Gulf of Alaska
Mt. St. Elias 5489
Mt. Logan 5959
YUKON TERRITORY
Whitehorse
Juneau
Mackenzie Mts
Inuvik
C. Bathurst
Mackenzie
Fort Simpson
Yellowknife
Great Bear Lake
NORTH
TERRIT
Back
Banks I.
McClure Strait
Victoria Island
Queen Elizabeth I.
Melville I.
Bathurst I.
Sverdrup Islands
Prince of Wales I.
180°
170°
160°
150°
140°
120°
100°
80°
70°
60°

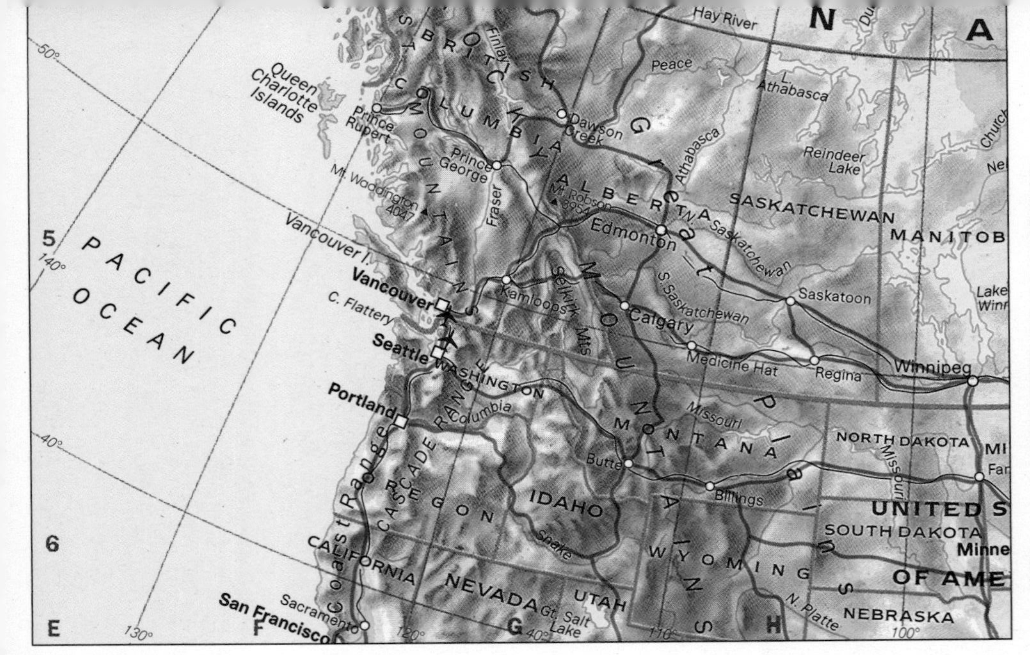
N A
MANITOB
UNITED S
OF AME
Minne
Hay River
L. Athabasca
Reindeer Lake
SASKATCHEWAN
Peace
Athabasca
Saskatoon
Winnipeg
Regina
Missouri
NORTH DAKOTA
SOUTH DAKOTA
NEBRASKA
N. Platte
N. Saskatchewan
S. Saskatchewan
Medicine Hat
Calgary
Edmonton
ALBERTA
Great Plains
ROCKY MOUNTAINS
MONTANA
Billings
Butte
WYOMING
Dawson Creek
Mt. Robson 3954
Selkirk Mts
Kamloops
Fraser
Prince George
Finlay
BRITISH COLUMBIA
COAST MOUNTAINS
Mt. Waddington 4047
Prince Rupert
Queen Charlotte Islands
Vancouver I.
Vancouver
C. Flattery
Seattle
WASHINGTON
Columbia
CASCADE RANGE
Portland
OREGON
IDAHO
Snake
UTAH
Gt. Salt Lake
NEVADA
Coast Range
CALIFORNIA
Sacramento
San Francisco
PACIFIC OCEAN
50°
40°
140°
130°
120°
110°
100°
5
6
E
F
G
H

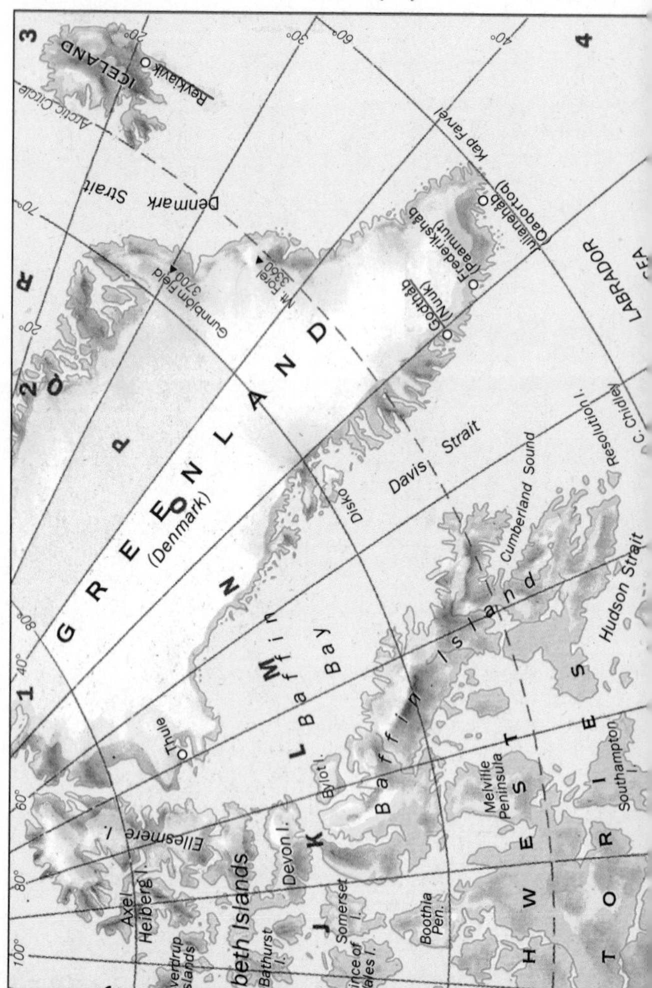

ICELAND
Reykjavik
Arctic Circle
Denmark Strait
Kap Farvel
Julianehåb
(Qaqortoq)
Frederikshåb
(Paamiut)
Godthåb
(Nuuk)
Mt. Forel
3360
Gunnbjørn Fjeld
3700
GREENLAND
(Denmark)
Disko
Davis Strait
Cumberland Sound
Resolution I.
C. Chidley
LABRADOR
Hudson Strait
Baffin Bay
Baffin Island
Thule
Bylot I.
Melville Peninsula
Southampton I.
Ellesmere I.
Devon I.
Axel Heiberg I.
Somerset I.
Boothia Pen.
Bathurst I.

Scale 1 : 25 200 000

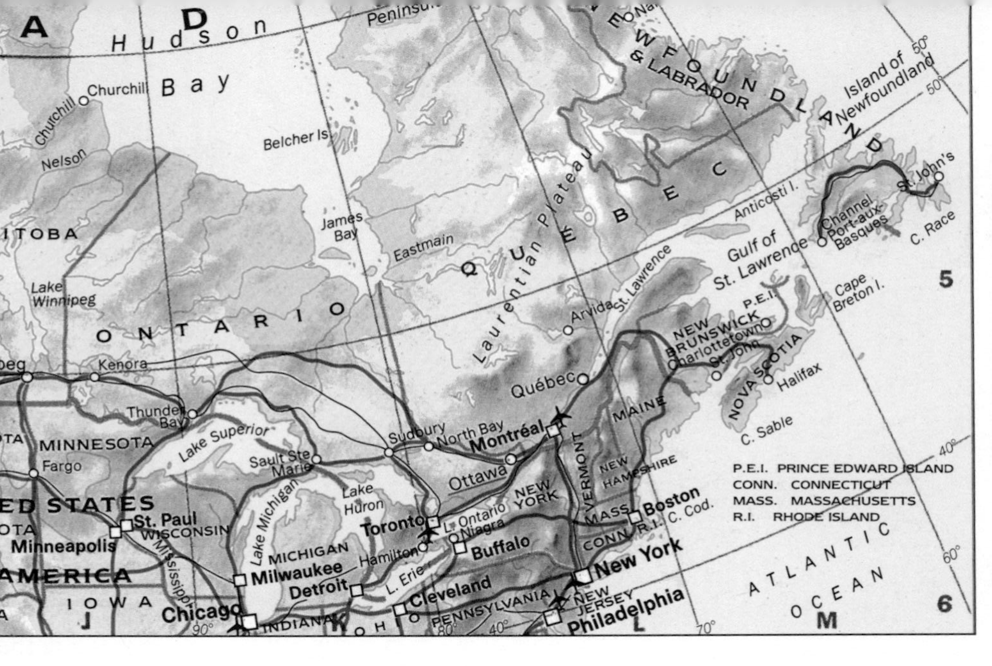

130°
C. Flattery
Vancouver
BRITISH
120°
WASHINGTON
Seattle
Olympia
Spokane
4392
Portland
Columbia
Salem
Snake
OREGON
Great
Sandy
Desert
40°
COAST
CASCADE
RANGE
Winnemucca
Sacramento
San Francisco
San Jose
Reno
Carson City
Stockton
NEVADA
Great
Basin
CALIFORNIA
Sierra Nevada
4397
1
2
130°
Fresno
Death Valley
Las Vegas
Colorado
Los Angeles
Pasadena
Channel
Islands
PACIFIC
San Diego
Tijuana
Mexicali
Sonora
Desert
30°
OC

B
C
D
110°
100°
Calgary
ALBERTA
SASKATCHEWAN
MANITOBA
Regina
Medicine Hat
Winnipeg
C A N
ROCKY MOUNTAINS
Great Plains
Missouri
MONTANA
NORTH DAKOTA
Helena
Butte
Yellowstone
Billings
Bismarck
Fargo
4202
Buffalo
SOUTH DAKOTA
Rapid City
Pierre
WYOMING
Casper
Missouri
Sioux Falls
Ogden
City
4114
NEBRASKA
Omaha
Cheyenne
Platte
Lincoln
UTAH
Richfield
Denver
4399
COLORADO
Colorado Springs
KANSAS
Topeka
San Juan Mts
Sangre de Cristo Mts
Arkansas
Wichita
4011
Flagstaff
SantaFe
Tulsa
OKLAHOMA
Albuquerque
3532
NEW MEXICO
Amarillo
Oklahoma City
Red
Lubbock
Pecos
Dallas
N I T E D
O F A M E R

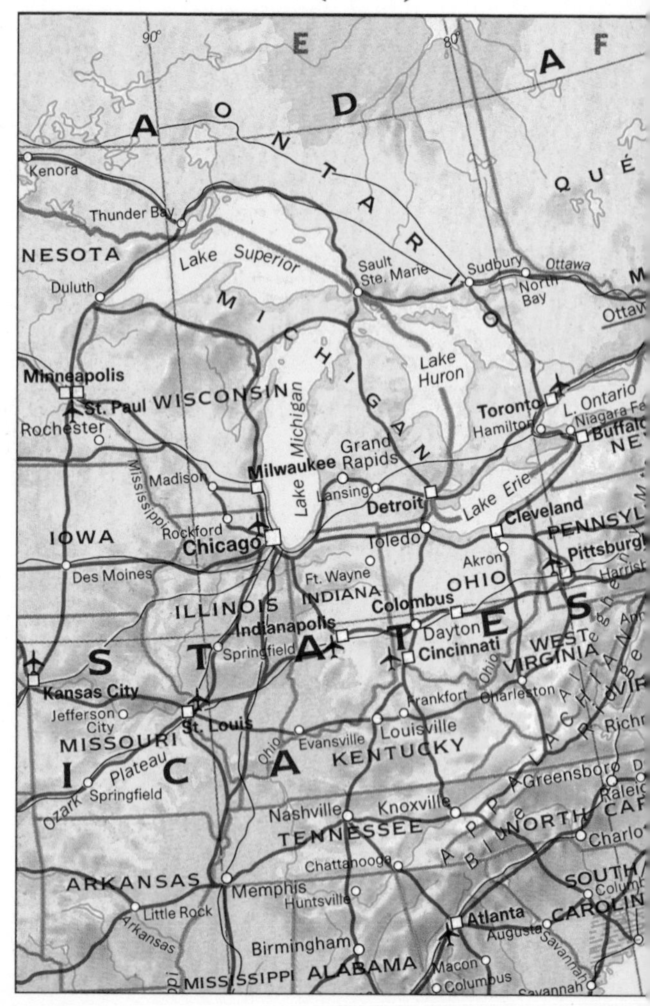

90°
80°
ONTARIO
QUÉ
Kenora
Thunder Bay
NESOTA
Lake Superior
Sault Ste. Marie
Sudbury
North Bay
Ottawa
Duluth
MICHIGAN
Lake Huron
Minneapolis
St. Paul
WISCONSIN
Lake Michigan
Toronto
Hamilton
L. Ontario
Buffalo
Rochester
Mississippi
Grand Rapids
Milwaukee
Madison
Lansing
Detroit
Lake Erie
Cleveland
IOWA
Rockford
Chicago
Toledo
PENNSYL
Akron
Pittsburgh
Des Moines
Ft. Wayne
OHIO
INDIANA
Columbus
ILLINOIS
Indianapolis
Dayton
Cincinnati
WEST VIRGINIA
UNITED STATES OF AMERICA
Springfield
Ohio
Kansas City
Frankfort
Charleston
Jefferson City
St. Louis
Louisville
MISSOURI
Evansville
KENTUCKY
Ozark Plateau
Springfield
APPALACHIAN MOUNTAINS
Greensboro
Nashville
Knoxville
TENNESSEE
NORTH
Blue Ridge
Chattanooga
ARKANSAS
Memphis
Huntsville
SOUTH CAROLINA
Little Rock
Arkansas
Atlanta
Augusta
Savannah
Birmingham
ALABAMA
Macon
Columbus
MISSISSIPPI
Savannah

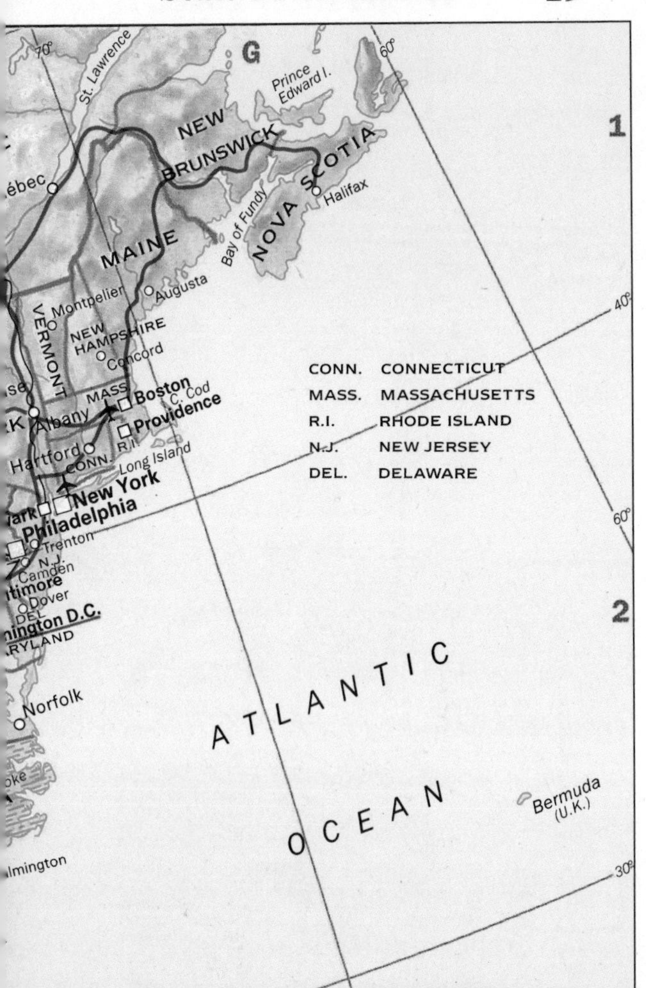
G
Prince Edward I.
St. Lawrence
NEW BRUNSWICK
NOVA SCOTIA
Halifax
Bay of Fundy
MAINE
Augusta
Montpelier
VERMONT
NEW HAMPSHIRE
Concord
MASS.
Boston
C. Cod
Providence
R.I.
Albany
Hartford
CONN.
Long Island
New York
Philadelphia
Trenton
N.J.
Camden
Dover
DEL.
Washington D.C.
MARYLAND
Norfolk
ATLANTIC
OCEAN
Bermuda (U.K.)
1
2
70°
60°
40°
30°
CONN. CONNECTICUT
MASS. MASSACHUSETTS
R.I. RHODE ISLAND
N.J. NEW JERSEY
DEL. DELAWARE

U.S.A. (S.E.) & WESTERN CARIBBEAN

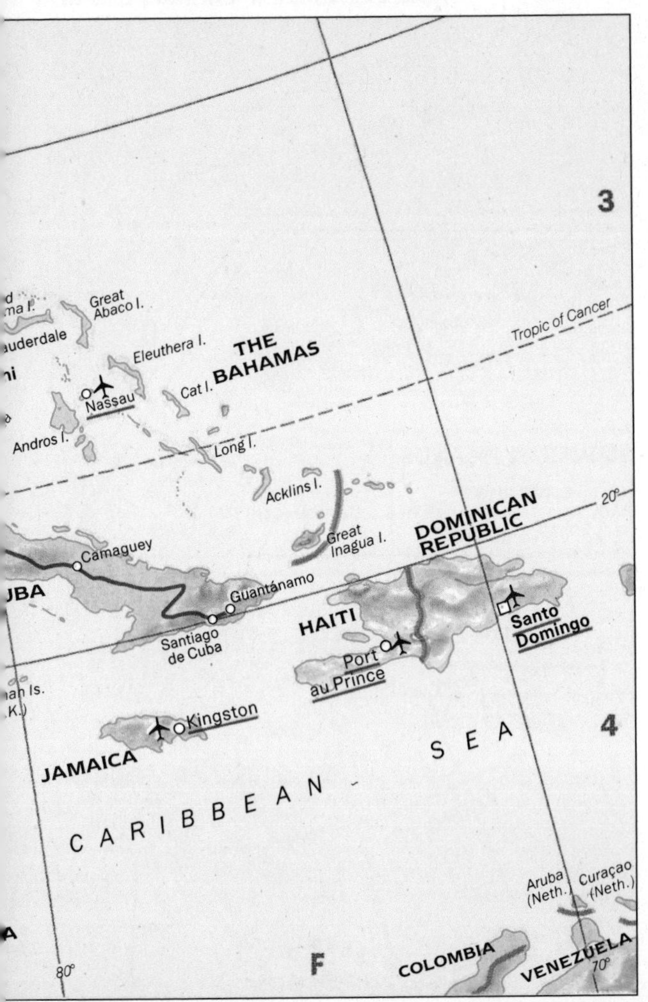
3
Great
Abaco I.
THE
BAHAMAS
Eleuthera I.
Nassau
Cat I.
Andros I.
Long I.
Tropic of Cancer
Acklins I.
Great
Inagua I.
DOMINICAN
REPUBLIC
20°
Camaguey
Guantánamo
Santiago
de Cuba
HAITI
Port
au Prince
Santo
Domingo
Kingston
JAMAICA
4
CARIBBEAN SEA
Aruba
(Neth.)
Curaçao
(Neth.)
COLOMBIA
VENEZUELA
F
80°
70°

U.S.A. (S.W.), MEXICO, ALASKA & HAWAIIAN I

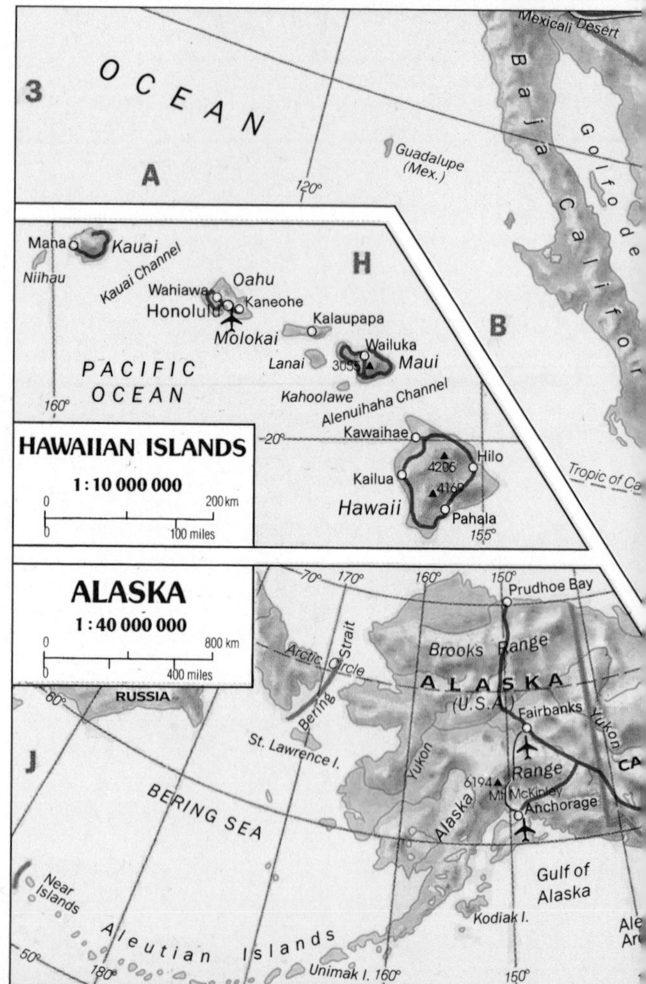

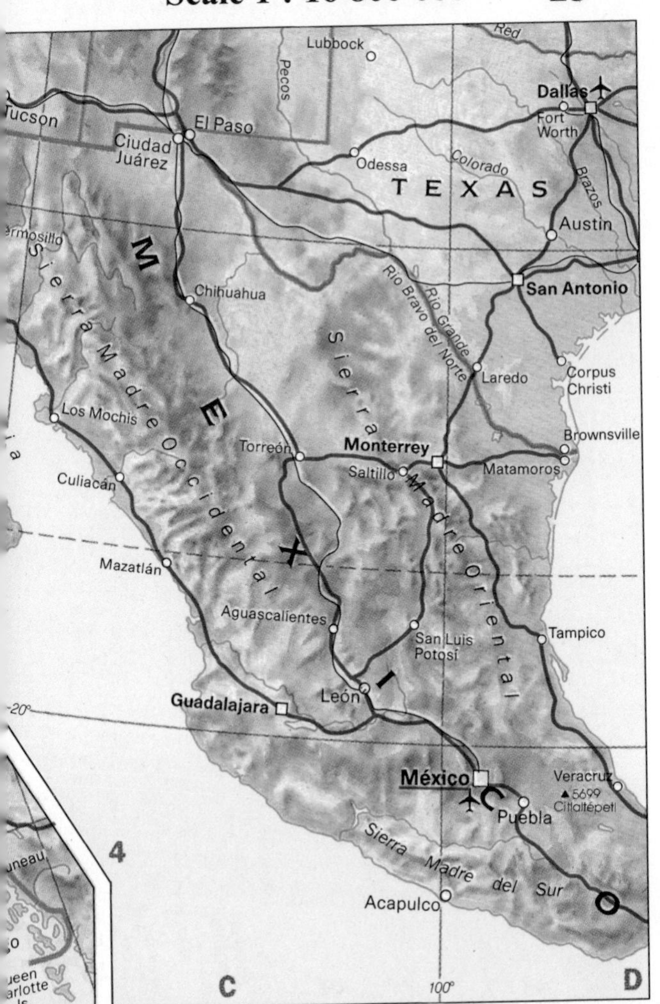
Lubbock
Pecos
Red
Dallas
Fort Worth
Tucson
El Paso
Ciudad Juárez
Odessa
Colorado
Brazos
TEXAS
Austin
ermosillo
Sierra Madre Occidental
M
E
X
I
C
O
Chihuahua
San Antonio
Rio Bravo del Norte
Rio Grande
Sierra Madre Oriental
Laredo
Corpus Christi
Los Mochis
Brownsville
Torreón
Monterrey
Saltillo
Matamoros
Culiacán
Mazatlán
Aguascalientes
Tampico
San Luis Potosí
León
Guadalajara
20°
México
Veracruz
5699
Citlaltépetl
Puebla
Sierra Madre del Sur
Acapulco
4
uneau
ueen
arlotte
Is.
C
100°
D

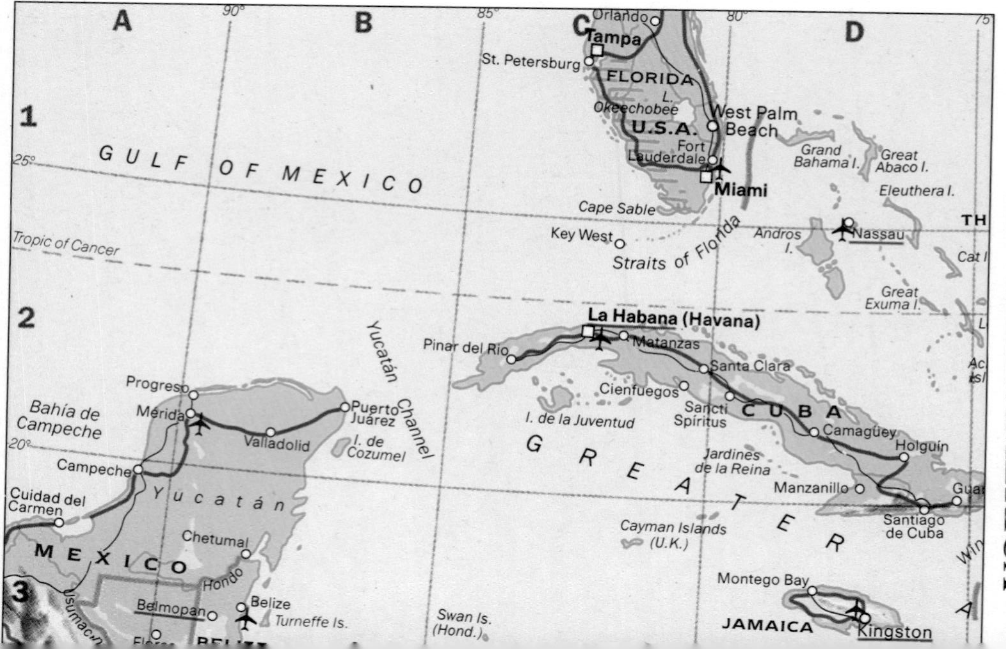

A
B
C
D
1
2
3
90°
85°
80°
75°
25°
20°
GULF OF MEXICO
Tropic of Cancer
Orlando
Tampa
St. Petersburg
FLORIDA
L. Okeechobee
U.S.A.
West Palm Beach
Fort Lauderdale
Miami
Cape Sable
Key West
Straits of Florida
Grand Bahama I.
Great Abaco I.
Eleuthera I.
Andros I.
Nassau
Great Exuma I.
La Habana (Havana)
Pinar del Río
Matanzas
Santa Clara
Cienfuegos
Sancti Spíritus
I. de la Juventud
CUBA
Camagüey
Holguín
Jardines de la Reina
Manzanillo
Santiago de Cuba
G R E A T E R
Cayman Islands (U.K.)
Montego Bay
JAMAICA
Kingston
Yucatán Channel
Progreso
Mérida
Puerto Juárez
Valladolid
I. de Cozumel
Bahía de Campeche
Campeche
Cuidad del Carmen
Yucatán
Chetumal
MEXICO
Hondo
Belmopan
Belize
Turneffe Is.
Swan Is. (Hond.)

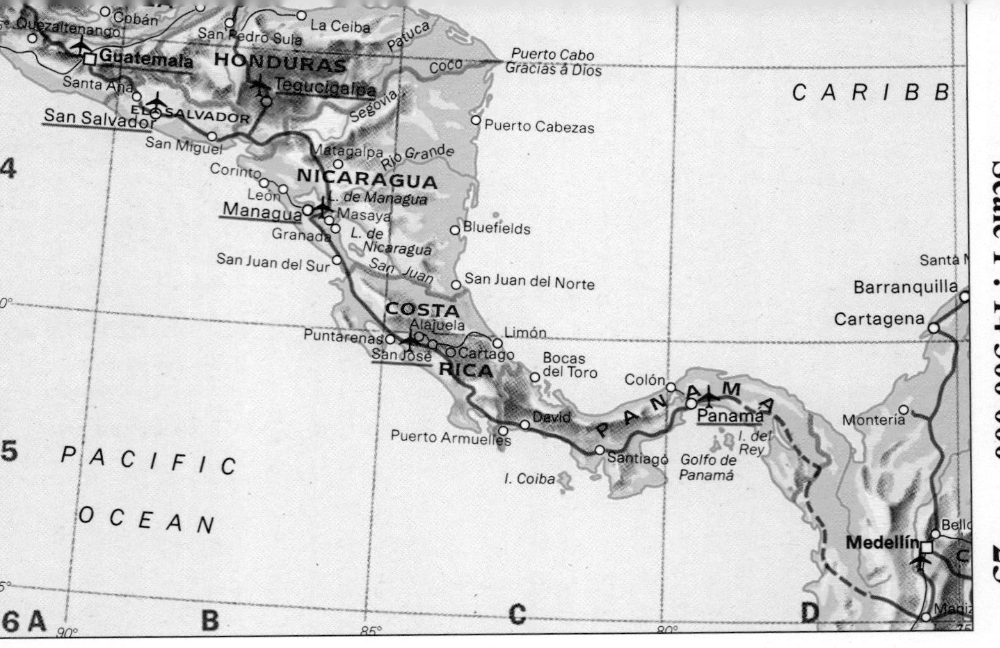
15°
Quezaltenango
Cobán
Guatemala
Santa Ana
San Salvador
EL SALVADOR
San Miguel
San Pedro Sula
La Ceiba
HONDURAS
Tegucigalpa
Patuca
Coco
Puerto Cabo
Gracias á Dios
Segovia
Puerto Cabezas
C A R I B B
Matagalpa
Río Grande
NICARAGUA
Corinto
León
L. de Managua
Managua
Masaya
Granada
L. de
Nicaragua
Bluefields
San Juan del Sur
San Juan
San Juan del Norte
Santa M
Barranquilla
Cartagena
10°
COSTA
RICA
Alajuela
Puntarenas
San José
Cartago
Limón
Bocas
del Toro
Colón
P A N A M A
Panamá
David
Puerto Armuelles
Santiago
I. del
Rey
Golfo de
Panamá
I. Coiba
Montería
Bello
Medellín
4
5
P A C I F I C
O C E A N
5°
6 A
B
C
D
90°
85°
80°

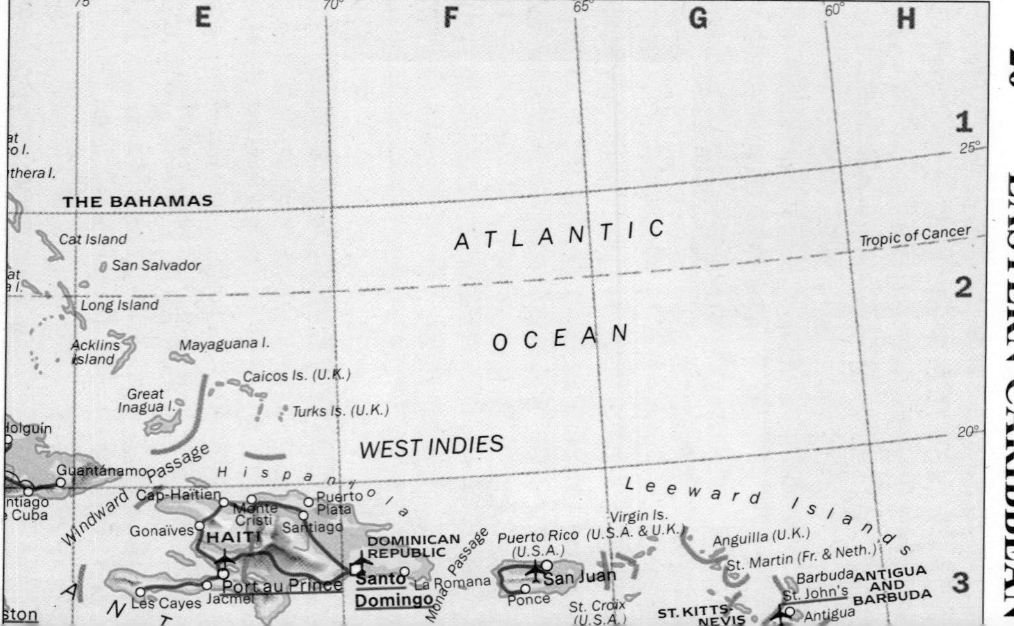
E
F
G
H
1
2
3
75°
70°
65°
60°
25°
20°
THE BAHAMAS
Cat Island
San Salvador
Long Island
Acklins Island
Mayaguana I.
Caicos Is. (U.K.)
Great Inagua I.
Turks Is. (U.K.)
ATLANTIC
OCEAN
Tropic of Cancer
WEST INDIES
Holguín
Guantánamo
Windward Passage
Hispaniola
Cap-Haïtien
Monte Cristi
Puerto Plata
Santiago
Gonaïves
HAITI
Port au Prince
Jacmel
Les Cayes
DOMINICAN REPUBLIC
Santo Domingo
La Romana
Mona Passage
Puerto Rico (U.S.A.)
San Juan
Ponce
Virgin Is. (U.S.A. & U.K.)
St. Croix (U.S.A.)
Leeward Islands
Anguilla (U.K.)
St. Martin (Fr. & Neth.)
Barbuda
ANTIGUA AND BARBUDA
St. John's
Antigua
ST. KITTS-NEVIS

SEA
LESSER
Roseau
Martinique (Fr.)
Fort-de-France
ST. LUCIA
Castries
BARBADOS
Bridgetown
ST. VINCENT & THE GRENADINES
Georgetown
GRENADA
St. George's
Tobago
TRINIDAD AND TOBAGO
Port of Spain
Trinidad
I. Blanquilla
I. Margarita
Güiria
Carúpano
Barcelona
Maturín
Ciudad Guayana
Orinoco
Ciudad Bolívar
La Tortuga
Is. Los Rogues
Caracas
Maracay
Valencia
Bonaire
Netherlands Antilles
Curaçao
Aruba
Coro
Barquisimeto
Cabimas
Lago de Maracaibo
Maracaibo
Pta. Gallinas
Santa Marta
Valledupar
Magdalena
San Cristóbal
Cúcuta
Bucaramanga
LLANOS
Meta
Bello
Manizales
Bogotá
VENEZUELA
COLOMBIA
GUYANA
BRAZIL
4
5
10°
60°
65°
70°
E
F
G

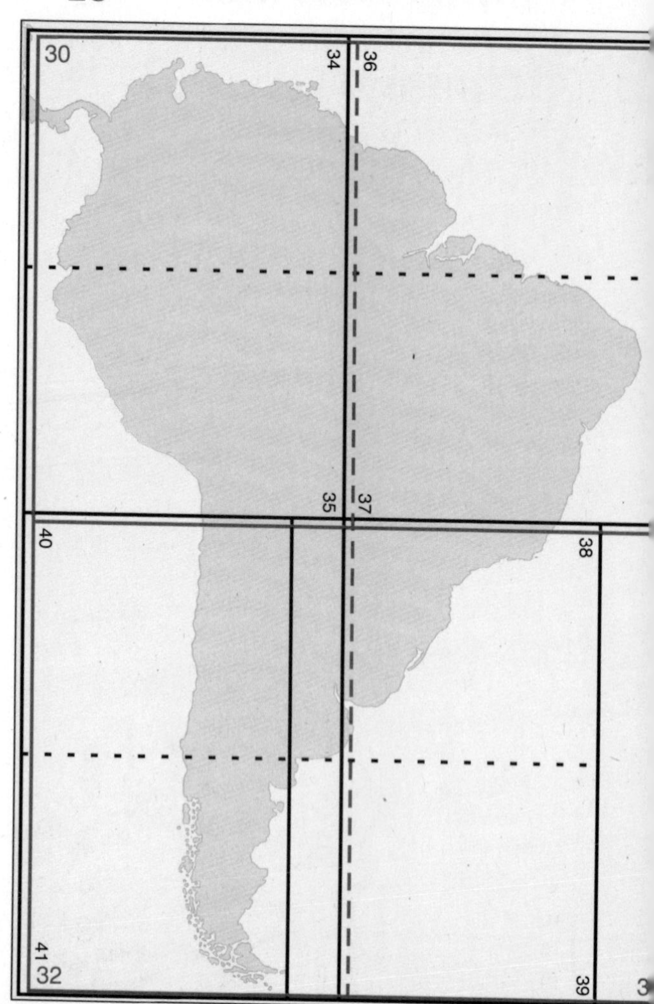
30
34
36
35
37
40
38
41
32
39

INDEX TO PAGES

30-31 SOUTH AMERICA POLITICAL (N)
32-33 SOUTH AMERICA POLITICAL (S)
34-35 SOUTH AMERICA (N.W.)
36-37 SOUTH AMERICA (N.E.)
38-39 SOUTH AMERICA (E)
40-41 SOUTH AMERICA (S)

SOUTH AMERICA POLITICAL (N)

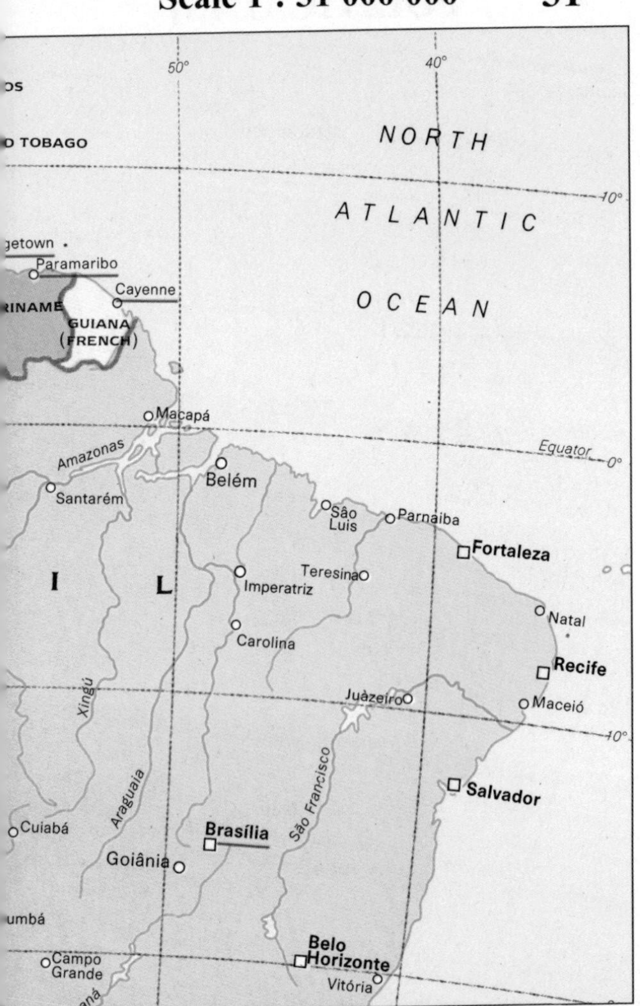
50°
40°
OS
O TOBAGO
NORTH
ATLANTIC
OCEAN
10°
getown
Paramaribo
Cayenne
RINAME
GUIANA
(FRENCH)
Macapá
Amazonas
Equator
0°
Belém
Santarém
São Luis
Parnaiba
Fortaleza
Teresina
Imperatriz
I
L
Natal
Carolina
Recife
Xingú
Juàzeiro
Maceió
10°
São Francisco
Araguaia
Salvador
Cuiabá
Brasília
Goiânia
umbá
Belo Horizonte
Campo Grande
Vitória
raná

SOUTH AMERICA POLITICAL (S)

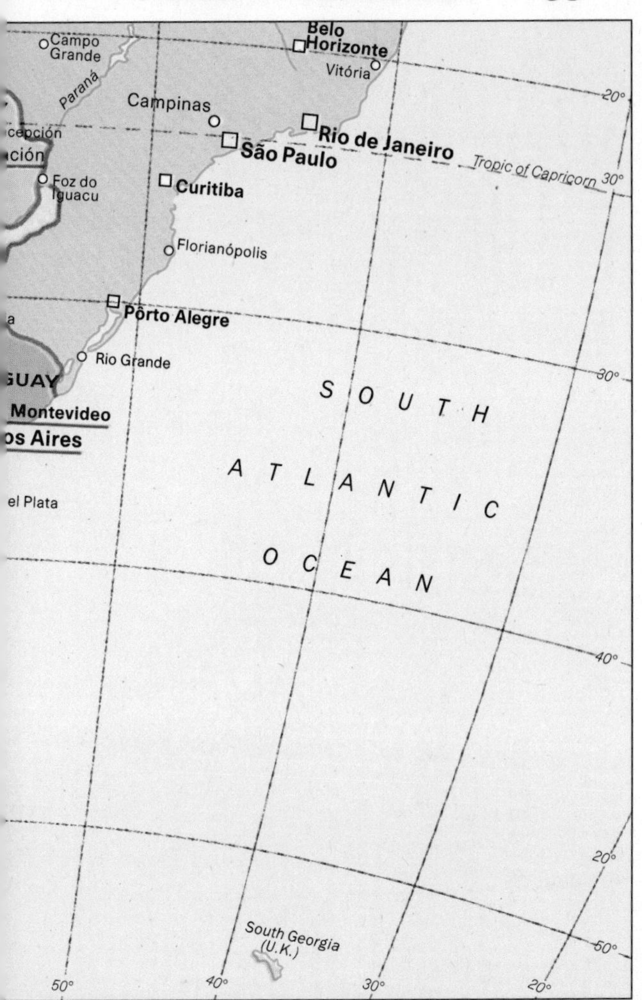
Campo Grande
Belo Horizonte
Vitória
Paraná
Campinas
Rio de Janeiro
São Paulo
Tropic of Capricorn
cepción
ción
Foz do Iguacu
Curitiba
Florianópolis
Pôrto Alegre
Rio Grande
GUAY
Montevideo
os Aires
el Plata
SOUTH ATLANTIC OCEAN
South Georgia (U.K.)
20°
30°
40°
50°
20°
30°
40°
50°

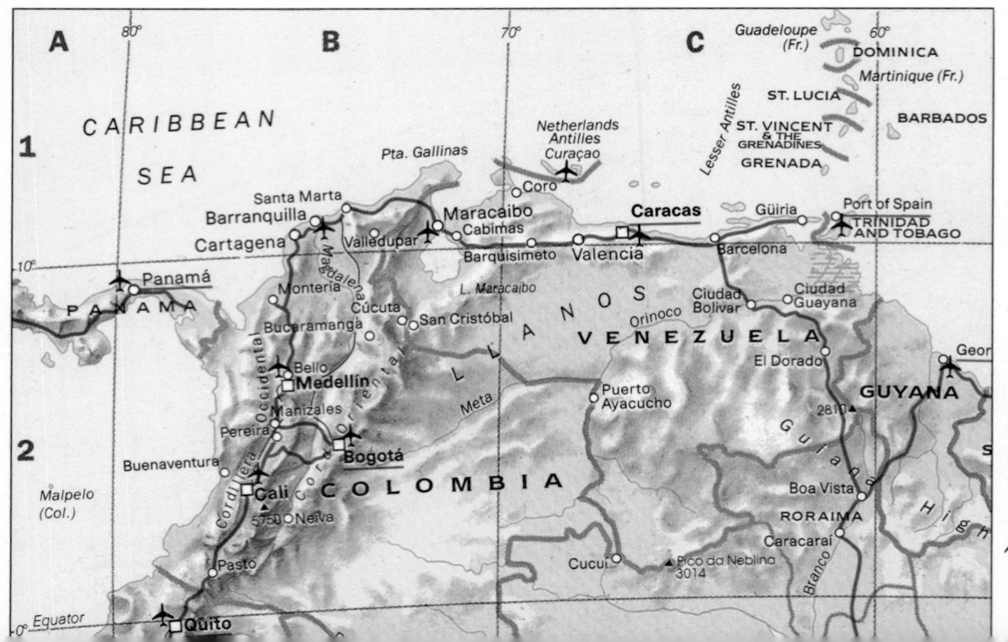

A
B
C
1
2
80°
70°
60°
10°
0°
Equator
CARIBBEAN SEA
Guadeloupe (Fr.)
DOMINICA
Martinique (Fr.)
ST. LUCIA
BARBADOS
ST. VINCENT & THE GRENADINES
GRENADA
Lesser Antilles
Netherlands Antilles
Curaçao
Pta. Gallinas
Coro
Santa Marta
Barranquilla
Cartagena
Valledupar
Maracaibo
Cabimas
Barquisimeto
Valencia
Caracas
Güiria
Port of Spain
TRINIDAD AND TOBAGO
Barcelona
Panamá
PANAMA
Montería
Magdalena
Cúcuta
L. Maracaibo
San Cristóbal
Bucaramanga
LLANOS
Orinoco
Ciudad Bolívar
Ciudad Guayana
VENEZUELA
El Dorado
Geor
GUYANA
Bello
Medellín
Manizales
Pereira
Occidental
Oriental
Meta
Puerto Ayacucho
2810
Guiana Highlands
Bogotá
Buenaventura
Cordillera
COLOMBIA
Cali
5750
Neiva
Malpelo (Col.)
Boa Vista
RORAIMA
Caracaraí
Branco
Pasto
Cucuí
Pico da Neblina 3014
Quito

Scale 1 : 21 400 000

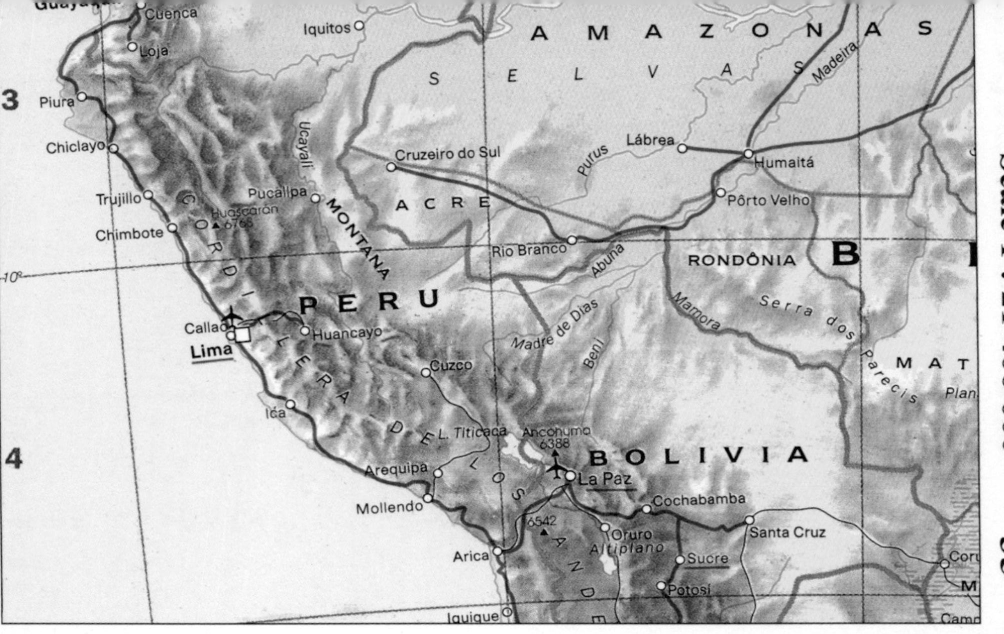

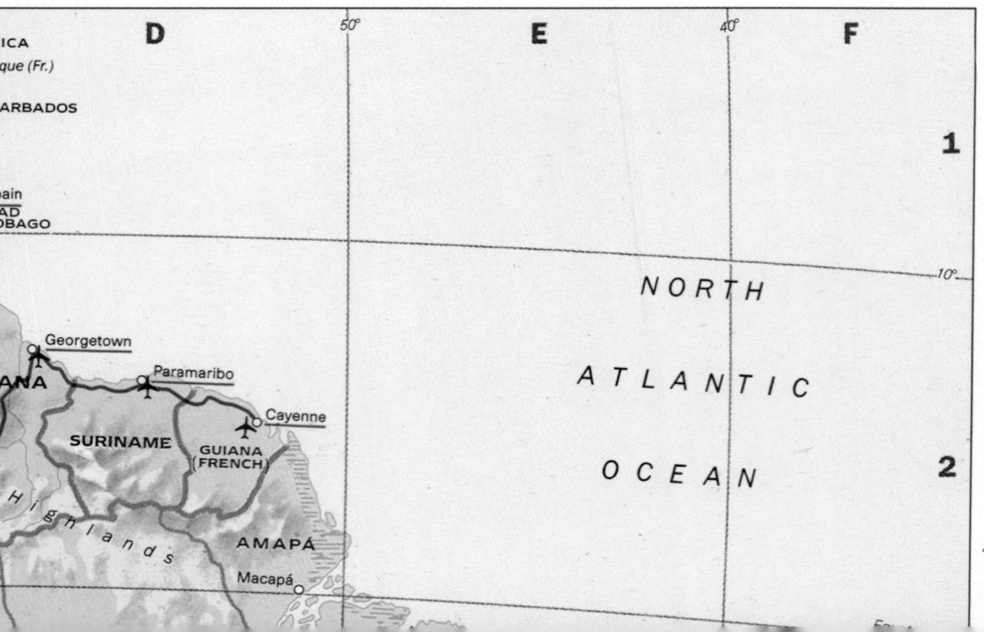

D
E
F
50°
40°
10°
1
2
NORTH
ATLANTIC
OCEAN
Georgetown
Paramaribo
Cayenne
SURINAME
GUIANA (FRENCH)
Highlands
AMAPÁ
Macapá

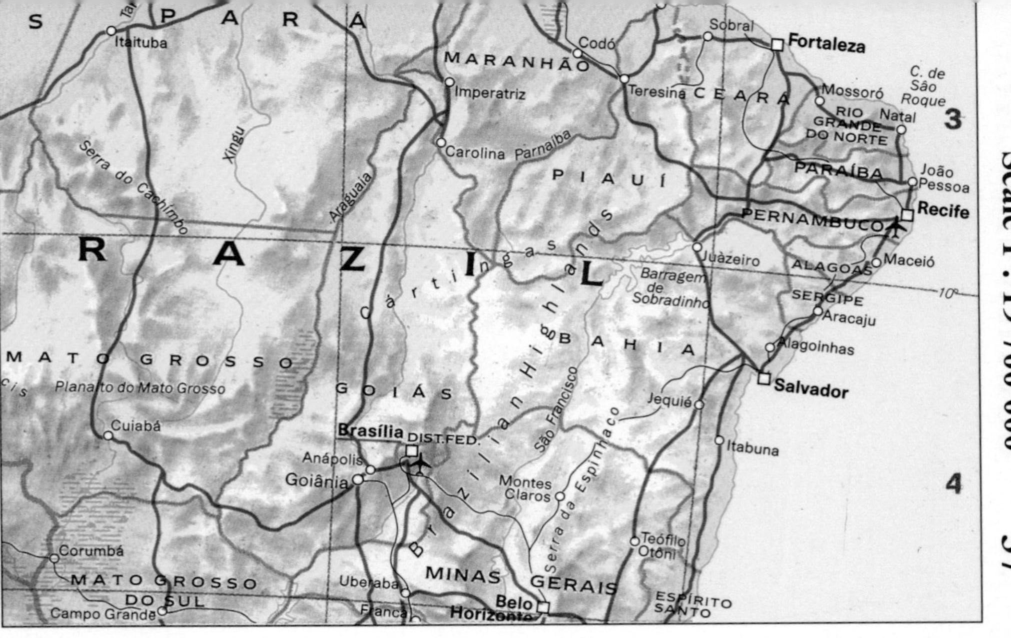
PARÁ
Itaituba
Codó
Sobral
Fortaleza
MARANHÃO
Imperatriz
Teresina
CEARÁ
C. de São Roque
Mossoró
RIO GRANDE DO NORTE
Natal
3
Serra do Cachimbo
Xingu
Carolina
Parnaíba
PIAUÍ
PARAÍBA
João Pessoa
Araguaia
Recife
PERNAMBUCO
Juàzeiro
ALAGOAS
Maceió
Barragem de Sobradinho
10°
SERGIPE
Aracaju
BAHIA
Alagoinhas
MATO GROSSO
Planalto do Mato Grosso
GOIÁS
Salvador
Brazilian Highlands
Jequié
Cuiabá
Brasília
DIST.FED.
São Francisco
Itabuna
Anápolis
Goiânia
Montes Claros
Serra da Espinhaço
4
Teófilo Otôni
Corumbá
MATO GROSSO DO SUL
Campo Grande
Uberaba
Franca
MINAS GERAIS
Belo Horizonte
ESPÍRITO SANTO

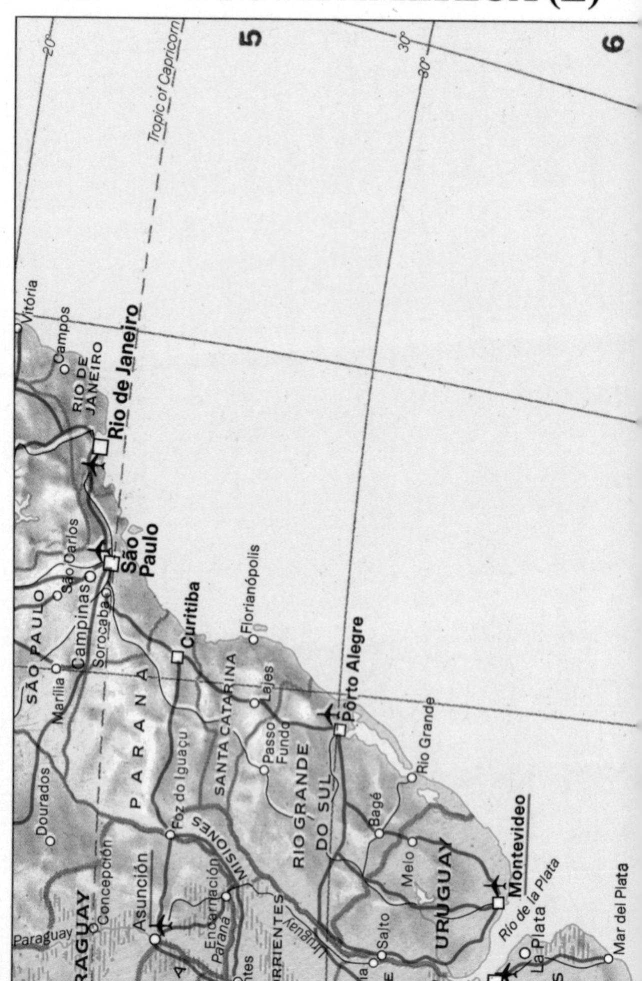
5
6
20°
30°
30°
Tropic of Capricorn
Vitória
Campos
RIO DE JANEIRO
Rio de Janeiro
São Paulo
São Carlos
Campinas
SÃO PAULO
Sorocaba
Marília
Curitiba
Florianópolis
P A R A N A
Pôrto Alegre
Lajes
SANTA CATARINA
Passo Fundo
RIO GRANDE DO SUL
Rio Grande
Dourados
Foz do Iguaçu
MISIONES
Bagé
Melo
URUGUAY
Montevideo
Río de la Plata
La Plata
Mar del Plata
Salto
Concepción
Asunción
Paraguay
Encarnación
Paraná
Uruguay

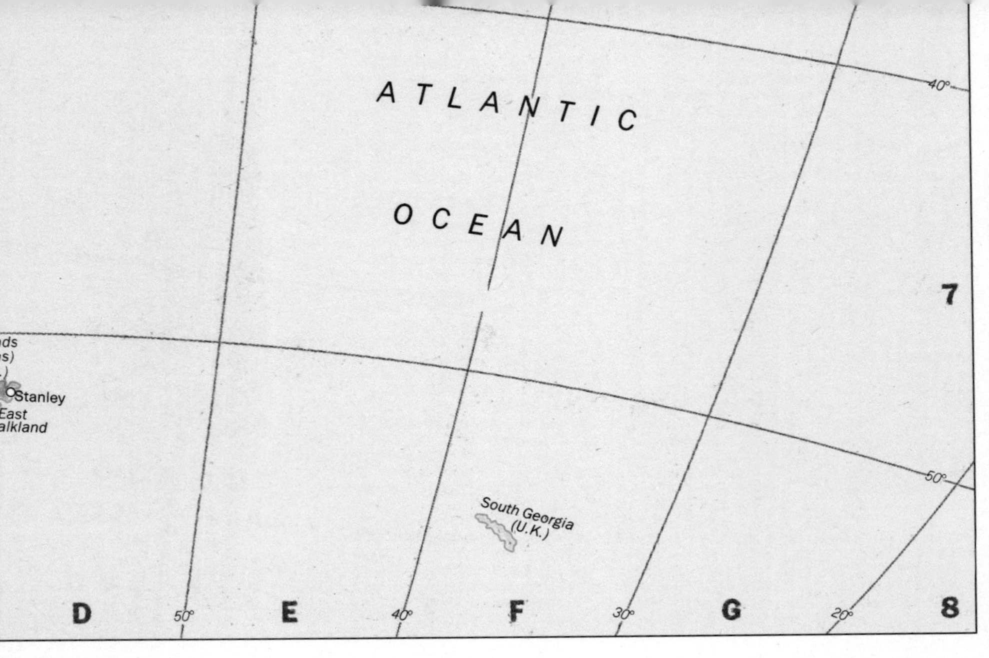
ATLANTIC
OCEAN
Stanley
East
South Georgia
(U.K.)
40°
7
50°
D
50°
E
40°
F
30°
G
20°
8

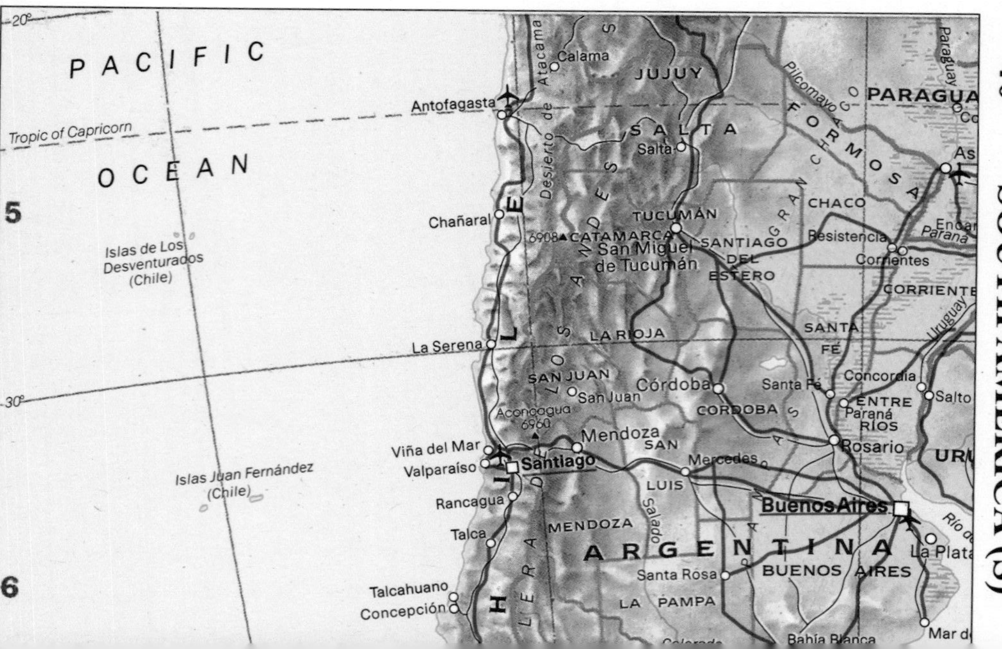
PACIFIC OCEAN
Tropic of Capricorn
Islas de Los Desventurados (Chile)
Islas Juan Fernández (Chile)
ARGENTINA
CHILE
GRAN CHACO
Paraguay
PARAGUAY
Pilcomayo
FORMOSA
CHACO
Resistencia
Corrientes
CORRIENTES
Paraná
Uruguay
Salto
Concordia
ENTRE RIOS
Rosario
Santa Fé
SANTA FÉ
SANTIAGO DEL ESTERO
TUCUMÁN
San Miguel de Tucumán
CATAMARCA
6908
Salta
SALTA
JUJUY
Calama
Desierto de Atacama
Antofagasta
Chañaral
La Serena
LA RIOJA
CÓRDOBA
Córdoba
SAN JUAN
San Juan
Mendoza
MENDOZA
SAN LUIS
Mercedes
Aconcagua 6960
Santiago
Viña del Mar
Valparaíso
Rancagua
Talca
Talcahuano
Concepción
Buenos Aires
BUENOS AIRES
La Plata
Bahía Blanca
Santa Rosa
LA PAMPA
Salado
20°
30°
5
6

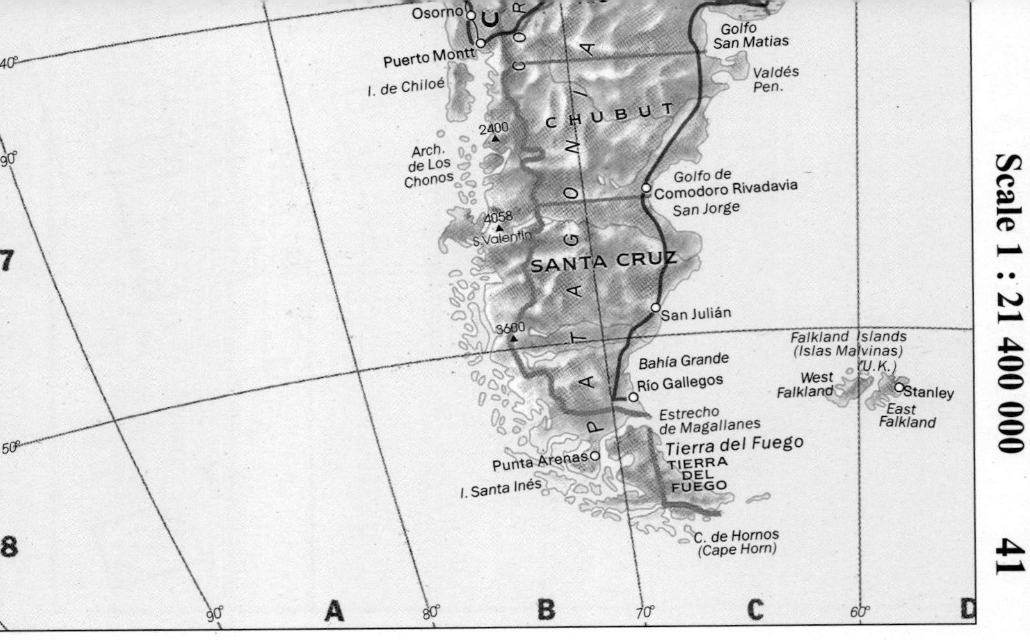

Osorno
Puerto Montt
I. de Chiloé
Golfo San Matias
Valdés Pen.
CHUBUT
PATAGONIA
2400
Arch. de Los Chonos
Golfo de San Jorge
Comodoro Rivadavia
4058
S.Valentín
SANTA CRUZ
San Julián
3600
Falkland Islands (Islas Malvinas) (U.K.)
West Falkland
East Falkland
Stanley
Bahía Grande
Río Gallegos
Estrecho de Magallanes
Tierra del Fuego
TIERRA DEL FUEGO
Punta Arenas
I. Santa Inés
C. de Hornos (Cape Horn)
40°
50°
60°
70°
80°
90°
7
8
A
B
C
D

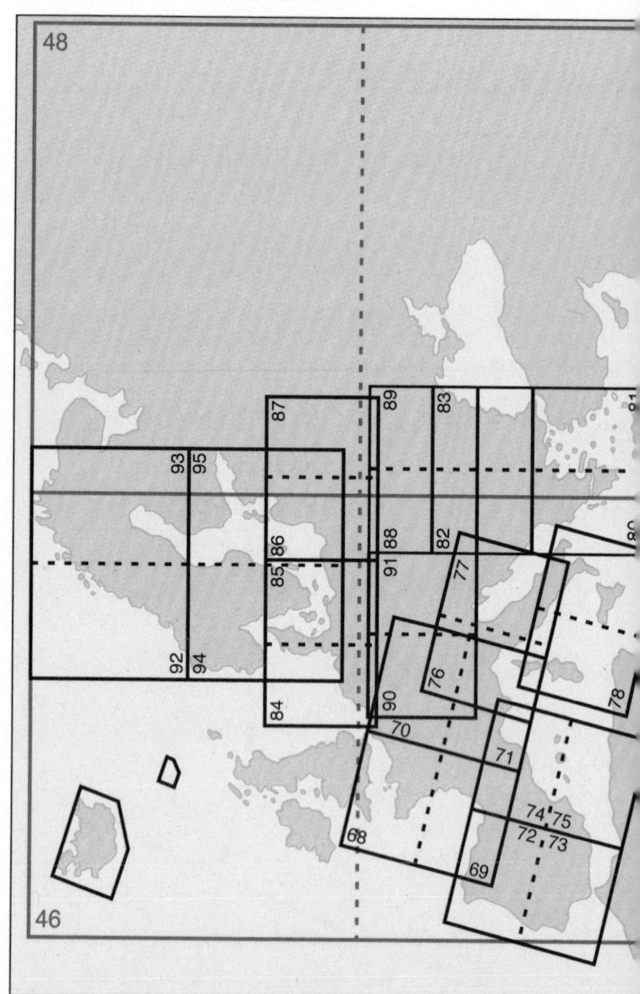
48
46
87
89
83
93
95
86
88
82
85
91
77
92
94
76
90
84
70
71
68
69
74
75
72
73
78

68-69 FRANCE (W)
70-71 FRANCE (E)
72-73 PORTUGAL & SPAIN (W)
74-75 SPAIN (E)
76-77 ITALY (N)
78-79 ITALY (S)
80-81 GREECE
82-83 S.E. EUROPE
84-85 CENTRAL EUROPE (N.W.)
86-87 CENTRAL EUROPE (N.E.)
88-89 CENTRAL EUROPE (S.E.)
90-91 CENTRAL EUROPE (S.W.)
92-93 SCANDINAVIA & THE BALTIC (N)
94-95 SCANDINAVIA & THE BALTIC (S)

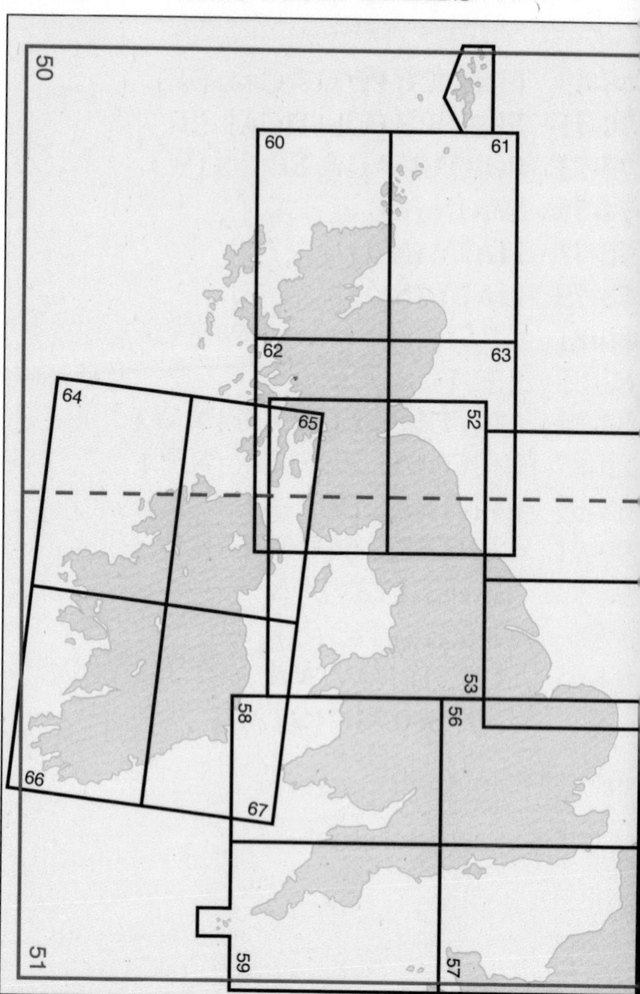
50
60
61
62
63
64
65
52
53
58
56
66
67
51
59
57

INDEX TO PAGES

46-47 EUROPE POLITICAL (W)
48-49 EUROPE POLITICAL (S)
50-51 BRITISH ISLES
52-53 ENGLAND & WALES (N.W.)
54-55 ENGLAND (N.E.)
56-57 ENGLAND (N.S.)
58-59 ENGLAND & WALES (N.S.)
60-61 SCOTLAND (N)
62-63 SCOTLAND (S)
64-65 IRELAND (N)
66-67 IRELAND (S)

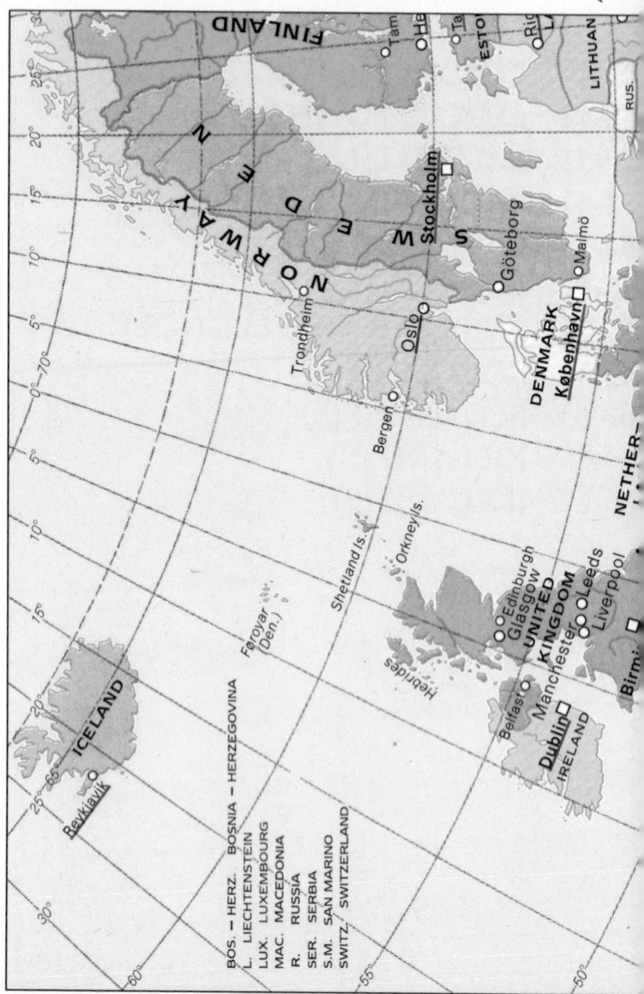
FINLAND
NORWAY
SWEDEN
ESTO
LITHUAN
RUS.
Stockholm
Göteborg
Malmö
Trondheim
Oslo
Bergen
DENMARK
København
NETHER-
Shetland Is.
Orkney Is.
Føroyar (Den.)
Hebrides
Edinburgh
Glasgow
UNITED KINGDOM
Leeds
Liverpool
Manchester
Belfast
Dublin
IRELAND
ICELAND
Reykjavik
BOS. – HERZ. BOSNIA – HERZEGOVINA
L. LIECHTENSTEIN
LUX. LUXEMBOURG
MAC. MACEDONIA
R. RUSSIA
SER. SERBIA
S.M. SAN MARINO
SWITZ. SWITZERLAND

Channel Is.
Paris
Luxembourg
Nantes
FRANCE
Bordeaux
Lyon
Toulouse
Marseille
Nice
MONACO
ANDORRA
Porto
Lisboa
PORTUGAL
SPAIN
Madrid
Zaragoza
Bilbao
Barcelona
Valencia
Islas Baleares
Sevilla
Malaga
Gibraltar (U.K.)
Rabat
Casablanca
MOROCCO
Oran
Alger
ALGERIA
Tunis
TUNISIA
MALTA
Palermo
Sicilia
Sardegna
Corse
ITALY
Roma
Napoli
Bari
S.M.
Firenze
Bologna
Genova
Torino
Milano
Venezia
Zürich
SWITZ.
Bern
L.
Essen
Köln
Bonn
LUX.
Frankfurt
Leipzig
Dresden
GERMANY
Stuttgart
München
Praha
CZECH REPUBLIC
Wien
AUSTRIA
Graz
SLOVENIA
Ljubljana
Zagreb
CROATIA
BOS.-HERZ.
Sarajevo
CRO.
SLOVAKIA
Bratislava
Miskolc
Budapest
HUNGARY
Łodz
Wrocław
Kraków
Timișoara
Beograd
SER.
YUGOSLAVIA
MONTENEGRO
Skopje
MAC.
Tiranë
ALBANIA
GREECE
45°
40°
35°
5°
0°
5°
10°
20°

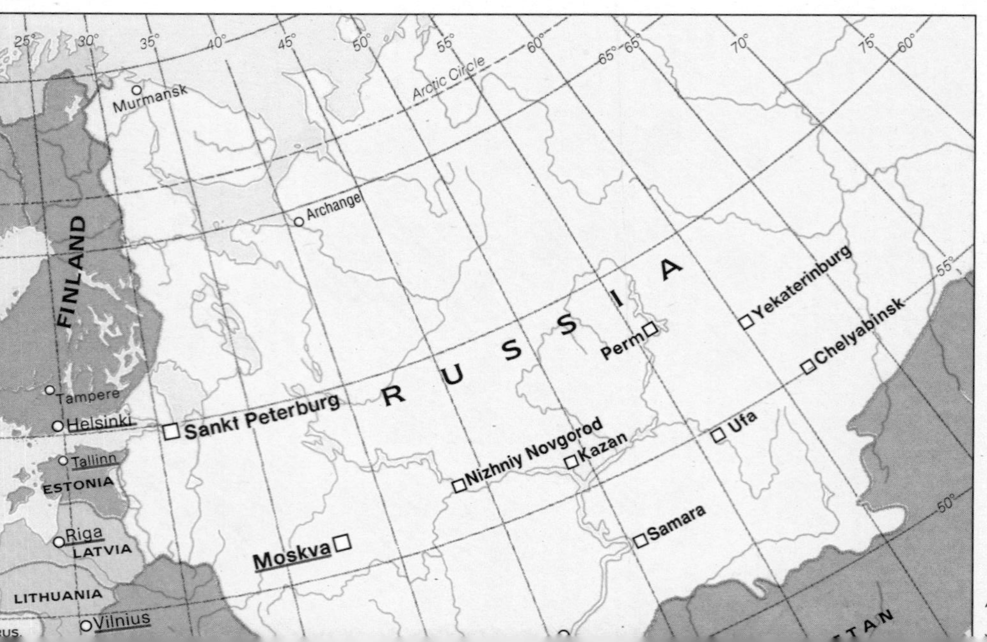
RUSSIA
FINLAND
ESTONIA
LATVIA
LITHUANIA
RUS.
TAN
Murmansk
Archangel
Arctic Circle
Tampere
Helsinki
Tallinn
Riga
Vilnius
Sankt Peterburg
Moskva
Nizhniy Novgorod
Kazan
Samara
Perm
Ufa
Yekaterinburg
Chelyabinsk
25°
30°
35°
40°
45°
50°
55°
60°
65°
65°
70°
75°
60°
55°
50°

Scale 1 : 51 200 000

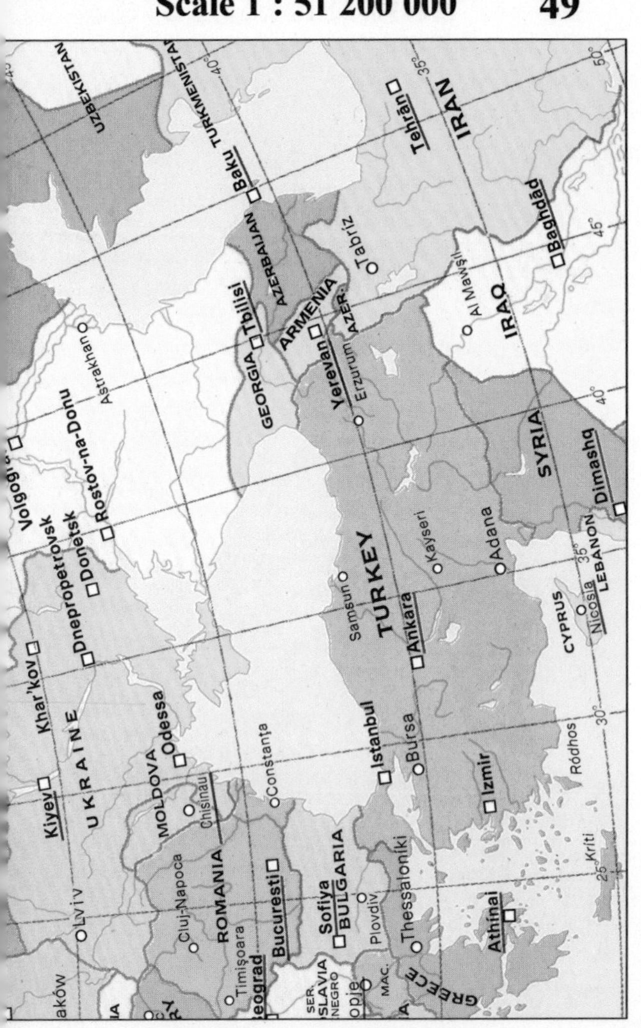

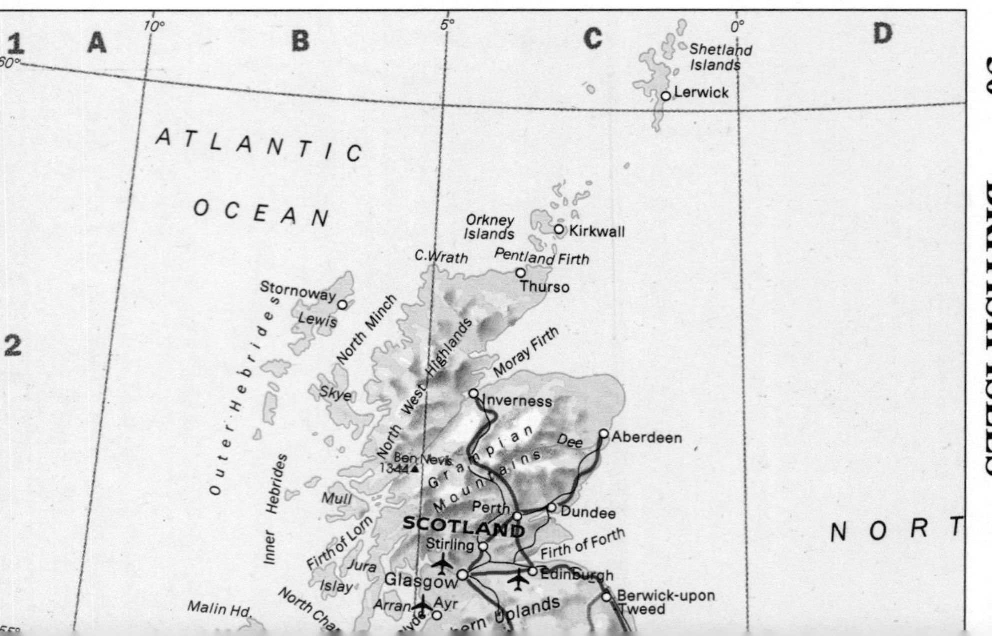
1
A
B
C
D
2
60°
10°
5°
0°
Shetland Islands
Lerwick
ATLANTIC
OCEAN
Orkney Islands
Kirkwall
C.Wrath
Pentland Firth
Thurso
Stornoway
Lewis
North Minch
Outer Hebrides
North West Highlands
Moray Firth
Skye
Inverness
Grampian Mountains
Dee
Aberdeen
Ben Nevis
1344
Inner Hebrides
Mull
Perth
Dundee
SCOTLAND
NORT
Firth of Lorn
Stirling
Firth of Forth
Jura
Glasgow
Edinburgh
Islay
Berwick-upon Tweed
Malin Hd.
Arran
Ayr
Uplands

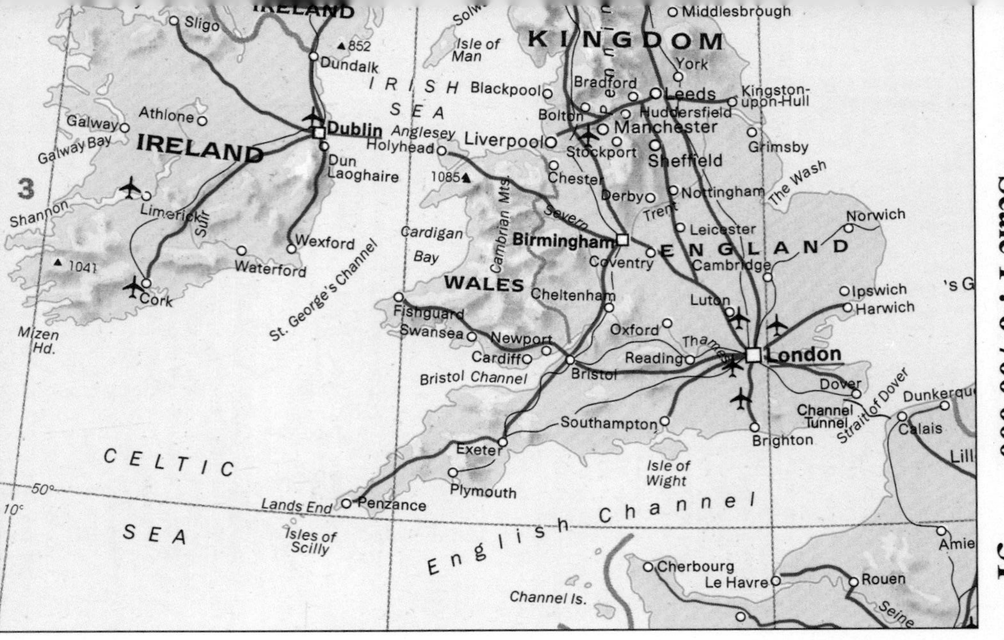

KINGDOM
ENGLAND
WALES
IRELAND
IRISH SEA
CELTIC SEA
English Channel
Middlesbrough
York
Leeds
Bradford
Huddersfield
Manchester
Stockport
Bolton
Blackpool
Liverpool
Chester
Derby
Sheffield
Nottingham
Leicester
Kingston-upon-Hull
Grimsby
The Wash
Norwich
Ipswich
Harwich
Cambridge
Luton
London
Thames
Birmingham
Coventry
Trent
Severn
Oxford
Reading
Cheltenham
Bristol
Newport
Cardiff
Swansea
Fishguard
Cardigan Bay
Cambrian Mts.
1085
Anglesey
Holyhead
Isle of Man
Bristol Channel
Exeter
Plymouth
Penzance
Lands End
Isles of Scilly
Southampton
Isle of Wight
Brighton
Channel Tunnel
Dover
Strait of Dover
Calais
Rouen
Seine
Le Havre
Cherbourg
Channel Is.
Dublin
Dun Laoghaire
Dundalk
852
Wexford
Waterford
St. George's Channel
Suir
Cork
Limerick
Athlone
Sligo
Galway
Galway Bay
Shannon
1041
Mizen Hd.
50°
10°
3

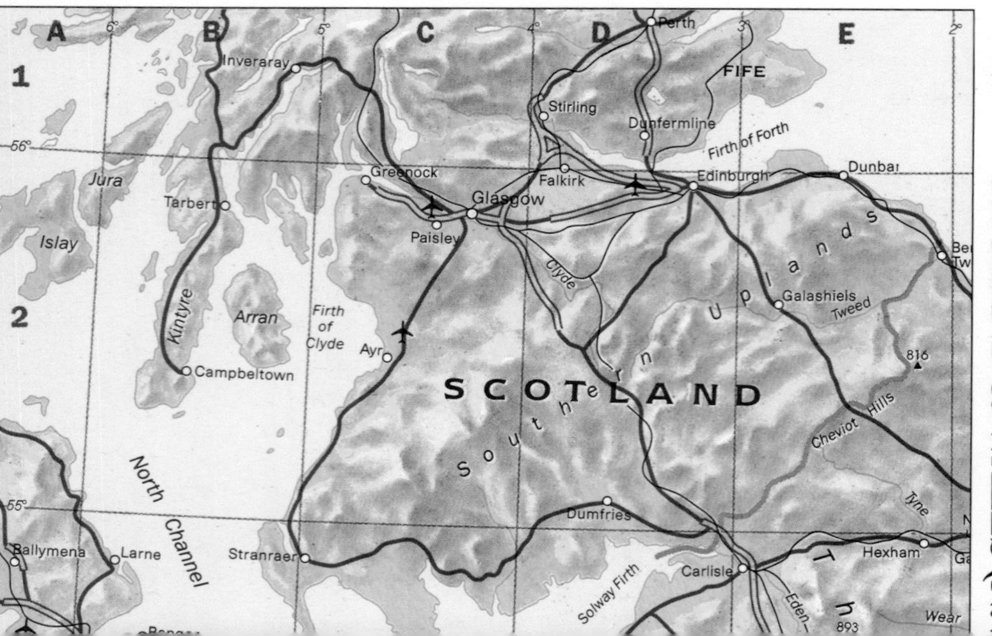
A
B
C
D
E
1
2
6°
5°
4°
3°
2°
56°
55°
Perth
FIFE
Stirling
Dunfermline
Firth of Forth
Inveraray
Jura
Tarbert
Islay
Greenock
Falkirk
Edinburgh
Dunbar
Glasgow
Paisley
Clyde
Kintyre
Arran
Firth of Clyde
Ayr
Campbeltown
Galashiels
Tweed
Southern Uplands
816
SCOTLAND
Cheviot Hills
Tyne
North Channel
Dumfries
Ballymena
Larne
Stranraer
Hexham
Carlisle
Solway Firth
Eden
Wear
893

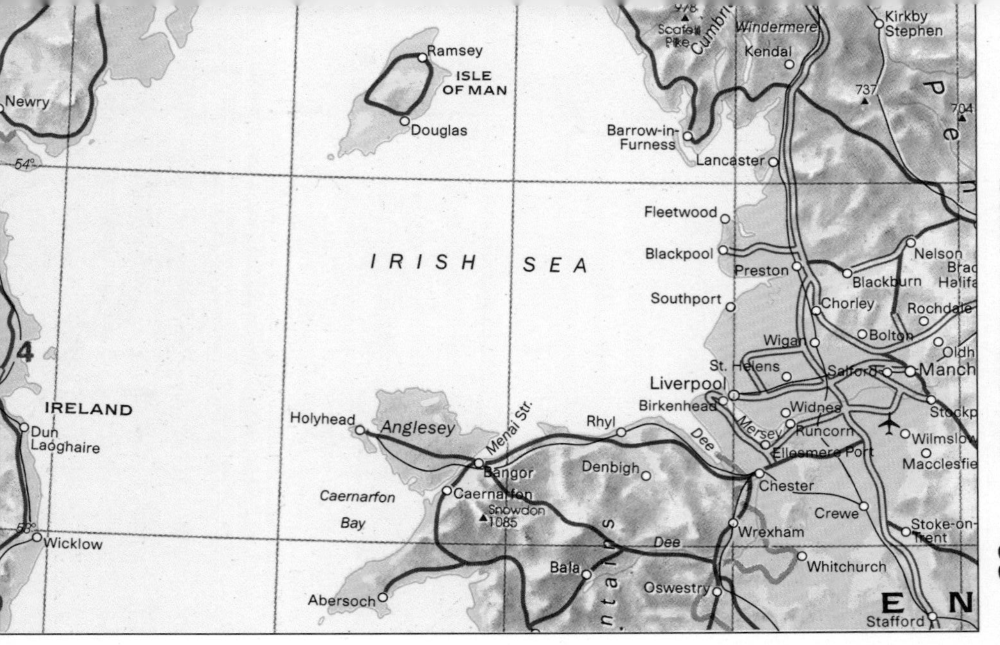
Ramsey
ISLE OF MAN
Douglas
Newry
Kendal
Windermere
Kirkby Stephen
737
704
Barrow-in-Furness
Lancaster
54°
Fleetwood
Blackpool
Preston
Nelson
Blackburn
IRISH SEA
Southport
Chorley
Rochdale
Bolton
Wigan
St. Helens
Salford
Liverpool
Birkenhead
Widnes
Mersey
Runcorn
Ellesmere Port
Wilmslow
IRELAND
Holyhead
Anglesey
Menai Str.
Rhyl
Dee
Dun Laoghaire
Bangor
Denbigh
Chester
Caernarfon
Caernarfon Bay
Snowdon
1085
Crewe
Wrexham
Stoke-on-Trent
Wicklow
Dee
Bala
Whitchurch
Oswestry
Abersoch
Stafford

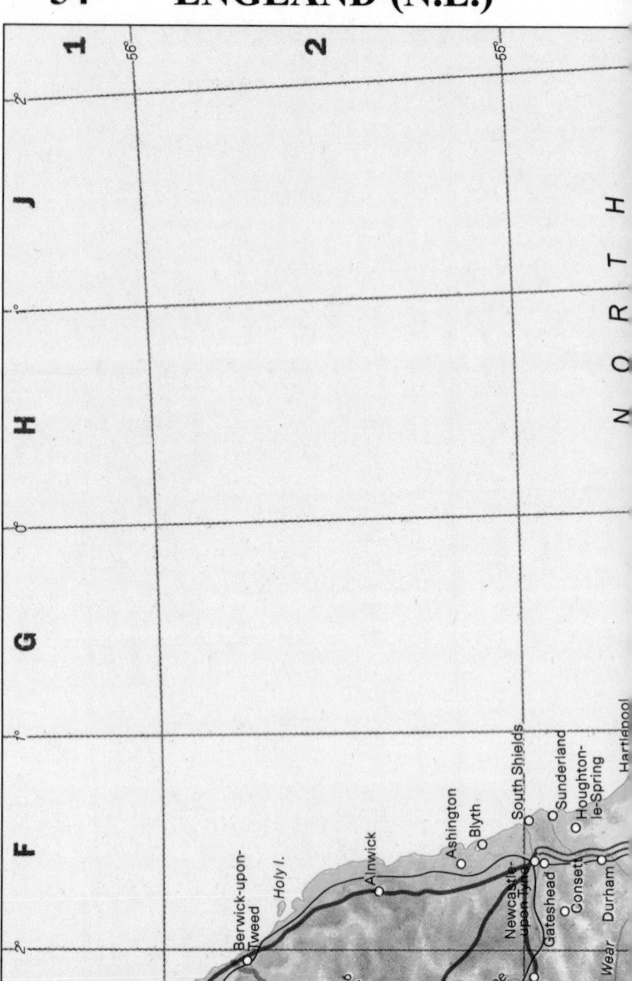

1
2
F
G
H
J
56°
55°
2°
1°
0°
1°
2°
N O R T H
Berwick-upon-Tweed
Holy I.
Alnwick
Ashington
Blyth
South Shields
Sunderland
Houghton-le-Spring
Hartlepool
Newcastle-upon-Tyne
Gateshead
Consett
Durham
Wear
Tyne
816

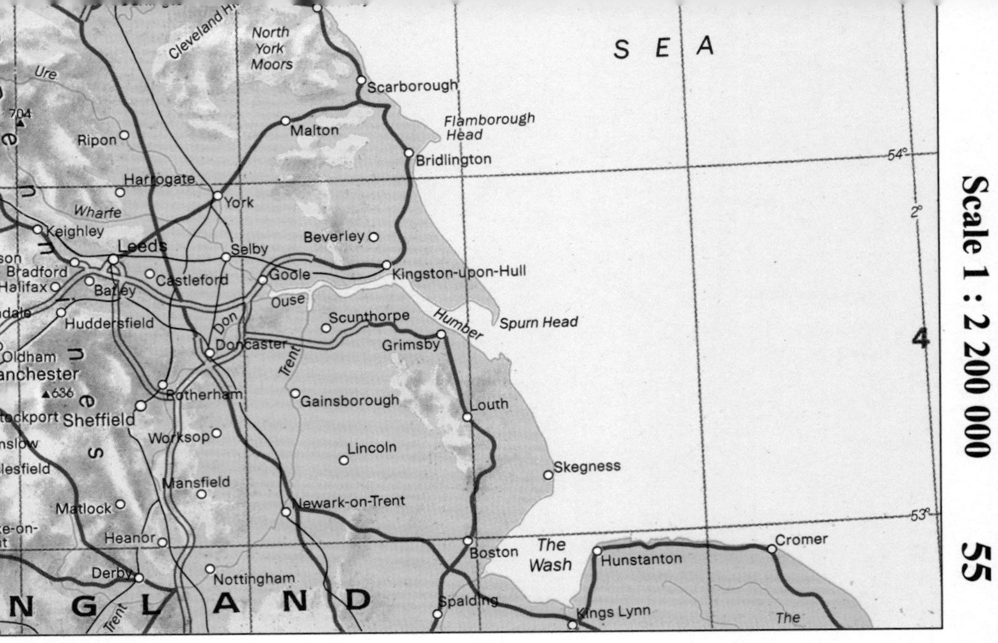

S E A
North York Moors
Ure
704
Ripon
Scarborough
Flamborough Head
Bridlington
54°
2°
4
53°
Malton
Harrogate
York
Wharfe
Keighley
Beverley
Leeds
Selby
Nelson
Bradford
Halifax
Batley
Castleford
Goole
Kingston-upon-Hull
Ouse
Rochdale
Huddersfield
Don
Scunthorpe
Humber
Spurn Head
Doncaster
Grimsby
Oldham
Trent
Manchester
636
Rotherham
Gainsborough
Louth
Stockport
Sheffield
Worksop
Lincoln
Wilmslow
Macclesfield
Skegness
Mansfield
Matlock
Newark-on-Trent
Stoke-on-Trent
Heanor
Boston
The Wash
Cromer
Hunstanton
Derby
Nottingham
N G L A N D
Spalding
Kings Lynn
P e n n i n e s

ENGLAND (S.E.)

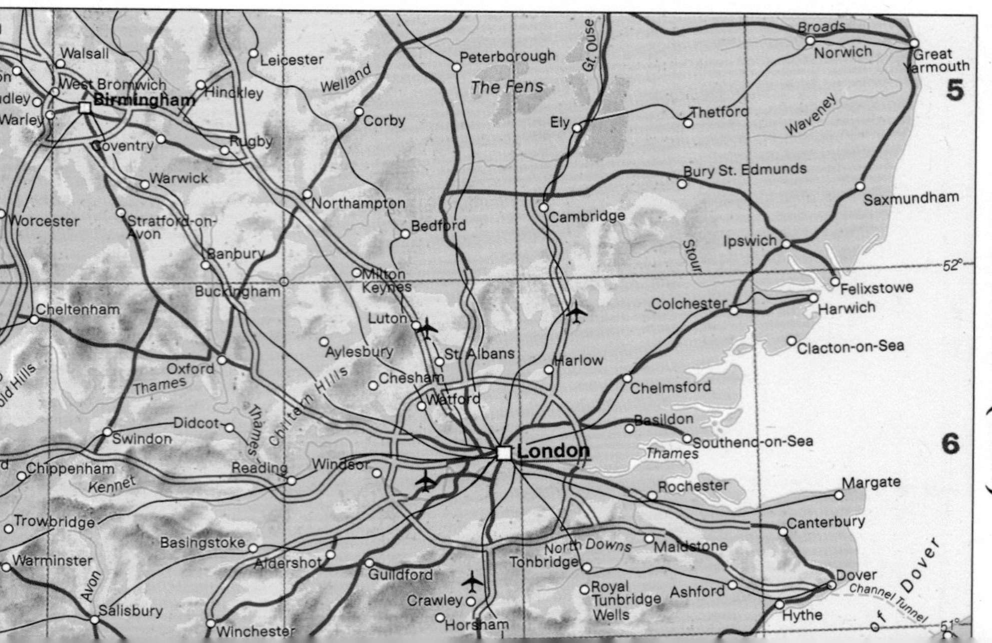
5
6
52°
51°
Walsall
West Bromwich
Birmingham
Warley
Hinckley
Leicester
Welland
Corby
Peterborough
The Fens
Gt. Ouse
Ely
Thetford
Broads
Norwich
Great Yarmouth
Waveney
Coventry
Rugby
Warwick
Northampton
Bury St. Edmunds
Saxmundham
Worcester
Stratford-on-Avon
Bedford
Cambridge
Ipswich
Stour
Banbury
Milton Keynes
Buckingham
Felixstowe
Harwich
Colchester
Cheltenham
Luton
Aylesbury
St. Albans
Harlow
Clacton-on-Sea
Oxford
Thames
Chiltern Hills
Chesham
Watford
Chelmsford
Didcot
Swindon
Basildon
Southend-on-Sea
London
Chippenham
Kennet
Reading
Windsor
Rochester
Margate
Trowbridge
Canterbury
Basingstoke
North Downs
Maidstone
Warminster
Aldershot
Guildford
Tonbridge
Dover
Royal Tunbridge Wells
Ashford
Avon
Crawley
Channel Tunnel
Salisbury
Horsham
Hythe
Winchester

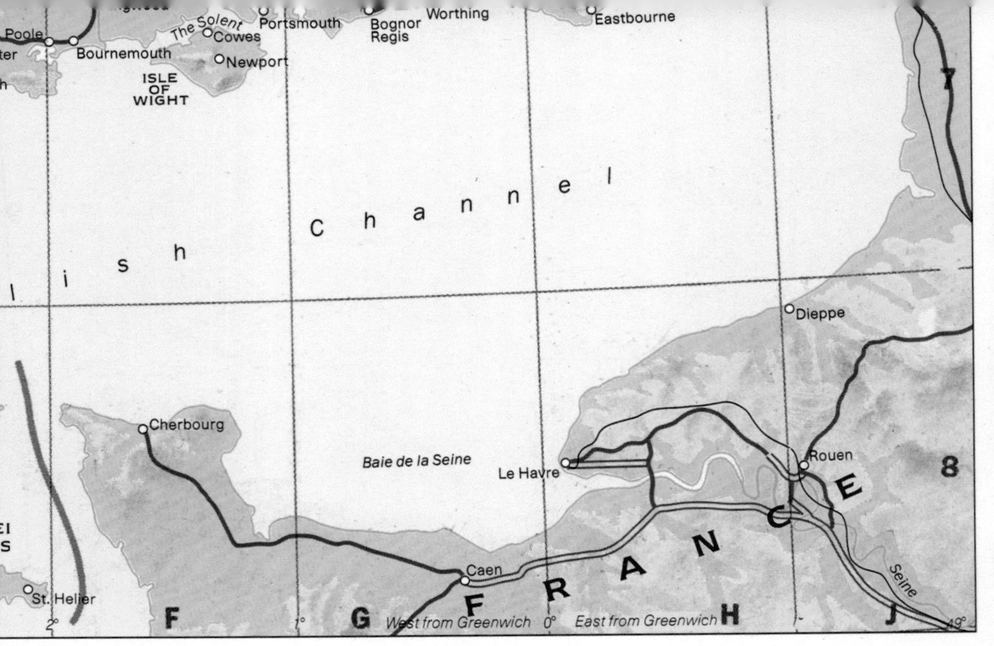
Poole
Bournemouth
The Solent
Cowes
Newport
ISLE OF WIGHT
Portsmouth
Bognor Regis
Worthing
Eastbourne
l i s h C h a n n e l
Dieppe
Cherbourg
Baie de la Seine
Le Havre
Rouen
Caen
Seine
St. Helier
F R A N C E
F
G
H
J
8
West from Greenwich 0° East from Greenwich

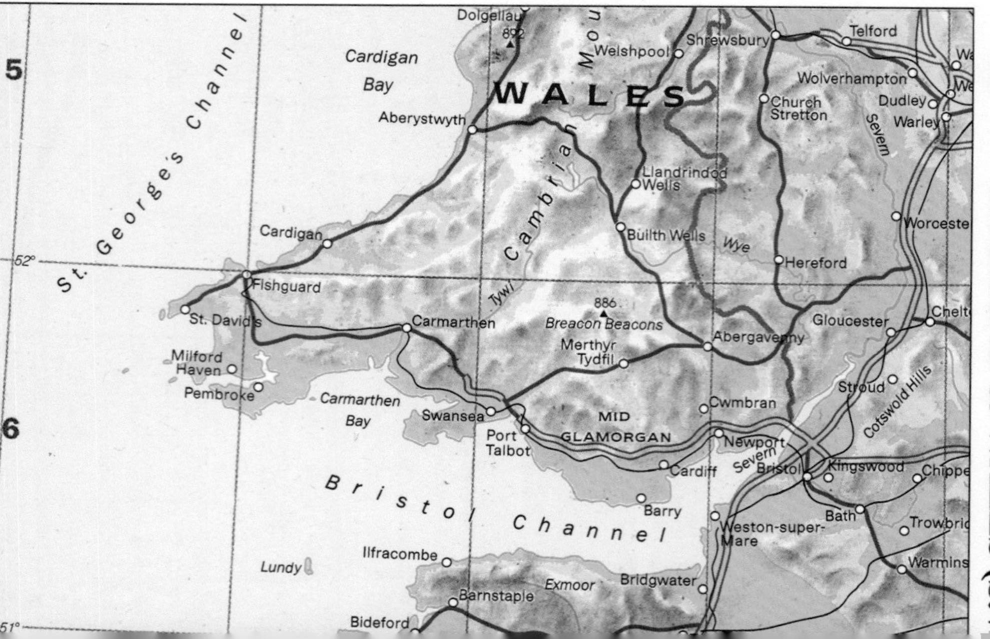
5
6
52°
51°
St. George's Channel
Cardigan Bay
Dolgellau
892
WALES
Cambrian Mountains
Aberystwyth
Cardigan
Fishguard
St. David's
Milford Haven
Pembroke
Carmarthen Bay
Carmarthen
Tywi
Swansea
Port Talbot
MID GLAMORGAN
886
Breacon Beacons
Merthyr Tydfil
Welshpool
Shrewsbury
Telford
Wolverhampton
Dudley
Warley
Severn
Church Stretton
Llandrindod Wells
Builth Wells
Wye
Hereford
Worcester
Abergavenny
Gloucester
Chelt
Stroud
Cotswold Hills
Cwmbran
Newport
Severn
Bristol
Kingswood
Chippe
Bath
Trowbrid
Warmins
Cardiff
Barry
Weston-super-Mare
Bristol Channel
Ilfracombe
Lundy
Exmoor
Bridgwater
Barnstaple
Bideford

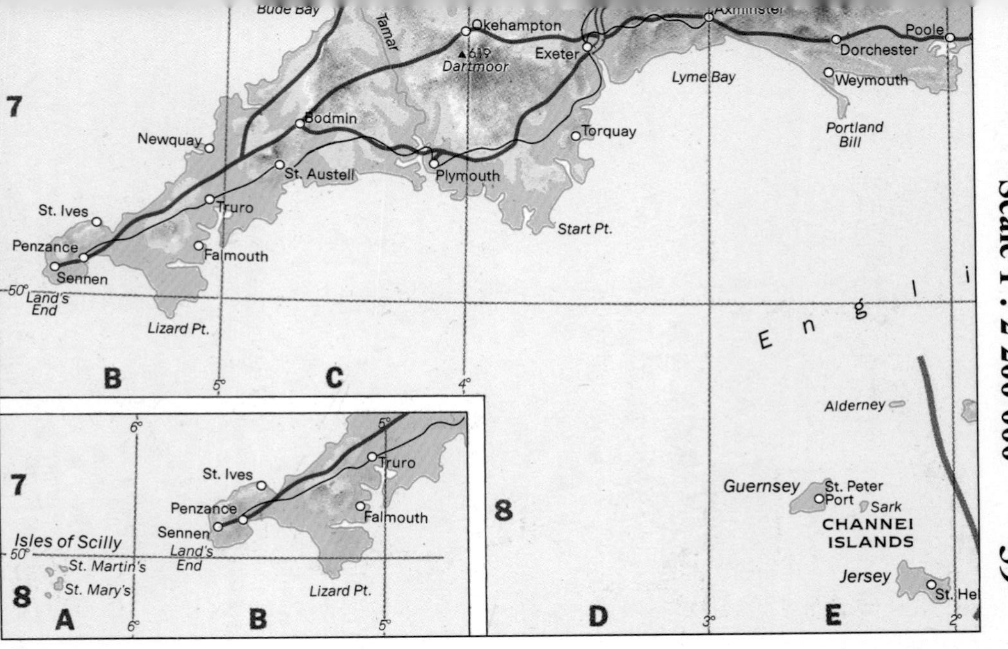
Bude Bay
Tamar
Okehampton
▲619
Dartmoor
Exeter
Poole
Dorchester
Weymouth
Lyme Bay
Portland Bill
Bodmin
Newquay
Torquay
St. Austell
Plymouth
St. Ives
Truro
Penzance
Falmouth
Sennen
Start Pt.
50°
Land's End
Lizard Pt.
E n g l i
B
C
5°
4°
7
Alderney
6°
St. Ives
Truro
Penzance
Falmouth
Sennen
Land's End
Isles of Scilly
St. Martin's
St. Mary's
Lizard Pt.
8
A
B
D
3°
E
2°
Guernsey
St. Peter Port
Sark
CHANNEL ISLANDS
Jersey
St. He

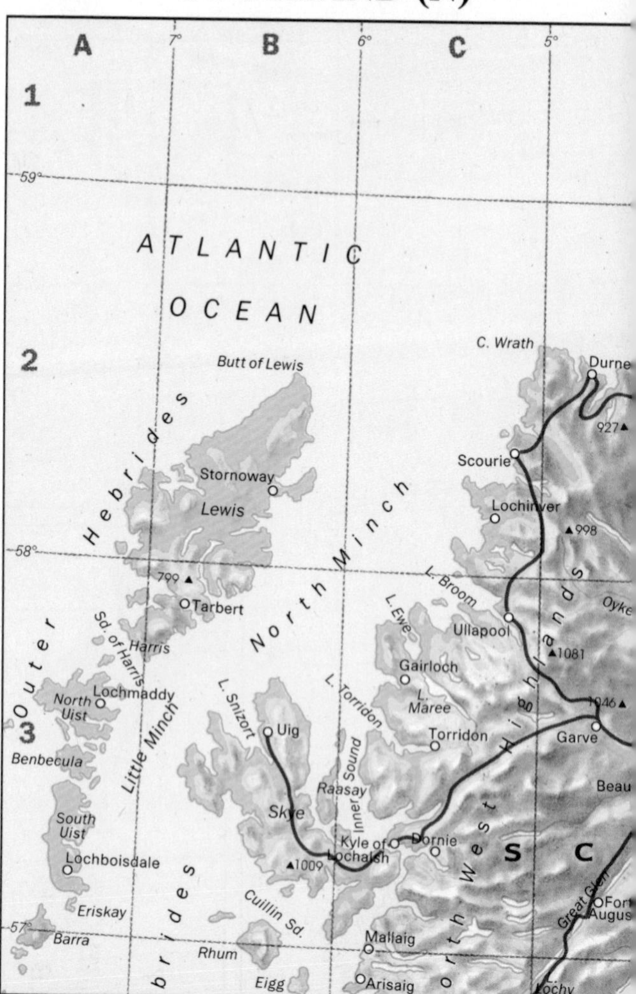
A
B
C
1
2
3
7°
6°
5°
59°
58°
57°
ATLANTIC
OCEAN
C. Wrath
Butt of Lewis
Stornoway
Lewis
Outer Hebrides
North Minch
Little Minch
Sd. of Harris
Harris
Tarbert
799
North Uist
Lochmaddy
Benbecula
South Uist
Lochboisdale
Eriskay
Barra
Hebrides
Rhum
Eigg
Cuillin Sd.
Skye
Uig
L. Snizort
Raasay
Inner Sound
L. Torridon
Torridon
Kyle of Lochalsh
Dornie
1009
Mallaig
Arisaig
Scourie
Lochinver
998
927
L. Broom
Ullapool
L. Ewe
Gairloch
L. Maree
North West Highlands
1081
1046
Garve
Beau
S
C
Great Glen
Fort Augus
Lochy
Durne
Oyke

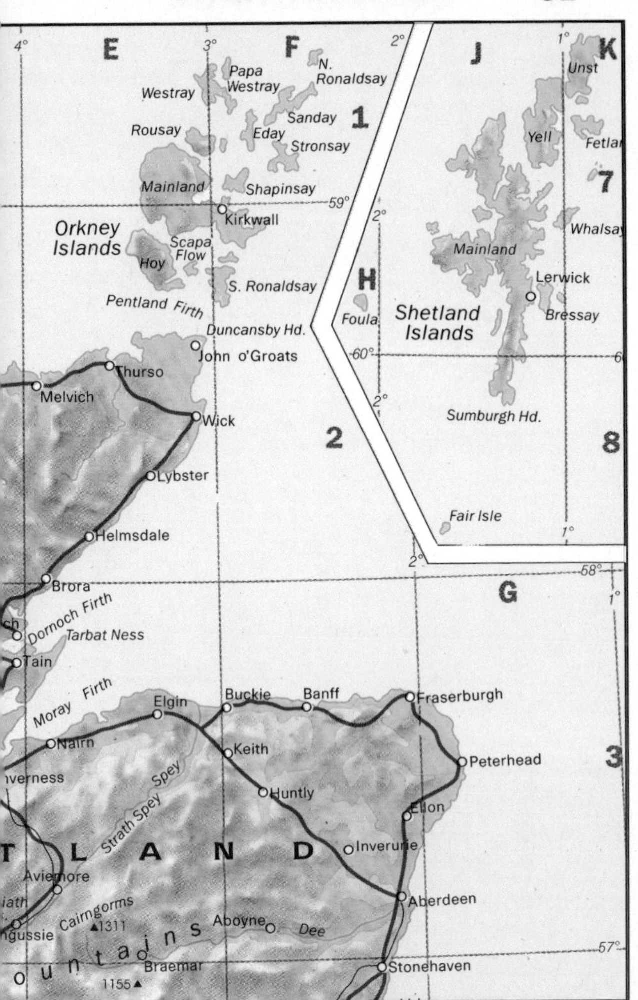
Papa Westray
N. Ronaldsay
Westray
Sanday
Rousay
Eday
Stronsay
Mainland
Shapinsay
Kirkwall
Orkney Islands
Scapa Flow
Hoy
S. Ronaldsay
Pentland Firth
Duncansby Hd.
John o'Groats
Thurso
Melvich
Wick
Lybster
Helmsdale
Brora
Dornoch Firth
Tarbat Ness
Tain
Moray Firth
Elgin
Buckie
Banff
Fraserburgh
Nairn
Keith
Peterhead
Spey
Huntly
Strath Spey
Ellon
Inverurie
Aviemore
Cairngorms
Aberdeen
Aboyne
Dee
Braemar
Stonehaven
Unst
Yell
Fetlar
Whalsay
Mainland
Lerwick
Foula
Shetland Islands
Bressay
Sumburgh Hd.
Fair Isle

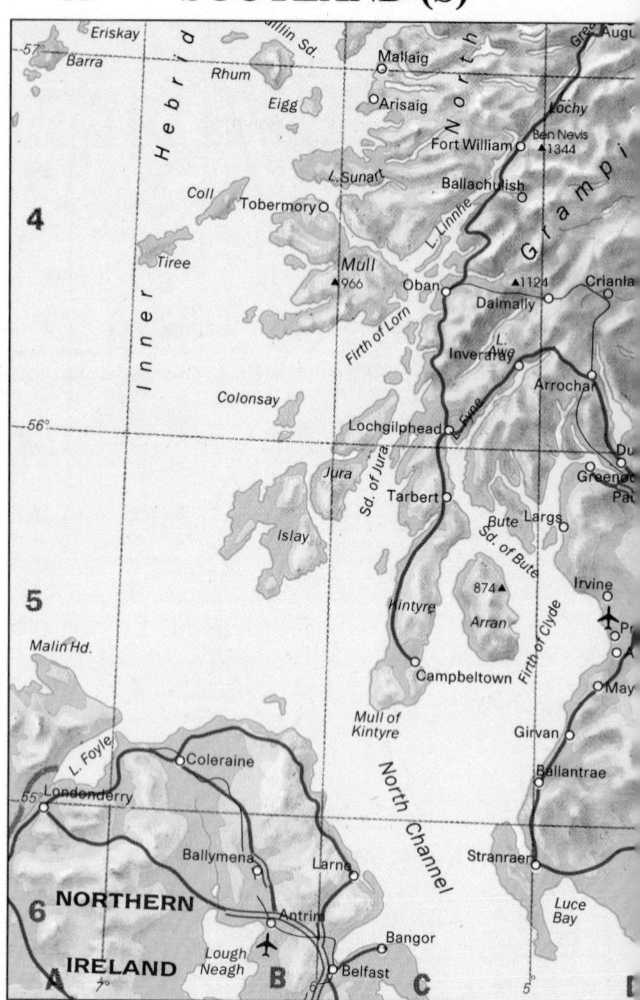

Eriskay
Barra
57°
Rhum
Eigg
Mallaig
Arisaig
Inner Hebrides
North
Lochy
Ben Nevis
1344
Fort William
L. Sunart
Ballachulish
Coll
Tobermory
L. Linnhe
Grampi
4
Tiree
Mull
966
Oban
1124
Dalmally
Firth of Lorn
L. Awe
Inveraray
Arrochar
Colonsay
56°
Lochgilphead
L. Fyne
Jura
Sd. of Jura
Tarbert
Islay
Bute
Largs
Sd. of Bute
874
Arran
Irvine
5
Kintyre
Firth of Clyde
Malin Hd.
Campbeltown
Mull of Kintyre
Girvan
L. Foyle
Coleraine
North Channel
Ballantrae
55°
Londonderry
Ballymena
Larne
Stranraer
6
NORTHERN
IRELAND
Antrim
Lough Neagh
Bangor
Belfast
Luce Bay
A
B
C
7°
6°
5°

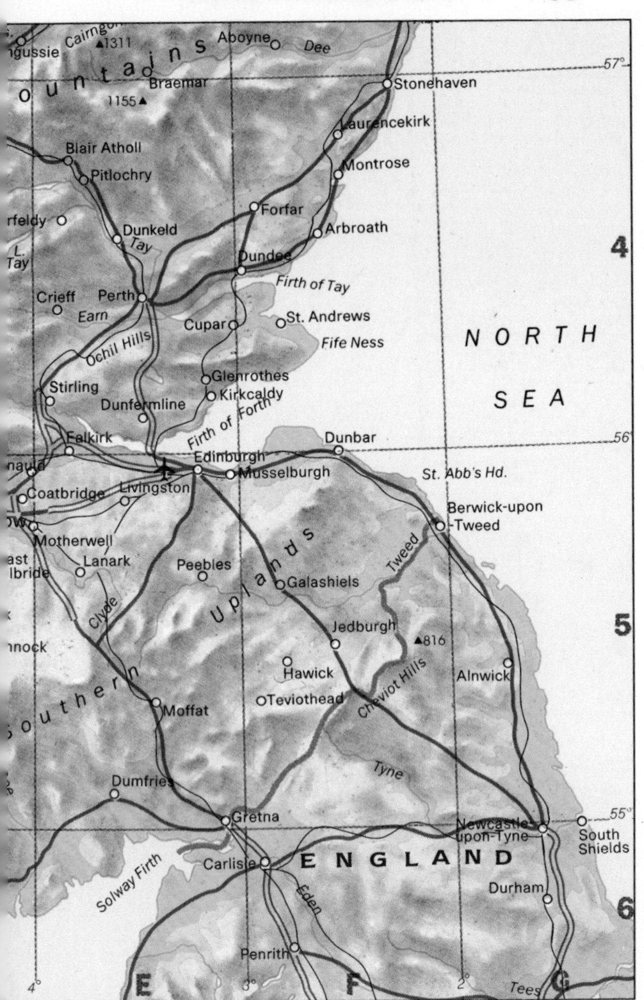
Cairngorm
1311
Aboyne
Dee
Mountains
Braemar
1155
57°
Stonehaven
Laurencekirk
Blair Atholl
Pitlochry
Montrose
Forfar
Dunkeld
Tay
Arbroath
Dundee
Firth of Tay
Crieff
Perth
Earn
Cupar
St. Andrews
Fife Ness
Ochil Hills
NORTH
SEA
Glenrothes
Kirkcaldy
Stirling
Dunfermline
Firth of Forth
Falkirk
Dunbar
56°
Edinburgh
Musselburgh
St. Abb's Hd.
Coatbridge
Livingston
Berwick-upon-Tweed
Motherwell
Lanark
Peebles
Southern Uplands
Tweed
Galashiels
Clyde
Jedburgh
816
Hawick
Alnwick
Teviothead
Cheviot Hills
Moffat
Tyne
Dumfries
Gretna
55°
Newcastle-upon-Tyne
South Shields
Solway Firth
Carlisle
ENGLAND
Eden
Durham
Penrith
Tees
4°
3°
2°
E
F
G
4
5
6

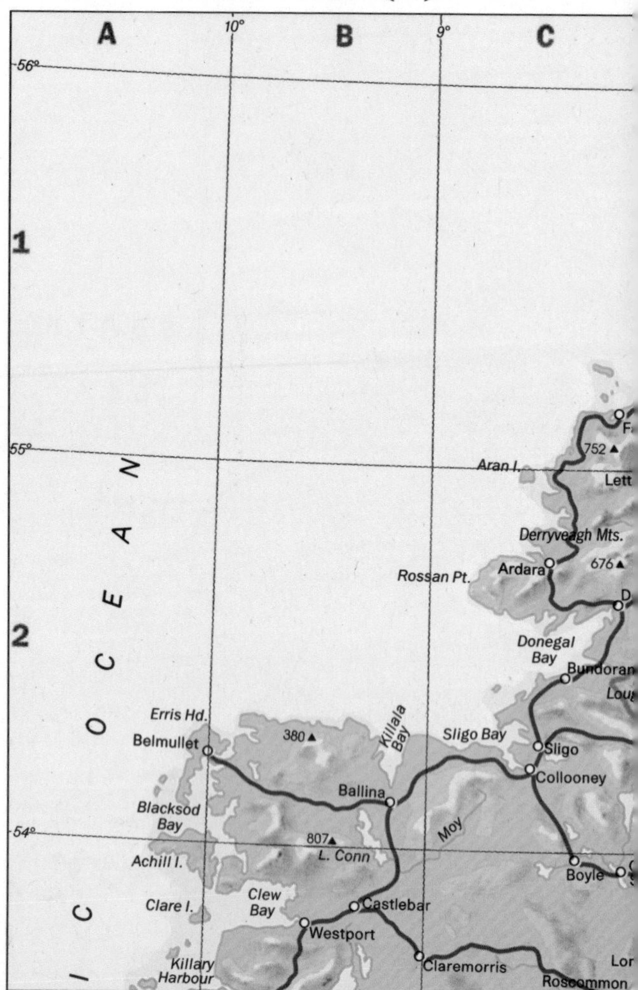
A
B
C
10°
9°
56°
55°
54°
1
2
OCEAN
Aran I.
752
Derryveagh Mts.
676
Ardara
Rossan Pt.
Donegal Bay
Bundoran
Erris Hd.
Belmullet
380
Killala Bay
Sligo Bay
Sligo
Collooney
Ballina
Blacksod Bay
Moy
807
L. Conn
Achill I.
Boyle
Clew Bay
Clare I.
Castlebar
Westport
Claremorris
Killary Harbour
Roscommon

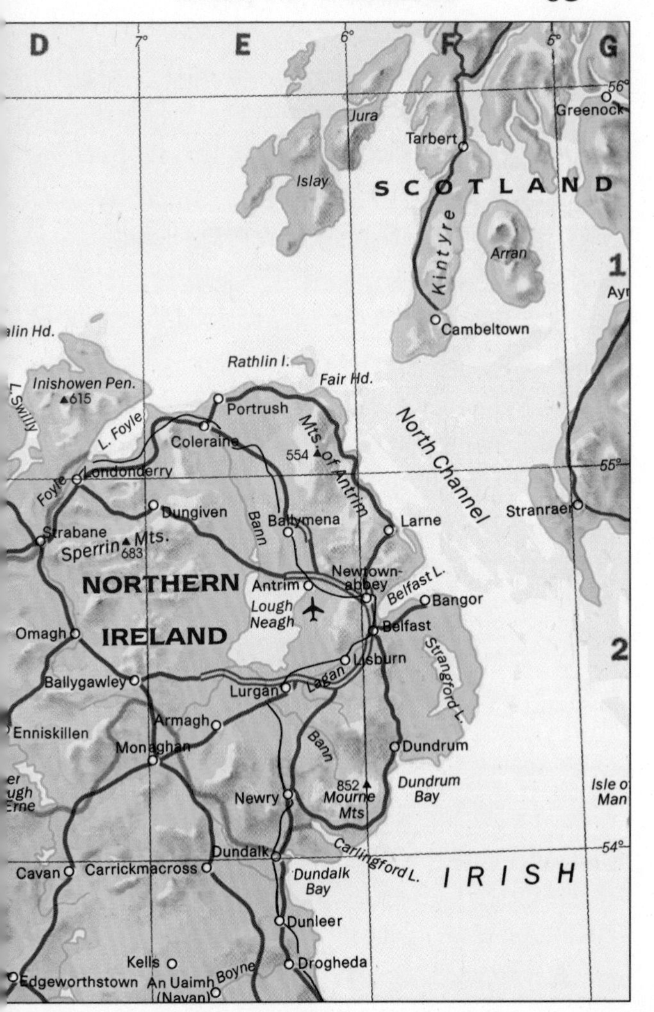
D
E
F
G
7°
6°
5°
56°
55°
54°
1
2
Jura
Greenock
Tarbert
Islay
SCOTLAND
Kintyre
Arran
Ayr
Cambeltown
alin Hd.
Rathlin I.
Fair Hd.
Inishowen Pen.
615
L. Swilly
L. Foyle
Portrush
Coleraine
Mts. of Antrim
554
North Channel
Londonderry
Foyle
Dungiven
Bann
Ballymena
Larne
Stranraer
Strabane
Sperrin Mts.
683
NORTHERN
IRELAND
Antrim
Newtown-abbey
Belfast L.
Bangor
Lough Neagh
Belfast
Omagh
Lisburn
Strangford L.
Ballygawley
Lurgan
Lagan
Armagh
Enniskillen
Monaghan
Bann
Dundrum
852
Mourne Mts
Dundrum Bay
Isle of Man
Newry
Dundalk
Carlingford L.
Cavan
Carrickmacross
Dundalk Bay
IRISH
Dunleer
Kells
Drogheda
Edgeworthstown
An Uaimh (Navan)
Boyne

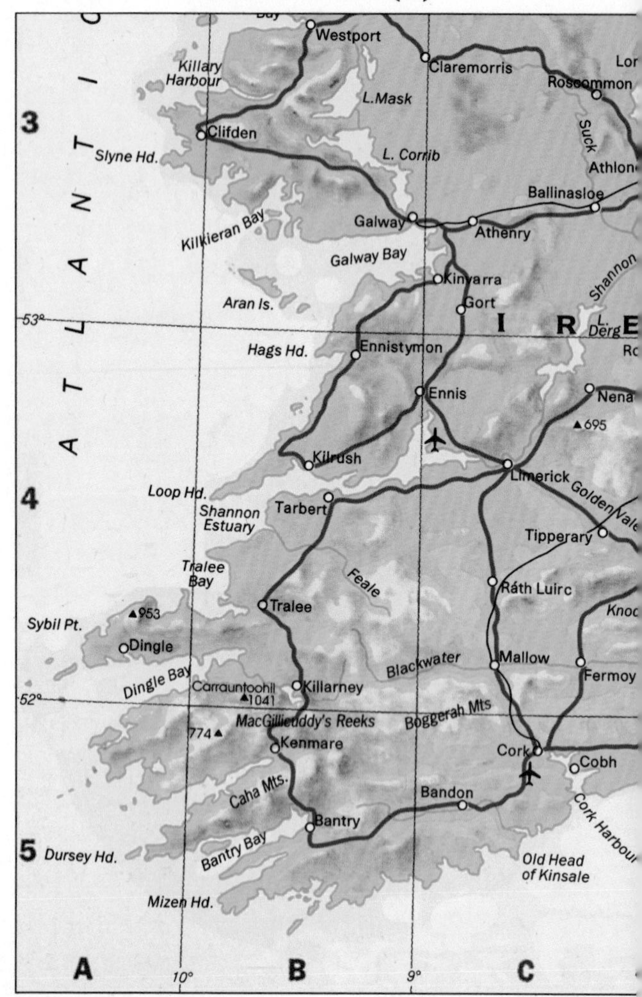

Westport
Claremorris
Roscommon
Killary Harbour
L. Mask
Clifden
Slyne Hd.
L. Corrib
Suck
Ballinasloe
Galway
Athenry
Kilkieran Bay
Galway Bay
Shannon
Kinvarra
Aran Is.
Gort
L. Derg
Hags Hd.
Ennistymon
Ennis
695
Kilrush
Limerick
Golden Vale
Loop Hd.
Tarbert
Shannon Estuary
Tipperary
Tralee Bay
Feale
Ráth Luirc
Tralee
Sybil Pt.
953
Dingle
Blackwater
Mallow
Fermoy
Dingle Bay
Carrauntoohil
1041
Killarney
MacGillicuddy's Reeks
Boggerah Mts
774
Kenmare
Cork
Cobh
Caha Mts.
Bandon
Cork Harbour
Bantry
Dursey Hd.
Bantry Bay
Old Head of Kinsale
Mizen Hd.
A T L A N T I
I R E
53°
52°
10°
9°
3
4
5
A
B
C

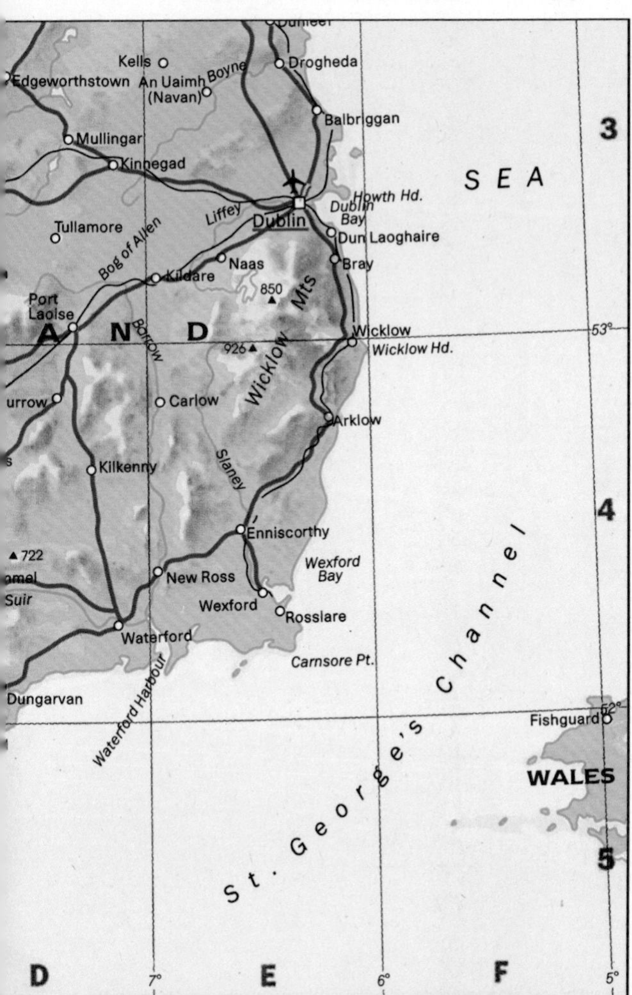
Drogheda
Kells
Edgeworthstown
An Uaimh
(Navan)
Boyne
Balbriggan
Mullingar
Kinnegad
SEA
Howth Hd.
Dublin Bay
Dublin
Liffey
Tullamore
Bog of Allen
Dun Laoghaire
Naas
Bray
Kildare
850
Wicklow Mts
Port Laoise
A N D
Barrow
Wicklow
Wicklow Hd.
926
53°
Carlow
Arklow
Kilkenny
Slaney
Enniscorthy
722
Wexford Bay
New Ross
Suir
Wexford
Rosslare
Waterford
Carnsore Pt.
Waterford Harbour
Dungarvan
St. George's Channel
Fishguard
52°
WALES
3
4
5
D
E
F
7°
6°
5°

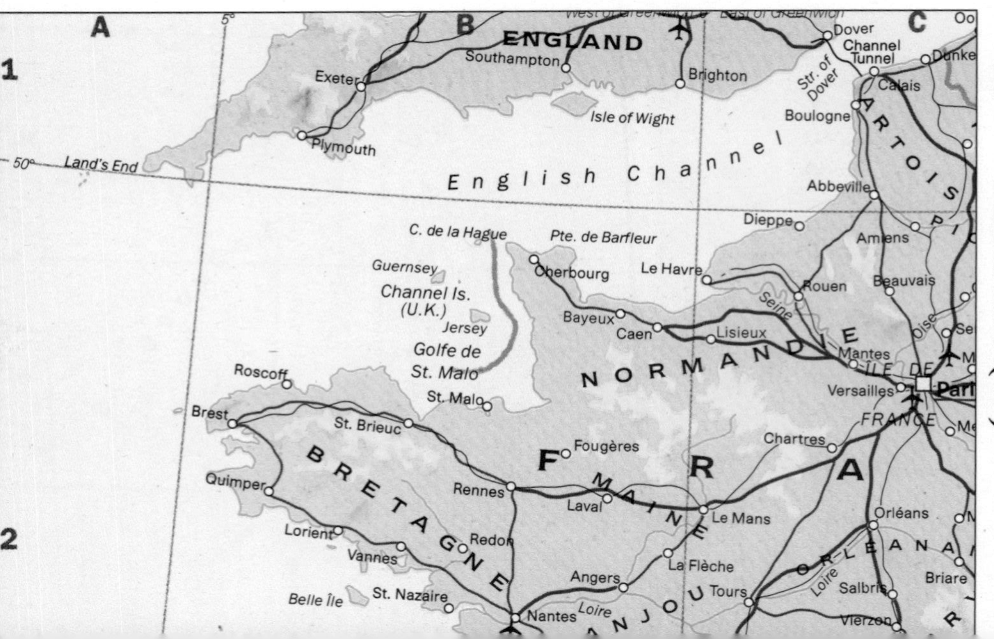
A
B
C
1
2
5°
50°
ENGLAND
Exeter
Plymouth
Land's End
Southampton
Brighton
Isle of Wight
Dover
Channel Tunnel
Str. of Dover
Calais
Boulogne
ARTOIS
English Channel
Abbeville
Dieppe
Amiens
Beauvais
Rouen
Seine
Oise
C. de la Hague
Pte. de Barfleur
Guernsey
Channel Is. (U.K.)
Jersey
Golfe de St. Malo
Cherbourg
Le Havre
Bayeux
Caen
Lisieux
NORMANDIE
Mantes
ÎLE DE FRANCE
Versailles
Roscoff
St. Malo
Brest
St. Brieuc
Fougères
Chartres
F R A
BRETAGNE
Quimper
Rennes
MAINE
Laval
Le Mans
Orléans
ORLÉANAIS
Lorient
Redon
Vannes
La Flèche
Angers
Briare
Loire
Salbris
Belle Île
St. Nazaire
ANJOU
Tours
Nantes
Vierzon

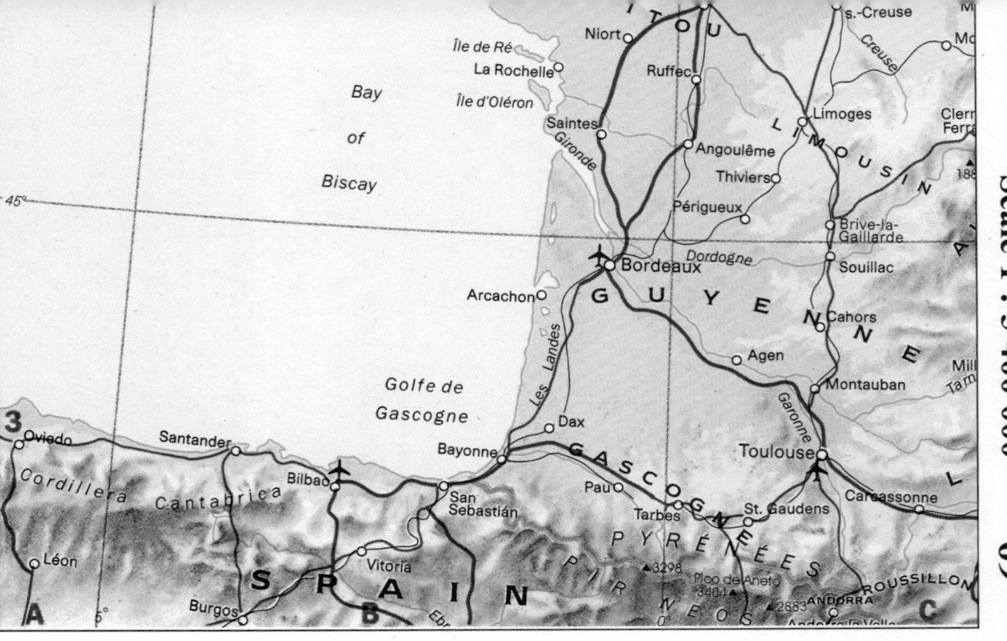
Bay
of
Biscay
Golfe de
Gascogne
Île de Ré
La Rochelle
Île d'Oléron
Niort
Saintes
Gironde
Ruffec
Angoulême
Limoges
Creuse
Thiviers
Périgueux
Bordeaux
Dordogne
Arcachon
Les Landes
Dax
Bayonne
Brive-la-Gaillarde
Souillac
Cahors
Montauban
Agen
Garonne
Toulouse
Carcassonne
St. Gaudens
Tarbes
Pau
San Sebastián
Vitoria
Bilbao
Santander
Burgos
Oviedo
Léon
Cordillera Cantabrica
Pico de Aneto
3404
3298
2883
ANDORRA
ROUSSILLON
LIMOUSIN
GUYENNE
GASCOGNE
PYRÉNÉES
PIRINEOS
SPAIN
Ebro
Tarn
45°
0°
5°
3
A
B
C

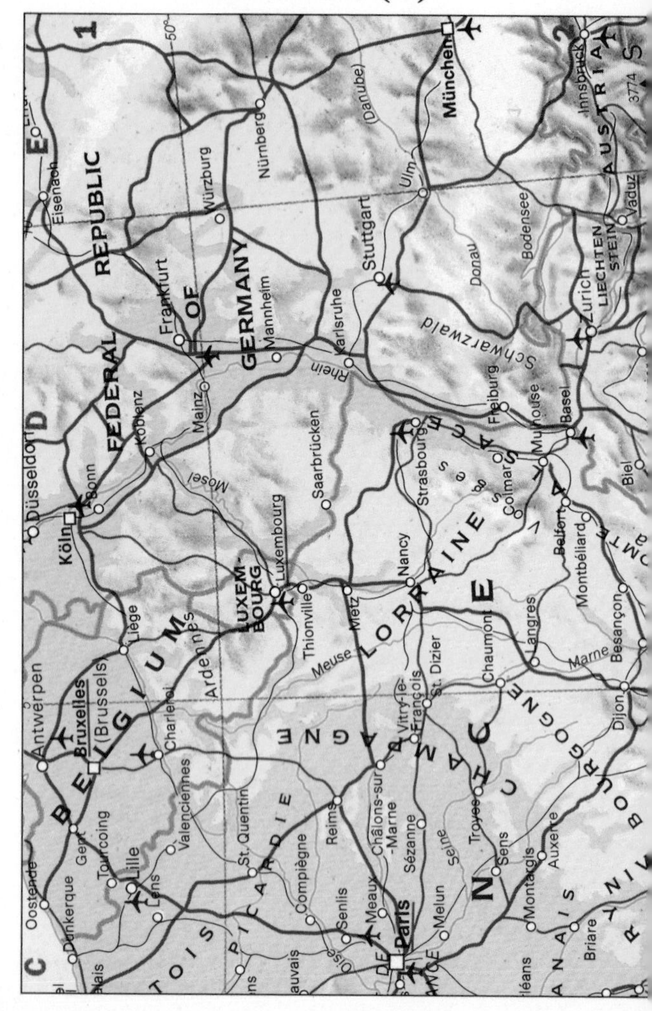

FEDERAL REPUBLIC OF GERMANY
BELGIUM
LUXEMBOURG
LORRAINE
ALSACE
CHAMPAGNE
PICARDIE
BOURGOGNE
AUSTRIA
LIECHTENSTEIN
München
Nürnberg
Würzburg
Eisenach
Frankfurt
Mannheim
Stuttgart
Ulm
Karlsruhe
Mainz
Koblenz
Bonn
Köln
Düsseldorf
Saarbrücken
Luxembourg
Thionville
Metz
Nancy
Strasbourg
Colmar
Freiburg
Mulhouse
Basel
Belfort
Montbéliard
Besançon
Biel
Zurich
Vaduz
Innsbruck
Bodensee
Donau
(Danube)
Schwarzwald
Rhein
Mosel
Meuse
Marne
Seine
Oise
Ardennes
Vosges
Liège
Antwerpen
Bruxelles
(Brussels)
Charleroi
Gent
Oostende
Dunkerque
Tourcoing
Lille
Lens
Valenciennes
St. Quentin
Compiègne
Senlis
Reims
Châlons-sur-Marne
Vitry-le-François
St. Dizier
Chaumont
Langres
Dijon
Sézanne
Troyes
Sens
Auxerre
Montargis
Briare
Meaux
Paris
Melun
3774

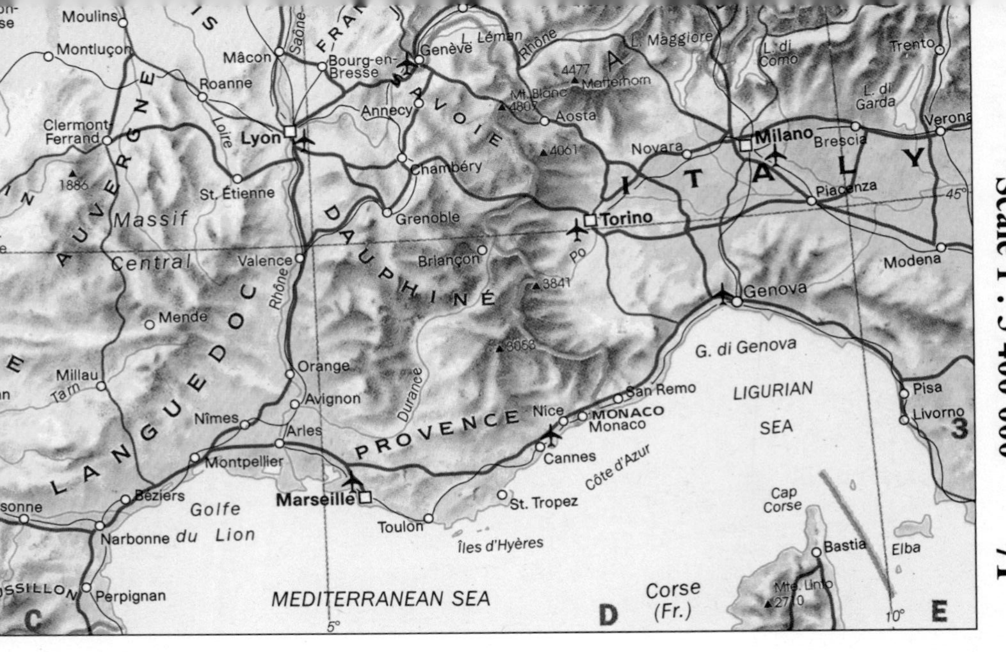
ITALY
FRANCE
SAVOIE
DAUPHINÉ
PROVENCE
LANGUEDOC
AUVERGNE
Massif Central
LIGURIAN SEA
MEDITERRANEAN SEA
Golfe du Lion
G. di Genova
Corse (Fr.)
Côte d'Azur
Îles d'Hyères
Cap Corse
Elba
Bastia
Mte. Cinto 2710
Milano
Torino
Lyon
Marseille
Genova
Brescia
Verona
Trento
Modena
Piacenza
Novara
Pisa
Livorno
L. di Garda
L. di Como
L. Maggiore
Matterhorn 4477
Mt. Blanc 4807
4061
3841
3058
1886
Aosta
L. Léman
Genève
Rhône
Annecy
Chambéry
Grenoble
Briançon
Bourg-en-Bresse
Saône
Mâcon
Roanne
Loire
St. Étienne
Valence
Orange
Avignon
Arles
Nîmes
Montpellier
Béziers
Narbonne
Perpignan
Mende
Millau
Tarn
Clermont-Ferrand
Montluçon
Moulins
Durance
Po
Toulon
St. Tropez
Cannes
Nice
MONACO
Monaco
San Remo
45°
5°
10°
3
C
D
E

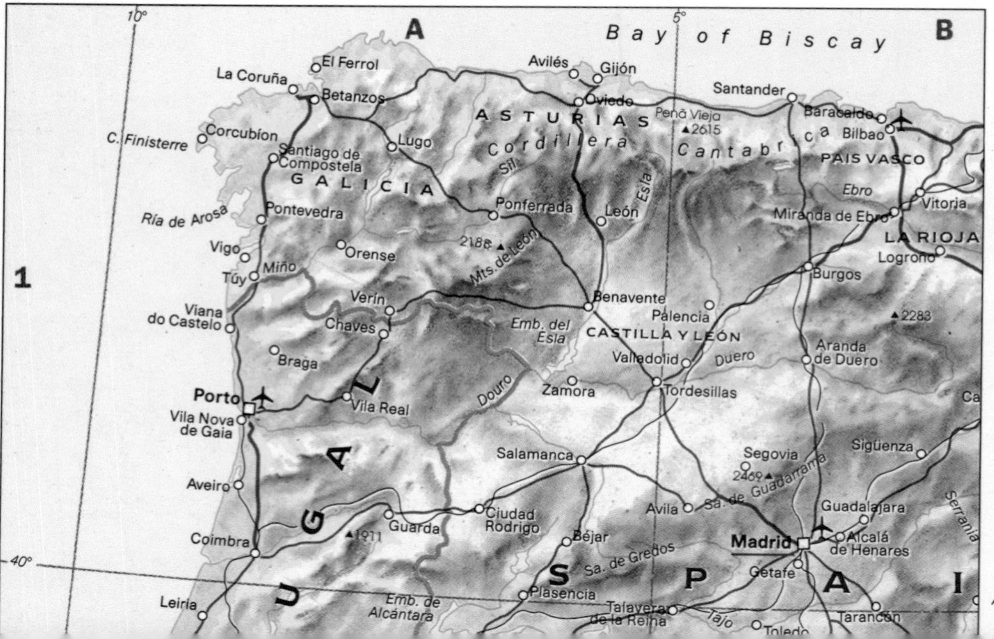
Bay of Biscay
A
B
1
ASTURIAS
Cordillera Cantabrica
PAIS VASCO
LA RIOJA
GALICIA
CASTILLA Y LEÓN
PORTUGAL
SPAI
El Ferrol
La Coruña
Betanzos
Avilés
Gijón
Oviedo
Santander
Baracaldo
Bilbao
Peña Vieja
2615
C. Finisterre
Corcubíon
Lugo
Santiago de Compostela
Sil
Esla
Ebro
Vitoria
Miranda de Ebro
Ría de Arosa
Pontevedra
Ponferrada
León
Logroño
Vigo
Orense
2188
Mts. de León
Miño
Túy
Burgos
Benavente
Palencia
2283
Viana do Castelo
Verín
Chaves
Emb. del Esla
Aranda de Duero
Valladolid
Duero
Braga
Zamora
Tordesillas
Douro
Porto
Vila Real
Vila Nova de Gaia
Ca
Salamanca
Segovia
Sigüenza
2469
Sa. de Guadarrama
Aveiro
Avila
Guadalajara
Serrania
Ciudad Rodrigo
Guarda
1911
Coimbra
Béjar
Madrid
Alcalá de Henares
Sa. de Gredos
40°
Getafe
Leiria
Emb. de Alcántara
Plasencia
Talavera de la Reina
Tajo
Toledo
Tarancón
10°
5°

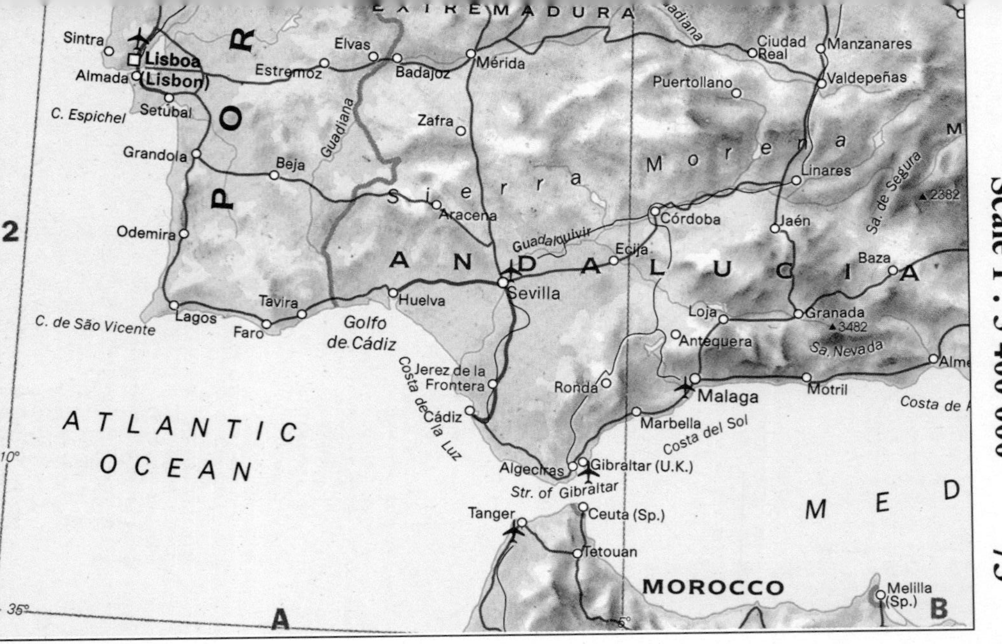
Sintra
Lisboa
(Lisbon)
Almada
Setúbal
C. Espichel
Grandola
Odemira
C. de São Vicente
Lagos
Faro
Tavira
Beja
Estremoz
Elvas
Badajoz
Guadiana
Zafra
Mérida
Aracena
Huelva
Golfo
de Cádiz
Sevilla
Guadalquivir
Jerez de la
Frontera
Cádiz
Costa de la Luz
Ecija
Córdoba
Puertollano
Ciudad
Real
Manzanares
Valdepeñas
Linares
Jaén
Granada
Baza
Sa. de Segura
2382
3482
Sa. Nevada
Motril
Loja
Antequera
Malaga
Marbella
Costa del Sol
Ronda
Gibraltar (U.K.)
Algeciras
Str. of Gibraltar
Tanger
Ceuta (Sp.)
Tetouan
MOROCCO
Melilla
(Sp.)
ATLANTIC
OCEAN
Sierra Morena
ANDALUCIA
EXTREMADURA
POR
MED
10°
35°
5°
2
A
B

B
C
D
1
0°
5°
40°
Toulouse
FRANCE
GASCOGNE
Montpellier
Nîmes
Marseille
Golfe du Lion
Narbonne
Perpignan
ROUSSILLON
ANDORRA
Andorra la Vella
2883
Bayonne
San Sebastián
Pamplona
Vitoria
RIOJA
NAVARRA
PYRÉNÉES
PIRINEOS
3298
Pico de Aneto 3404
Viella
C. Creus
Costa Brava
Figueras
Gerona
CATALUÑA
Calahorra
Tudela
Ebro
2283
Cinca
ARAGÓN
Zaragoza
Fraga
Lérida
Tarrasa
Sabadell
Badalona
Barcelona
Calatayud
Valls
Caspe
Tarragona
Daroca
Ebro
Alcañiz
Tortosa
Amposta
C. de Tortosa
Costa Dorada
Monreal del Campo
Serranía de Cuenca
Tajo
Teruel
2019
Benicarló
Sarrión
Cuenca
Castellón de la Plana
Menorca (Minorca)
Mahón
Mallorca (Majorca)

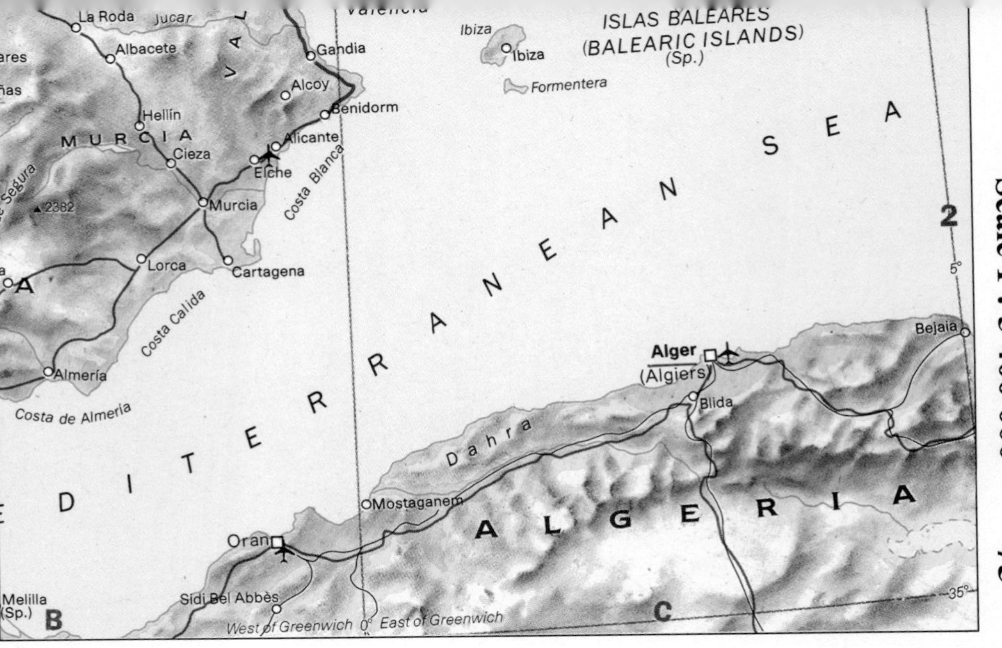
ISLAS BALEARES
(BALEARIC ISLANDS)
(Sp.)
Ibiza
Ibiza
Formentera
MEDITERRANEAN SEA
La Roda
Jucar
Albacete
Gandia
Alcoy
Benidorm
Hellín
MURCIA
Cieza
Alicante
Elche
Costa Blanca
Murcia
2382
Lorca
Cartagena
Costa Calida
Almería
Costa de Almería
Alger
(Algiers)
Blida
Bejaia
Dahra
Mostaganem
Oran
ALGERIA
Sidi Bel Abbès
Melilla
(Sp.)
West of Greenwich 0° East of Greenwich
5°
35°
2
B
C

A
B
1
2
Dijon
FRANCHE-COMTE
Jura
Biel
Zurich
Luzern
Bern
LIECHTENSTEIN
Vaduz
Rhein
SWITZERLAND
Mâcon
Saône
Lausanne
L. Léman
Genève
Rhône
Domodossola
Lyon
SAVOIE
Mt Blanc 4807
4477
Matterhorn
L. Maggiore
L. di Como
Aosta
Como
4061
Monza
Bergamo
FRANCE
Novara
Milano
Brescia
45°
Grenoble
Valence
DAUPHINÉ
Torino
Po
Piacenza
Alessandria
Rhône
Mondovi
Cuneo
Genova
Avignon
Savona
Durance
G. di Genova
La Spezia
PROVENCE
Nice
San Remo
Massa
Monaco
MONACO
LIGURIAN SEA
Marseille
Cannes
Pisa
Toulon
St. Tropez
Cecina
C. Corse
Piombino
Bastia
Elba
Calvi
Mt. Cinto 2710
Ajaccio
Cateraggio
CORSE (Fr.)
Porto Vecchio
Strait of Bonifacio
Porto

Salzburg
Bruck an der Mur
Graz
AUSTRIA
Brenner P.
3798 Grossglockner
3342
Dolomiti
Adige
Rovereto
Villach
Tarvisio
Klagenfurt
Maribor
Nagykanizsa
Varazdin
Kranj
Ljubljana
Udine
Sava
SLOVENIA
Zagreb
Monfalcone
Treviso
Vicenza
Padova
Venezia
Trieste
Karlovac
Sisak
Vrbovsko
Rijeka
CROATIA
G. di Venezia
Istra
Rovigo
Po
Krk
Senj
Ferrara
Pula
Cres
Rab
Banja Luka
Reno
Bologna
Ravenna
Lošinj
Karlobag
Gospić
Pag
Jajce
Forli
Rimini
SAN MARINO
San Marino
Prato
Fano
Zadar
Dugi
Firenze
Kornat
Šibenik
Livno
Ancona
Citta di Castello
Arezzo
Siena
Civitanova Marche
Split
Brač
Makarska
Perugia
San Benedetto del Tronto
Vis
Hvar
1738
Foligno
Korčula
Grosseto
Terni
Lastovo
Tevere
Viterbo
Pescara
L'Aquila
Vasto
Termoli
ADRIATIC
Roma (Rome)
Avezzano
Ostia
Frosinone
S. Severo
Manfredonia
Cassino
2050
Latina
Foggia
Barletta
Formia

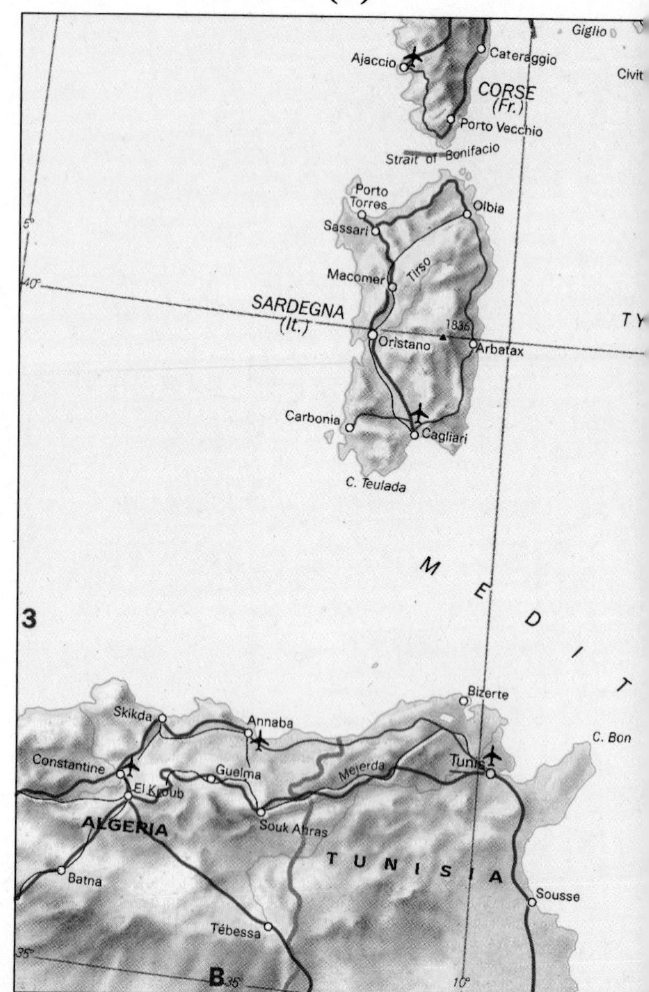
Giglio
Cateraggio
Ajaccio
Civit
CORSE
(Fr.)
Porto Vecchio
Strait of Bonifacio
Porto
Torres
Olbia
Sassari
5°
Tirso
Macomer
40°
SARDEGNA
(It.)
1835
TY
Oristano
Arbatax
Carbonia
Cagliari
C. Teulada
M
E
D
I
T
3
Bizerte
Skikda
Annaba
C. Bon
Constantine
Guelma
Mejerda
Tunis
El Kroub
ALGERIA
Souk Ahras
TUNISIA
Batna
Sousse
Tébessa
35°
B
10°

Pescara
L'Aquila
Vasto
Termoli
Kotor
Roma
(Rome)
Avezzano
Ostia
Frosinone
Latina
Cassino
2050
S. Severo
Manfredonia
Foggia
Barletta
Formia
Caserta
Benevento
Cerignola
Bari
Monopoli
Napoli
Avellino
Ischia
Vesuvio
1277
Salerno
Potenza
Brindisi
Capri
Sorrento
Eboli
Polia
Taranto
Agropoli
IAN SEA
Sapri
Golfo
di
Taranto
Gallipoli
G. di Policastro
2248
Castrovillari
Corigliano
C. Sta Maria
di Leuca
Cosenza
1929
Crotone
C. Rizzuto
Vibo
Valentia
Catanzaro
1423
I. Lipari
(Eolie)
Palmi
Messina
Locri
Palermo
Reggio di
Calabria
IONIAN
Cefalù
Mti Nebrodi
Str. di Messina
C. Spartivento
Mt. Etna
3323
Enna
SICILIA
Catania
Agrigento
Gela
Siracusa
C. Passero
Malta Channel
Gozo
MALTA
Valletta
Linosa (It.)
Lampedusa (It.)
SEA
C
15°
D

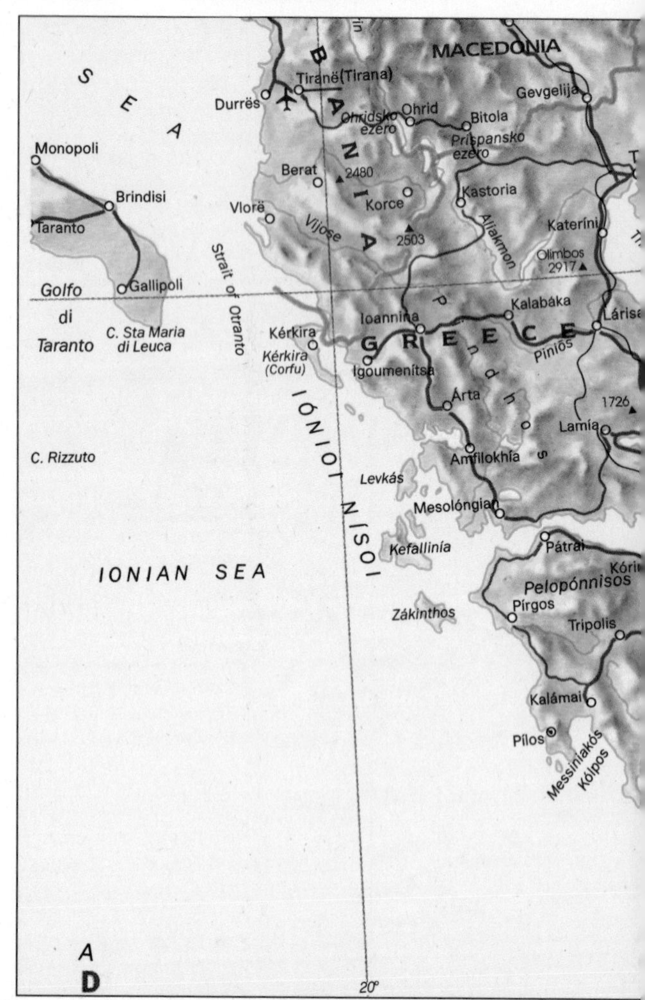
MACEDONIA
Tiranë (Tirana)
Durrës
Ohrid
Ohridsko ezero
Bitola
Gevgelija
Prispansko ezero
Monopoli
Brindisi
Taranto
Berat
2480
Korce
Kastoria
Vlorë
Vijose
2503
Aliakmon
Katerini
Olimbos 2917
Golfo di Taranto
Gallipoli
Strait of Otranto
C. Sta Maria di Leuca
Kérkira
Kérkira (Corfu)
Ioannina
Kalabáka
Lárisa
Igoumenítsa
Piniós
GREECE
Árta
1726
Lamía
Amfilokhía
C. Rizzuto
Levkás
IÓNIOI NÍSOI
Mesolóngion
Kefallinía
Pátrai
IONIAN SEA
Pelopónnisos
Pírgos
Zákinthos
Tripolis
Kalámai
Pílos
Messiniakós Kólpos
20°

Planina
Néstos
Dráma
Xánthi
Komotini
Kavála
Alexandroúpolis
Kesan
Sea of Marmara
Marmara
Bandirma
Bursa
Thásos
K. Strimonikós
Samothráki
Gelibolu
Eceabat
Çanakkale
Gökçeada
2033
K. Singitikós
Límnos
Simav
Balikesir
Edremit
Ayvalik
Áyios Evstrátios
Akhisar
TURKEY
Iliodhrómia
Lésvos
Skópelos
Skiros
Manisa
Gediz
Évvoia
AEGEAN SEA
Izmir
Khalkis
Khíos
Selçuk
Deniz
Athínai (Athens)
Ándros
Sámos
Ikaría
Kéa
Tinos
Mikonos
Muğla
Síros
DHODHEKÁNISOS
Léros
Bodrum
Kíthnos
KIKLÁDHES
Kálimnos
Ídhra
Sérifos
Páros
Náxos
Marmaris
Mirtoan Sea
Sífnos
Kós
Amorgós
Ródhos
Síkinos
Íos
Mílos
Astípálaia
Tílos
Ródhos (Rhodes)
Thíra
Anáfi
Kárpathos
Sea of Crete
Kríti (Crete)
Khaniá
Akr. Sídheros
Kásos
Iráklion
2456
Timbákion
35°
25°
40°
F

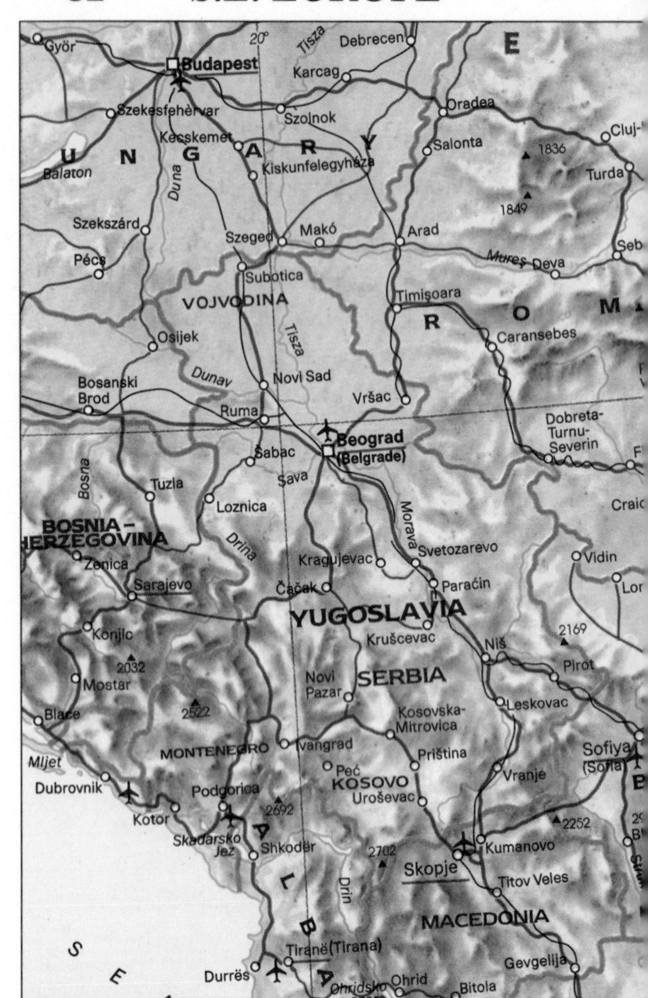
Györ
Budapest
Debrecen
Karcag
Szolnok
Szekesfehèrvar
Kecskemet
Oradea
Salonta
Cluj-
Turda
Kiskunfelegyháza
Balaton
Duna
Tisza
Szekszárd
Szeged
Makó
Arad
Pécs
Subotica
Mureș
Deva
VOJVODINA
Timișoara
Caransebes
Osijek
Dunav
Novi Sad
Vršac
Bosanski
Brod
Ruma
Dobreta-
Turnu-
Severin
Beograd
(Belgrade)
Šabac
Sava
Bosna
Tuzla
Loznica
Morava
BOSNIA-
HERZEGOVINA
Drina
Kragujevac
Svetozarevo
Vidin
Zenica
Sarajevo
Čačak
Paraćin
YUGOSLAVIA
Kruščevac
Konjic
2032
2169
Niš
Pirot
Mostar
Novi
Pazar
SERBIA
Leskovac
Blace
2522
Kosovska-
Mitrovica
MONTENEGRO
Ivangrad
Priština
Sofiya
(Sofia)
Mljet
Peć
KOSOVO
Vranje
Dubrovnik
Podgorica
2692
Uroševac
Kotor
2252
Skadarsko
Jez
Shkodër
2702
Kumanovo
Skopje
Drin
Titov Veles
MACEDONIA
Tiranë(Tirana)
Gevgelija
Durrës
Ohridsko
Ohrid
Bitola
1836
1849
U N G A R Y
R O M
A L B A
S E A

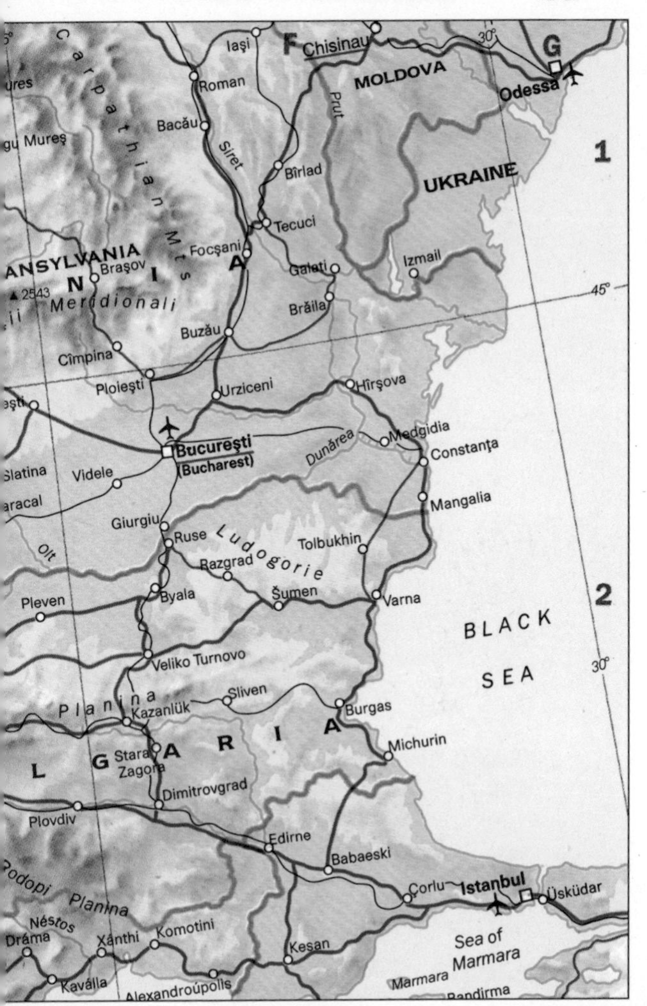

Iaşi
F
Chisinau
30°
G
Odessa
MOLDOVA
Roman
Prut
Bacău
gu Mureş
Siret
1
Bîrlad
UKRAINE
Carpathian Mts
Tecuci
TRANSYLVANIA
Focşani
A
Izmail
Braşov
N
I
Galati
45°
▲2543
Meridionali
Brăila
Buzău
Cîmpina
Ploieşti
Urziceni
Hîrşova
Bucureşti
(Bucharest)
Dunărea
Medgidia
Constanţa
Slatina
Videle
Caracal
Mangalia
Giurgiu
Ruse
Ludogorie
Olt
Tolbukhin
Razgrad
Šumen
Byala
Varna
2
Pleven
BLACK
SEA
30°
Veliko Turnovo
Sliven
Planina
Kazanlük
Burgas
A
I
R
A
G
L
Stara Zagora
Michurin
Dimitrovgrad
Plovdiv
Edirne
Babaeski
Rodopi Planina
Çorlu
Istanbul
Üsküdar
Néstos
Dráma
Xánthi
Komotini
Keşan
Sea of Marmara
Kavalla
Alexandroúpolis
Marmara
Bandirma

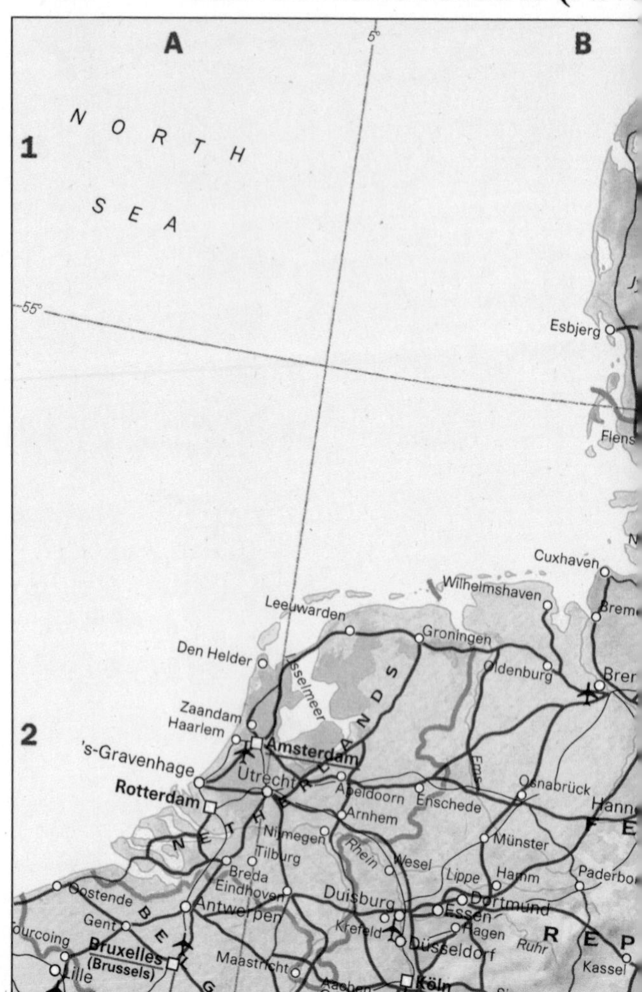
A
B
1
2
NORTH SEA
55°
5°
Esbjerg
Flens
Cuxhaven
Wilhelmshaven
Brem
Leeuwarden
Groningen
Den Helder
IJsselmeer
Oldenburg
Bren
Zaandam
Haarlem
Amsterdam
's-Gravenhage
Utrecht
Rotterdam
Apeldoorn
Enschede
Osnabrück
Hann
Arnhem
NETHERLANDS
Ems
Nijmegen
Münster
Tilburg
Rhein
Wesel
Breda
Eindhoven
Lippe
Hamm
Paderbo
Oostende
Duisburg
Dortmund
Antwerpen
Essen
Gent
Krefeld
Hagen
Tourcoing
Bruxelles
(Brussels)
Düsseldorf
Ruhr
Lille
Maastricht
Kassel
Aachen
Köln
Siegen
BELG
REP

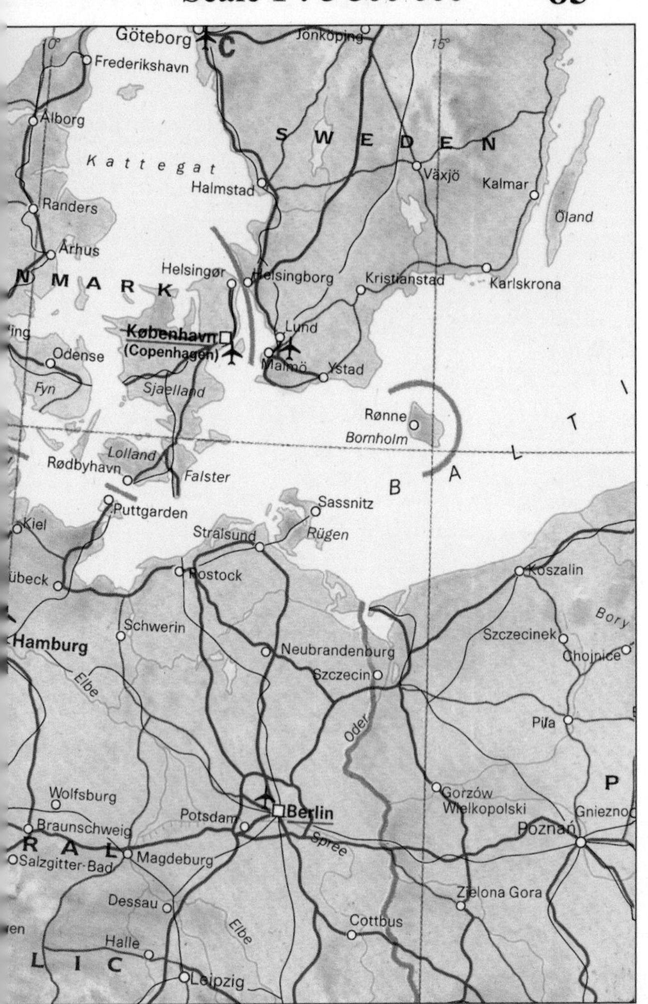
Göteborg
Jönköping
Frederikshavn
Ålborg
Kattegat
SWEDEN
Växjö
Kalmar
Halmstad
Öland
Randers
Århus
Helsingør
Helsingborg
Kristianstad
Karlskrona
MARK
København
(Copenhagen)
Lund
Malmö
Odense
Ystad
Fyn
Sjælland
Rønne
Bornholm
Lolland
Rødbyhavn
Falster
BALTI
Puttgarden
Sassnitz
Kiel
Stralsund
Rügen
Rostock
Koszalin
übeck
Schwerin
Bory
Hamburg
Szczecinek
Neubrandenburg
Chojnice
Elbe
Szczecin
Oder
Piła
Wolfsburg
Gorzów
Wielkopolski
P
Braunschweig
Potsdam
Berlin
Gniezno
Poznań
RAL
Spree
Salzgitter-Bad
Magdeburg
Zielona Gora
Dessau
Cottbus
Elbe
Halle
LIC
Leipzig

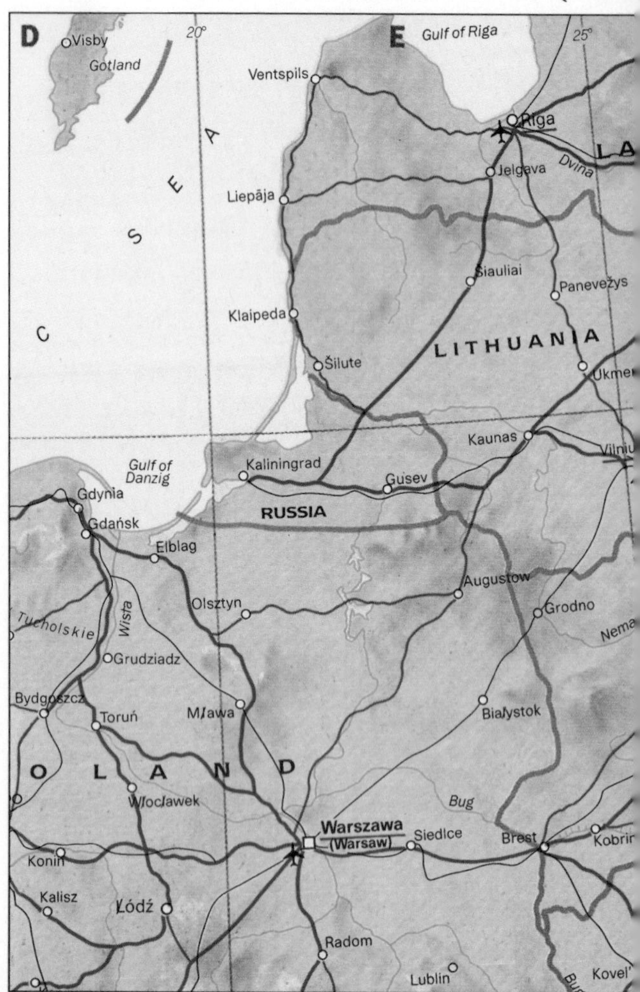
D
E
20°
25°
Visby
Gotland
Gulf of Riga
Ventspils
Riga
Jelgava
Dvina
Liepāja
S
E
A
C
Šiauliai
Panevežys
Klaipeda
Šilute
LITHUANIA
Kaunas
Vilniu
Kaliningrad
Gulf of Danzig
Gdynia
Gdańsk
Gusev
RUSSIA
Elblag
Augustow
Olsztyn
Grodno
Tucholskie
Wisła
Grudziadz
Bydgoszcz
Toruń
Mława
Białystok
O L A N D
Włocławek
Bug
Warszawa
(Warsaw)
Siedlce
Brest
Konin
Kalisz
Łódź
Radom
Lublin
Kovel'

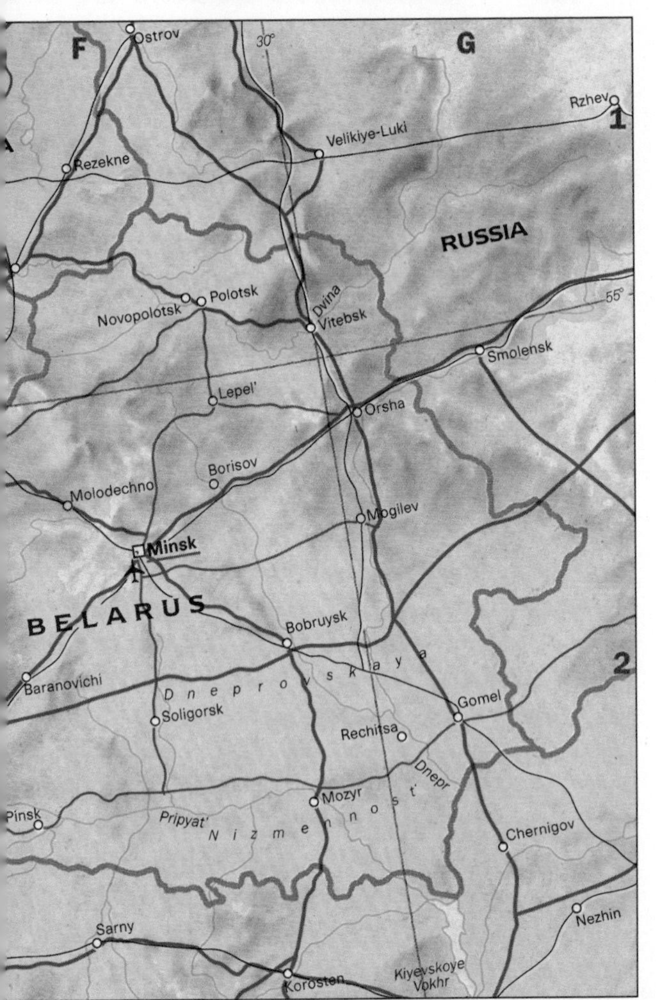

F
G
30°
55°
1
2
Ostrov
Rzhev
Velikiye-Luki
Rezekne
RUSSIA
Novopolotsk
Polotsk
Dvina
Vitebsk
Smolensk
Lepel'
Orsha
Borisov
Molodechno
Mogilev
Minsk
BELARUS
Bobruysk
Baranovichi
Dneprovskaya
Gomel
Soligorsk
Rechitsa
Dnepr
Mozyr
Pinsk
Pripyat'
Nizmennost'
Chernigov
Nezhin
Sarny
Korosten
Kiyevskoye Vdkhr

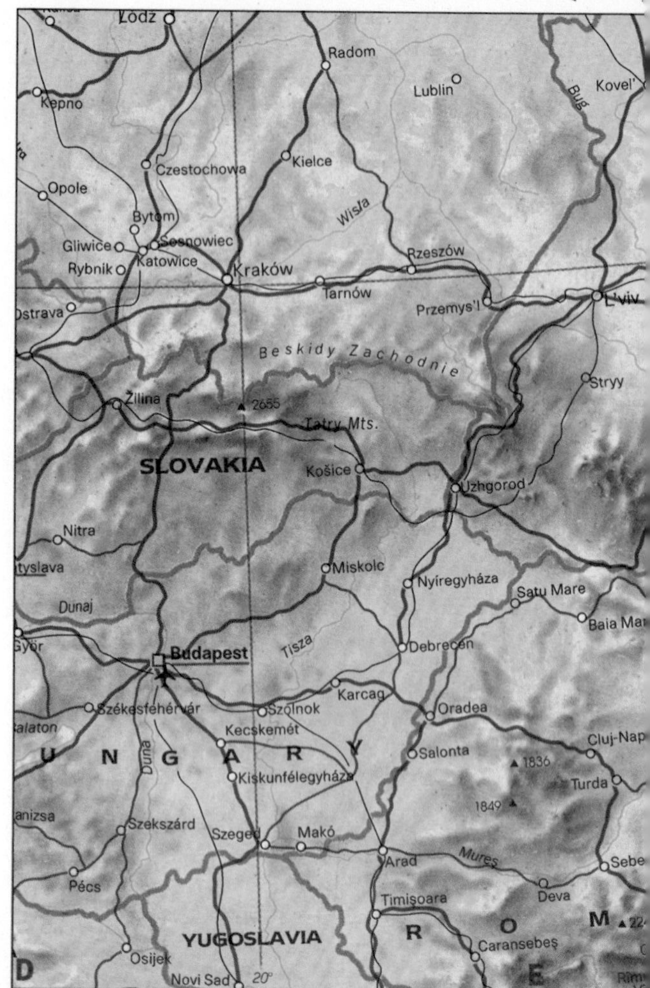

Lodz
Radom
Lublin
Kovel'
Bug
Kepno
Czestochowa
Kielce
Opole
Wisła
Bytom
Sosnowiec
Gliwice
Katowice
Rybnik
Kraków
Rzeszów
Tarnów
Przemys'l
L'viv
Ostrava
Beskidy Zachodnie
Stryy
Žilina
2655
Tatry Mts.
SLOVAKIA
Košice
Uzhgorod
Nitra
Miskolc
Nyíregyháza
Satu Mare
Baia Mar
Dunaj
Györ
Budapest
Tisza
Debrecen
Karcag
Székesfehérvár
Szolnok
Oradea
Kecskemét
Salonta
Cluj-Nap
HUNGARY
Duna
1836
Kiskunfélegyháza
Turda
1849
anizsa
Szekszárd
Szeged
Makó
Arad
Mureş
Sebe
Pécs
Deva
Timişoara
M
YUGOSLAVIA
R
O
Caransebeş
Osijek
Novi Sad
20°
Rim

89

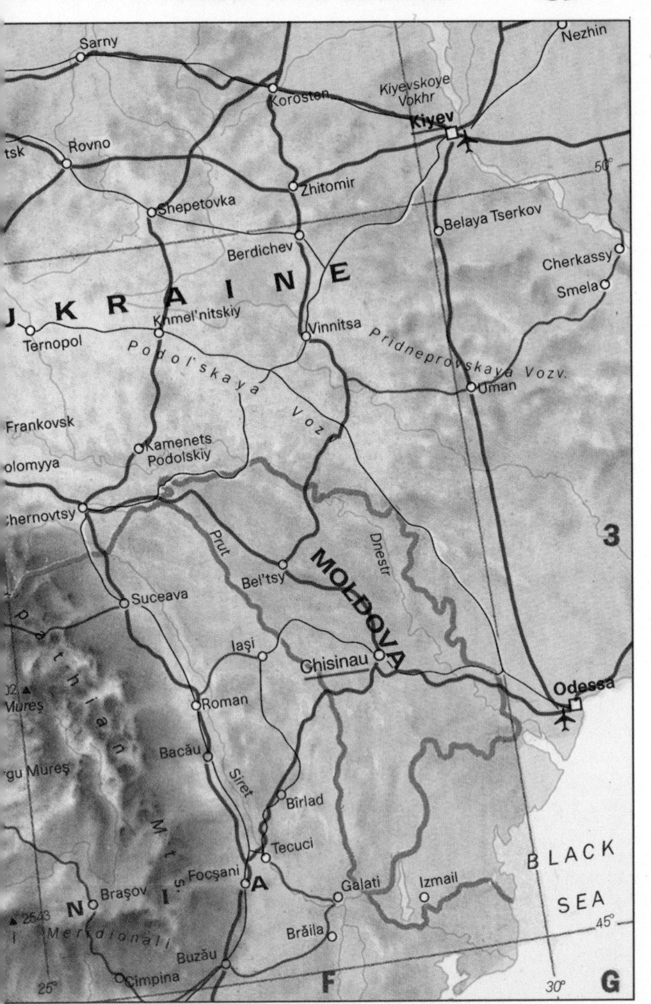
Sarny
Nezhin
Korosten
Kiyevskoye Vokhr
Kiyev
Rovno
Zhitomir
50°
Shepetovka
Belaya Tserkov
Berdichev
Cherkassy
Smela
U K R A I N E
Khmel'nitskiy
Ternopol
Vinnitsa
Pridneprovskaya Vozv.
Podol'skaya Vozv.
Uman
Frankovsk
Kamenets Podolskiy
Kolomyya
Chernovtsy
Prut
Dnestr
MOLDOVA
Bel'tsy
3
Suceava
Iaşi
Chisinau
Odessa
Roman
Mureş
Bacău
Tîrgu Mureş
Siret
Bîrlad
Tecuci
BLACK
SEA
Focşani
A
Galati
Izmail
Braşov
N
I
2543
Meridionali
Brăila
45°
Buzău
Cîmpina
25°
F
30°
G

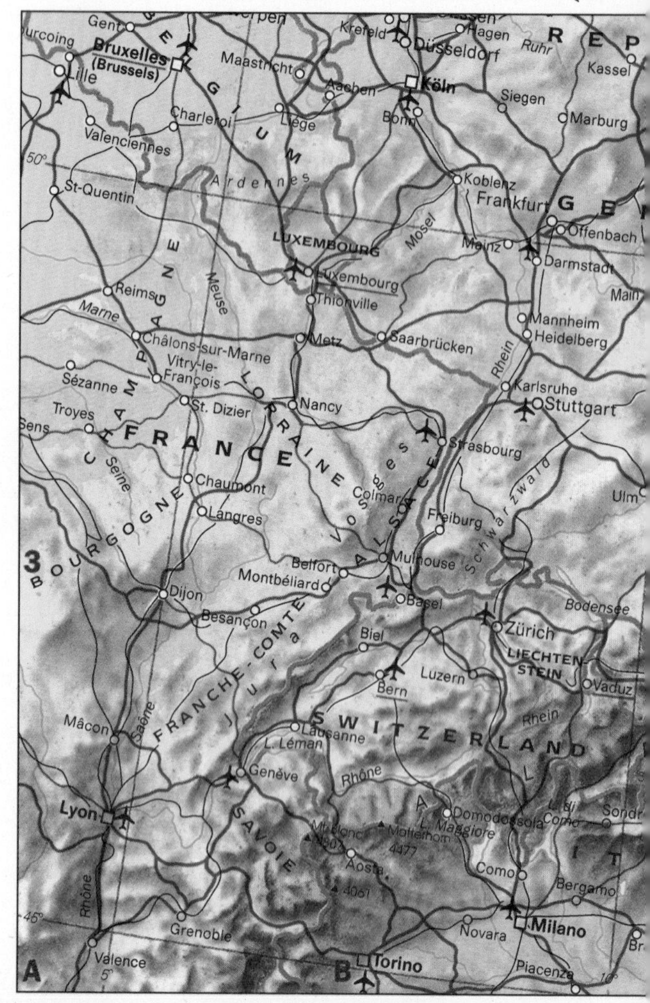
Gent
Bruxelles
(Brussels)
Lille
Maastricht
Aachen
Krefeld
Hagen
Düsseldorf
Ruhr
Kassel
Köln
Siegen
Bonn
Marburg
Charleroi
Liège
Valenciennes
50°
St-Quentin
Ardennes
Koblenz
Frankfurt
Offenbach
Mosel
LUXEMBOURG
Mainz
Darmstadt
Luxembourg
Thionville
Main
Reims
Marne
Meuse
Mannheim
Heidelberg
Châlons-sur-Marne
Metz
Saarbrücken
Rhein
Vitry-le-François
Sézanne
Karlsruhe
Stuttgart
Troyes
St. Dizier
Nancy
Sens
FRANCE
CHAMPAGNE
LORRAINE
Strasbourg
Seine
Schwarzwald
Chaumont
Colmar
Ulm
Langres
Vosges
ALSACE
Freiburg
3
BOURGOGNE
Belfort
Mulhouse
Montbéliard
Dijon
Basel
Besançon
Bodensee
Zürich
Biel
Jura
LIECHTENSTEIN
FRANCHE-COMTÉ
Luzern
Vaduz
Bern
Mâcon
Saône
Lausanne
Rhein
L. Léman
SWITZERLAND
Genève
Rhône
Lyon
SAVOIE
Domodossola
L. di Como
Mt Blanc
Matterhorn
4477
L. Maggiore
Aosta
Como
4061
Bergamo
Rhône
45°
Grenoble
Novara
Milano
Valence
5°
Torino
Piacenza
10°
A
B

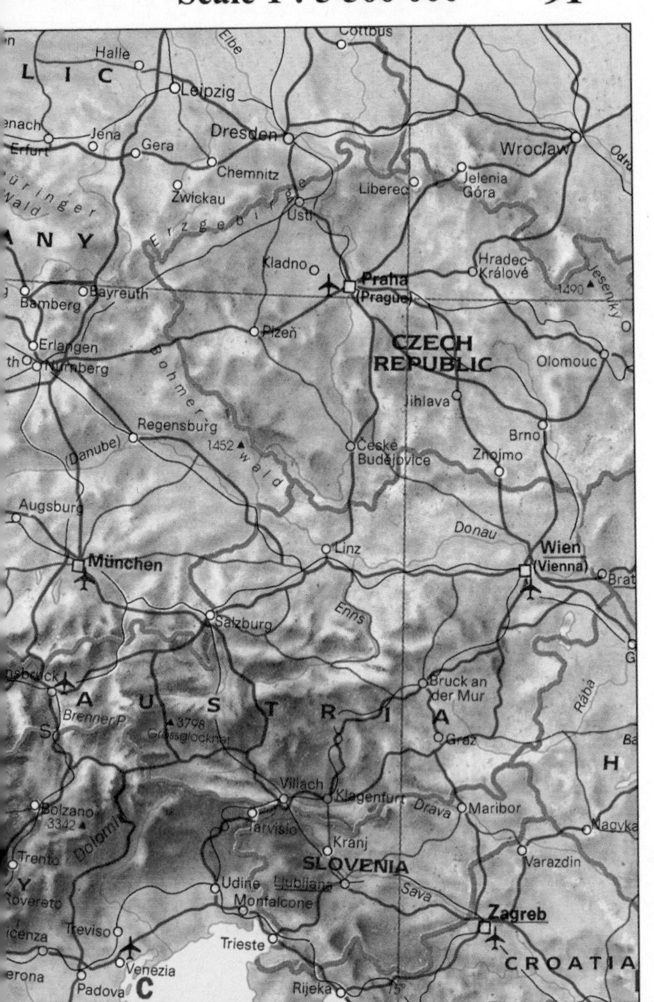
Cottbus
Elbe
Halle
Leipzig
Dresden
Jena
Erfurt
Gera
Chemnitz
Zwickau
Erzgebirge
Ústí
Liberec
Jelenia Góra
Wroclaw
Oder
Kladno
Praha (Prague)
Hradec-Králové
Jesenicky
1490
Bamberg
Bayreuth
Plzeň
Erlangen
Nürnberg
CZECH REPUBLIC
Olomouc
Jihlava
Brno
Regensburg
(Danube)
1452
České Budějovice
Znojmo
Augsburg
Donau
Linz
Wien (Vienna)
München
Salzburg
Enns
Bruck an der Mur
Rába
A U S T R I A
Brenner P.
3798
Grossglockner
Graz
H
Villach
Klagenfurt
Drava
Maribor
Bolzano
3342
Dolomiti
Tarvisio
Kranj
Nagyka
Trento
SLOVENIA
Varazdin
Udine
Ljubljana
Sava
Rovereto
Monfalcone
Zagreb
Treviso
Trieste
CROATIA
Venezia
Padova
Rijeka
C

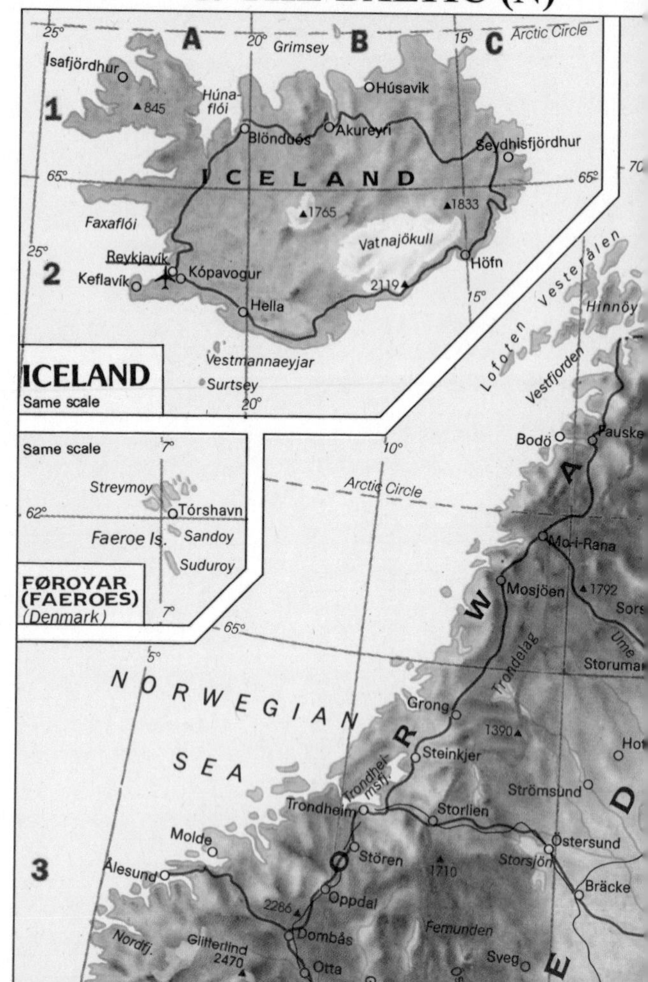

ICELAND
Same scale
Arctic Circle
Grimsey
Ísafjördhur
Húsavik
Húna-flói
845
Blönduós
Akureyri
Seydhisfjördhur
ICELAND
1765
1833
Faxaflói
Vatnajökull
Reykjavík
Kópavogur
Höfn
Keflavík
2119
Hella
Vestmannaeyjar
Surtsey
Same scale
Streymoy
Tórshavn
Faeroe Is.
Sandoy
Suduroy
FØROYAR (FAEROES) (Denmark)
Vesterålen
Hinnøy
Lofoten
Vestfjorden
Bodö
Arctic Circle
Mo-i-Rana
Mosjöen
1792
Storuman
NORWEGIAN SEA
Trondelag
Grong
1390
Steinkjer
Trondheimsfj.
Trondheim
Strömsund
Storlien
Molde
Östersund
Stören
Storsjön
Ålesund
1710
Bräcke
Oppdal
2286
Femunden
Dombås
Nordfj.
Glitterlind 2470
Sveg
Otta

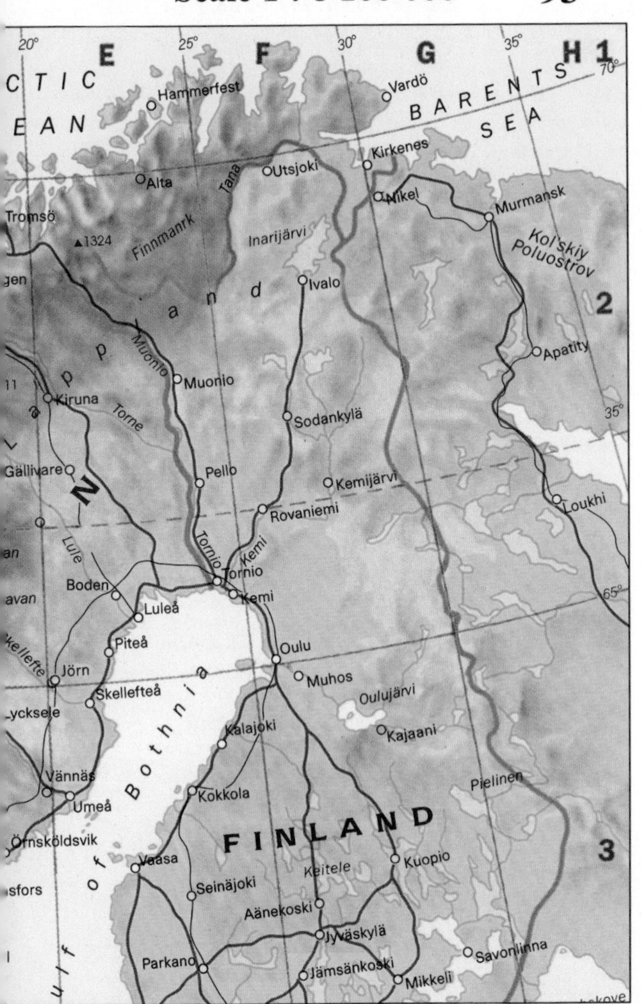

20°
25°
30°
35°
E
F
G
H
1
2
3
70°
65°
35°
CTIC
EAN
BARENTS
SEA
Hammerfest
Vardö
Kirkenes
Utsjoki
Alta
Tana
Nikel
Murmansk
Tromsö
1324
Finnmanrk
Inarijärvi
Kol'skiy Poluostrov
Ivalo
Lappland
Muonio
Muonio
Apatity
Kiruna
Torne
Sodankylä
Gällivare
Pello
Kemijärvi
Loukhi
Rovaniemi
Lule
Tornio
Kemi
Tornio
Boden
Kemi
Luleå
Piteå
Oulu
Jörn
Muhos
Skellefteå
Oulujärvi
Lycksele
Kajaani
Kalajoki
Vännäs
Umeå
Kokkola
Pielinen
FINLAND
Örnsköldsvik
Vaasa
Kuopio
Keitele
Seinäjoki
Äänekoski
Jyväskylä
Savonlinna
Parkano
Jämsänkoski
Mikkeli
Gulf of Bothnia

SCANDINAVIA & THE BALTIC (S)

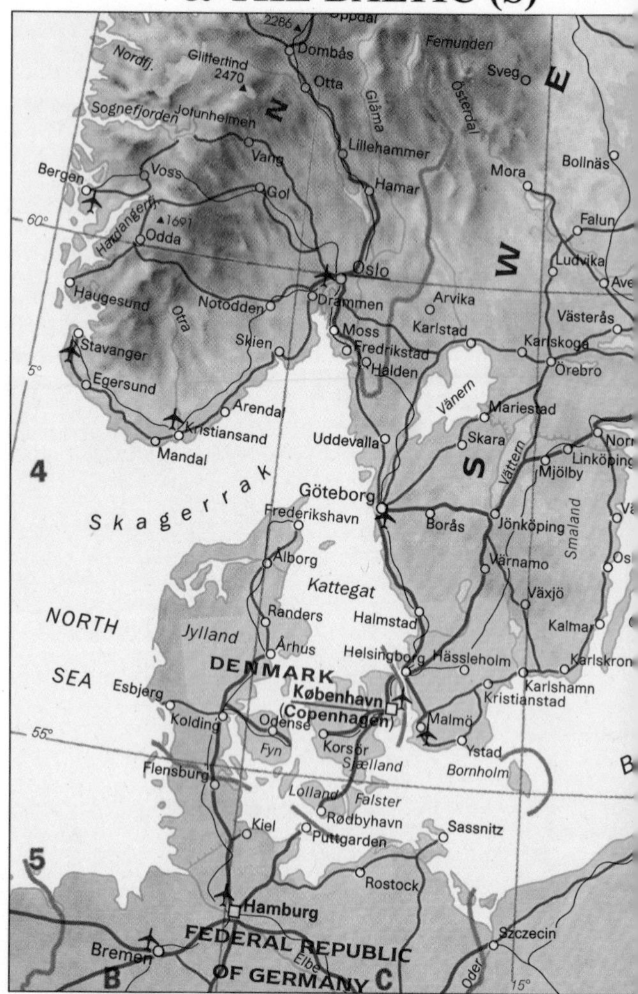

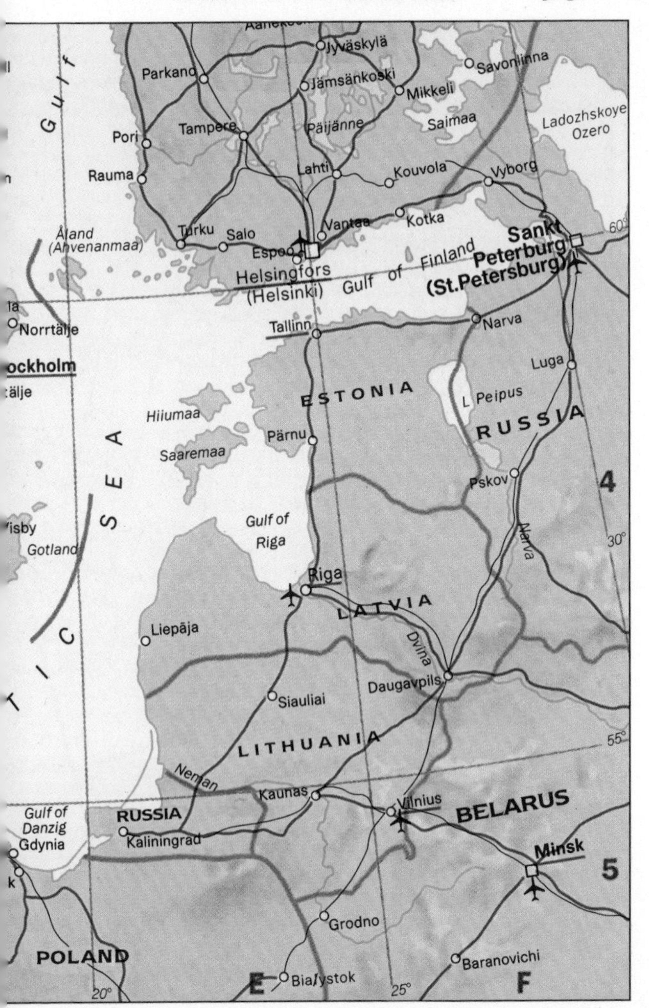
Jyväskylä
Parkano
Savonlinna
Jämsänkoski
Mikkeli
Saimaa
Ladozhskoye Ozero
Tampere
Päijänne
Pori
Rauma
Lahti
Kouvola
Vyborg
Kotka
Vantaa
Turku
Salo
Åland (Ahvenanmaa)
Espoo
Sankt Peterburg (St.Petersburg)
Helsingfors (Helsinki)
Gulf of Finland
Norrtälje
Tallinn
Narva
Luga
ESTONIA
L. Peipus
RUSSIA
Hiiumaa
Saaremaa
Pärnu
Pskov
Gulf of Riga
Gotland
Riga
LATVIA
Narva
Liepāja
Dvina
Daugavpils
Siauliai
LITHUANIA
Neman
Kaunas
Vilnius
BELARUS
Gulf of Danzig
Gdynia
RUSSIA
Kaliningrad
Minsk
Grodno
POLAND
Baranovichi
Bialystok
Gulf
SEA
60°
30°
55°
20°
25°
4
5
E
F

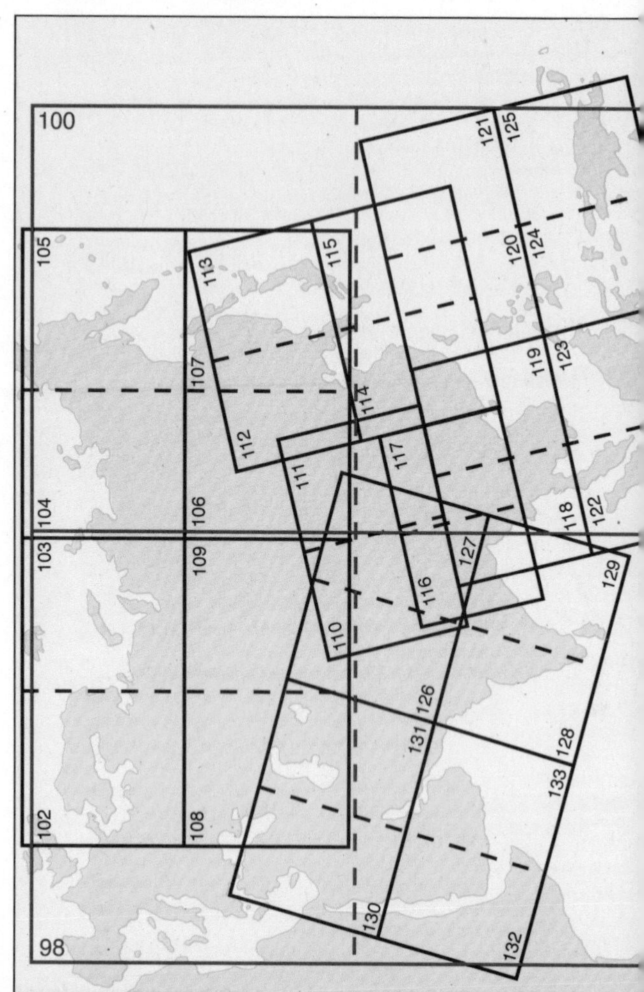
100
105
104
103
102
98
107
106
109
108
113
115
112
111
110
114
117
116
127
121
125
120
124
119
123
118
122
129
126
131
128
133
130
132

INDEX TO PAGES

98-99 ASIA POLITICAL (W)
100-101 ASIA POLITICAL (E)
102-103 RUSSIA (N.W.)
104-105 RUSSIA (N.E.)
106-107 RUSSIA (S.E.)
108-109 RUSSIA (S.W.)
110-111 EASTERN ASIA (N.W.)
112-113 EASTERN ASIA (N.E.)
114-115 EASTERN ASIA (S.E.), CENTRAL JAPAN
116-117 EASTERN ASIA (S.W.)
118-119 S.E. ASIA (W)
120-121 S.E. ASIA (E)
122-123 MALAYSIA & INDONESIA (W)
124-125 INDONESIA (E)
126-127 NORTHERN INDIA & THE HIMALAYAS
128-129 SOUTHERN INDIA
130-131 MIDDLE EAST (N)
132-133 MIDDLE EAST (S)

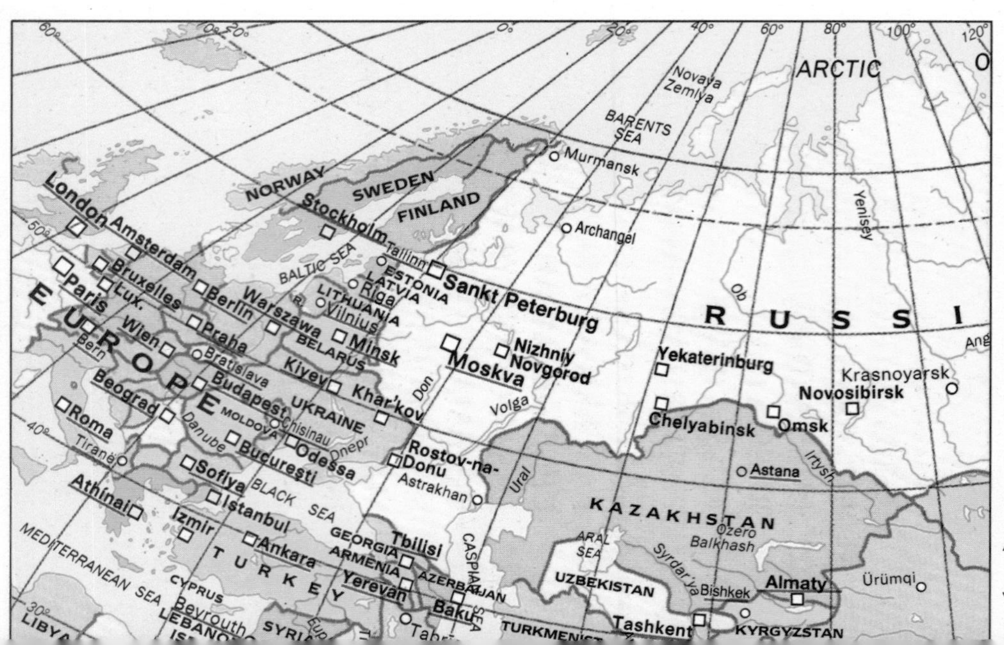
ARCTIC
RUSSIA
EUROPE
KAZAKHSTAN
UZBEKISTAN
KYRGYZSTAN
TURKMENISTAN
TURKEY
SWEDEN
FINLAND
NORWAY
ESTONIA
LATVIA
LITHUANIA
BELARUS
UKRAINE
MOLDOVA
GEORGIA
ARMENIA
AZERBAIJAN
CYPRUS
SYRIA
LEBANON
LIBYA
Novaya Zemlya
BARENTS SEA
BALTIC SEA
BLACK SEA
CASPIAN SEA
ARAL SEA
MEDITERRANEAN SEA
Yenisey
Ob
Irtysh
Volga
Ural
Don
Dnepr
Danube
Syrdar'ya
Ozero Balkhash
Krasnoyarsk
Novosibirsk
Omsk
Astana
Almaty
Bishkek
Tashkent
Ürümqi
Yekaterinburg
Chelyabinsk
Murmansk
Archangel
Sankt Peterburg
Nizhniy Novgorod
Moskva
Rostov-na-Donu
Astrakhan
Tbilisi
Yerevan
Baku
Tallinn
Riga
Vilnius
Minsk
Khar'kov
Kiyev
Odessa
Chisinau
Bucuresti
Stockholm
Warszawa
Berlin
Praha
Bratislava
Budapest
Wien
Beograd
Sofiya
Istanbul
Ankara
Izmir
Beyrouth
Athinai
Tiranë
Roma
Bern
Paris
Lux.
Bruxelles
Amsterdam
London
120°
100°
80°
60°
40°
20°
0°
50°
30°

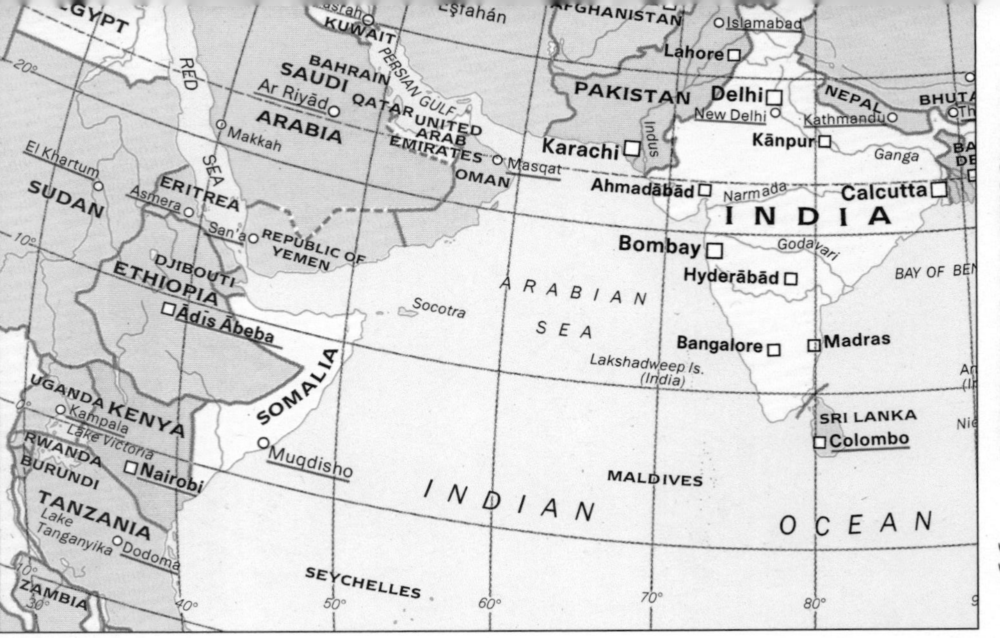

KUWAIT
Islamabad
Lahore
BAHRAIN
PERSIAN GULF
SAUDI ARABIA
Ar Riyāḍ
QATAR
RED SEA
PAKISTAN
Delhi
New Delhi
NEPAL
Kathmandu
Makkah
UNITED ARAB EMIRATES
Karachi
Indus
Kānpur
Ganga
El Khartum
Masqat
OMAN
Ahmadābād
Narmada
Calcutta
SUDAN
ERITREA
Asmera
INDIA
San'a
REPUBLIC OF YEMEN
Bombay
Godavari
DJIBOUTI
ETHIOPIA
Hyderābād
Ādīs Ābeba
ARABIAN SEA
Socotra
Bangalore
Madras
Lakshadweep Is.
(India)
SOMALIA
UGANDA
KENYA
Kampala
Lake Victoria
SRI LANKA
Colombo
RWANDA
BURUNDI
Nairobi
Muqdisho
MALDIVES
INDIAN OCEAN
TANZANIA
Lake Tanganyika
Dodoma
SEYCHELLES
ZAMBIA
20°
10°
0°
10°
30°
40°
50°
60°
70°
80°

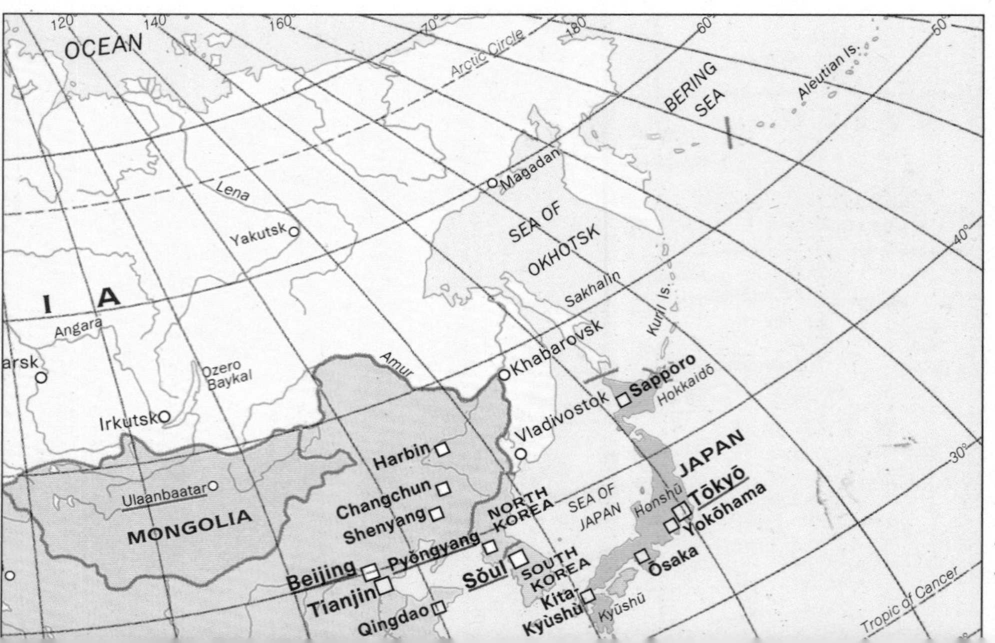

OCEAN
Arctic Circle
BERING SEA
Aleutian Is.
Lena
Magadan
Yakutsk
SEA OF OKHOTSK
Sakhalin
Kuril Is.
I A
Angara
arsk
Ozero Baykal
Amur
Khabarovsk
Sapporo
Hokkaidō
Irkutsk
Vladivostok
Harbin
JAPAN
Ulaanbaatar
Changchun
NORTH KOREA
SEA OF JAPAN
Honshū
Tōkyō
Yokohama
MONGOLIA
Shenyang
Pyŏngyang
Beijing
Sŏul
SOUTH KOREA
Ōsaka
Tianjin
Kita-Kyūshū
Kyūshū
Qingdao
Tropic of Cancer

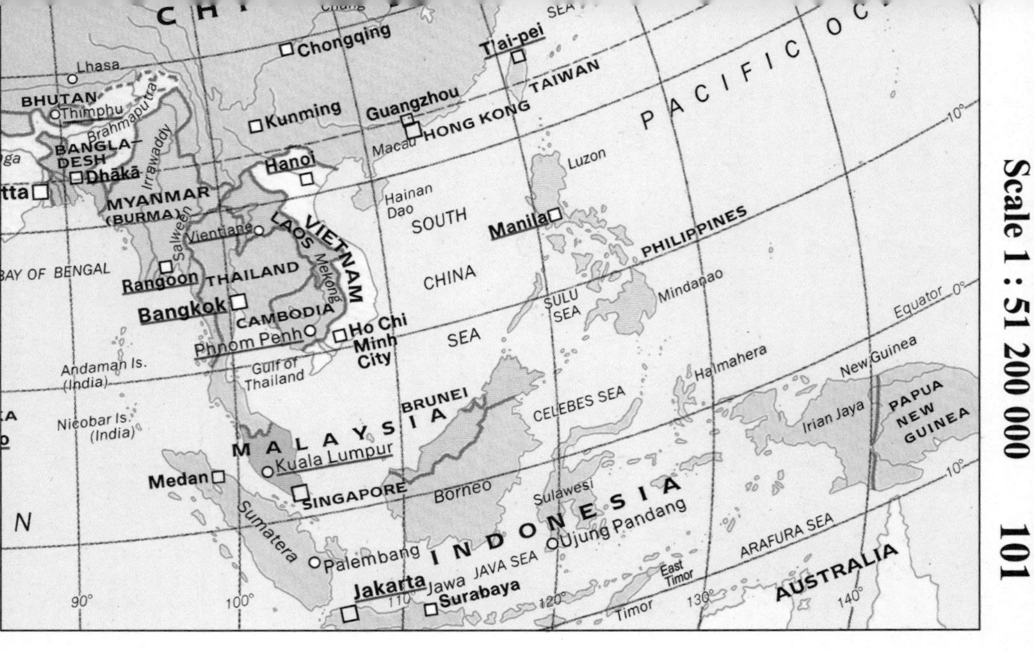
C H
Chongqing
T'ai-pei
SEA
P A C I F I C O C
Lhasa
BHUTAN
Thimphu
Brahmaputra
Kunming
Guangzhou
TAIWAN
HONG KONG
Macau
BANGLA-DESH
Dhākā
Irrawaddy
Hanoi
Luzon
tta
MYANMAR (BURMA)
Hainan Dao
SOUTH
Manila
Salween
Vientiane
LAOS
VIETNAM
PHILIPPINES
BAY OF BENGAL
Rangoon
THAILAND
Mekong
CHINA
Bangkok
CAMBODIA
SULU SEA
Mindanao
Phnom Penh
Ho Chi Minh City
SEA
Equator 0°
Andaman Is. (India)
Gulf of Thailand
Halmahera
New Guinea
BRUNEI
CELEBES SEA
Nicobar Is. (India)
M A L A Y S I A
Irian Jaya
PAPUA NEW GUINEA
Kuala Lumpur
10°
Medan
SINGAPORE
Borneo
Sulawesi
I N D O N E S I A
N
Sumatera
Ujung Pandang
ARAFURA SEA
Palembang
JAVA SEA
East Timor
Jakarta
Jawa
AUSTRALIA
Surabaya
90°
100°
110°
120°
130°
140°
Timor

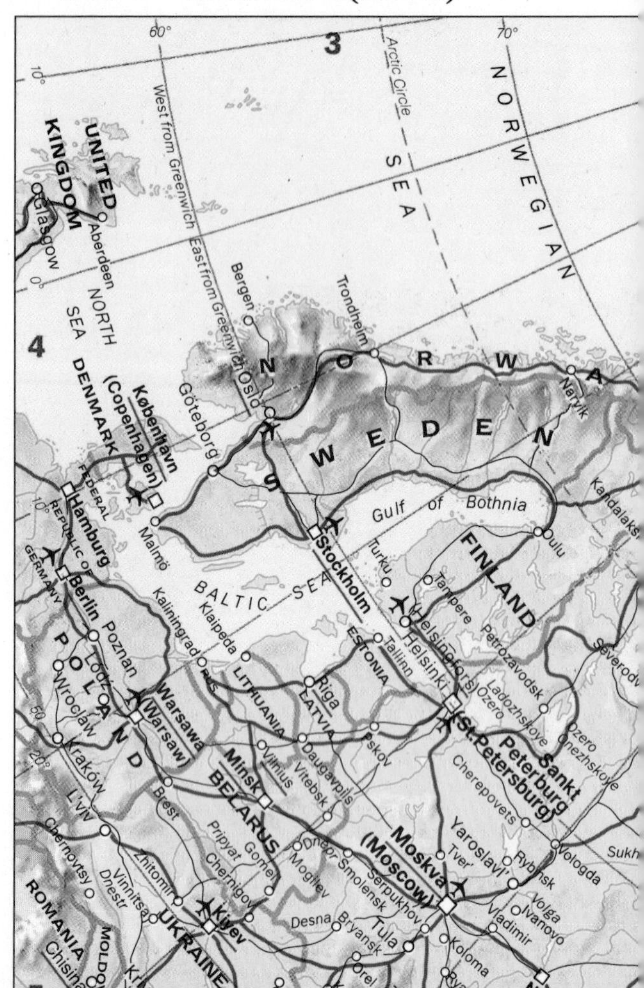

3
4
60°
70°
10°
0°
20°
50°
Arctic Circle
West from Greenwich
East from Greenwich
NORWEGIAN SEA
NORTH SEA
UNITED KINGDOM
Glasgow
Aberdeen
Bergen
Trondheim
NORWAY
Oslo
Göteborg
Narvik
SWEDEN
Gulf of Bothnia
Stockholm
Oulu
Kandalaksha
DENMARK
København (Copenhagen)
Malmö
FEDERAL REPUBLIC OF GERMANY
Hamburg
Berlin
BALTIC SEA
Turku
Tampere
FINLAND
Helsinki
Helsingfors
Tallinn
ESTONIA
Kaliningrad
RUS.
Klaipeda
LITHUANIA
Riga
LATVIA
Petrozavodsk
Ladozhskoye Ozero
Onezhskoye Ozero
Severodvinsk
Sankt Peterburg (St.Petersburg)
Poznan
POLAND
Lódź
Wrocław
Warsawa (Warsaw)
Kraków
Pskov
Daugavpils
Vilnius
Minsk
BELARUS
Vitebsk
Cherepovets
Vologda
Sukh
Yaroslavl'
Rybinsk
Tver'
Moskva (Moscow)
Brest
L'viv
Chernovtsy
Pripyat
Gomel
Dnepr
Mogilev
Smolensk
Serpukhov
Chernigov
Zhitomir
Vinnitsa
Dnestr
Kiyev
UKRAINE
Desna
Bryansk
Tula
Volga
Ivanovo
Vladimir
Koloma
Orel
ROMANIA
MOLDOVA
Chisinau

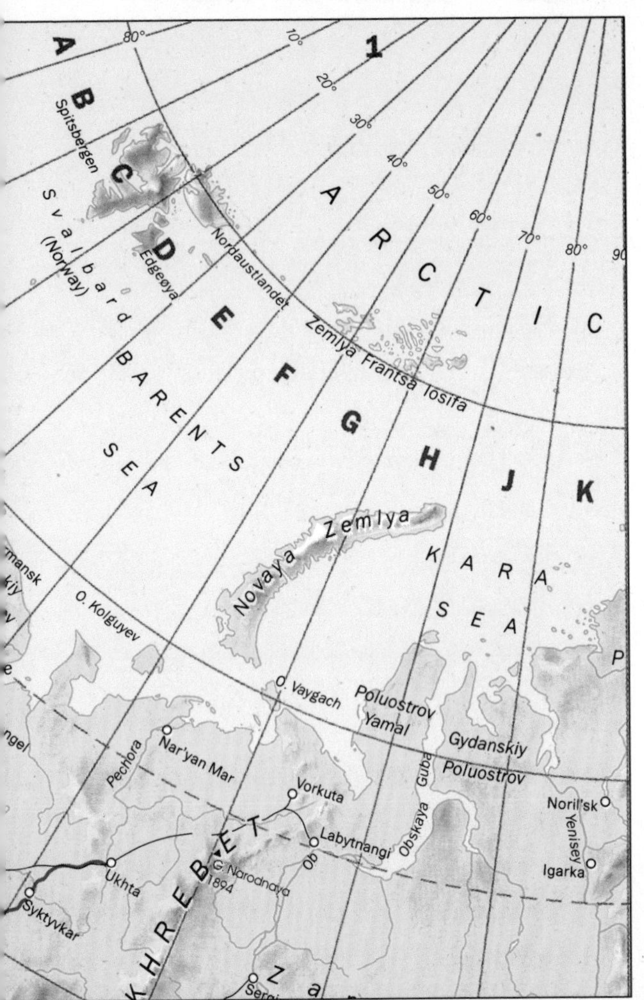

ARCTIC
BARENTS SEA
KARA SEA
Svalbard (Norway)
Spitsbergen
Edgeøya
Nordaustlandet
Zemlya Frantsa Iosifa
Novaya Zemlya
O. Kolguyev
O. Vaygach
Poluostrov Yamal
Gydanskiy Poluostrov
Obskaya Guba
Nar'yan Mar
Pechora
Vorkuta
Labytnangi
Ob
G. Narodnaya 1894
Ukhta
Syktyvkar
Noril'sk
Yenisey
Igarka

OCEAN
LAPTEV SEA
EAST
1
L M N O P Q R S T U
100°
110°
120°
130°
140°
150°
160°
170°
80°
O. Komsomolets
O. Oktyabr'skoy Revolyutsii
Severnaya Zemlya
O. Bol'shevik
Novosibirskiye Ostrova
O. Faddeyevskiy
O. Novaya Sibir
O. Bol'shoy Lyakhovskiy
O. Kotel'nyy
Gory Byrranga
Ozero Taymyr
Poluostrov Taymyr
Lena
Khrebet Orulgan
Gory Putorana
Verkhoyanski
Yakutsk
Suntar
Tunguska
Sredne

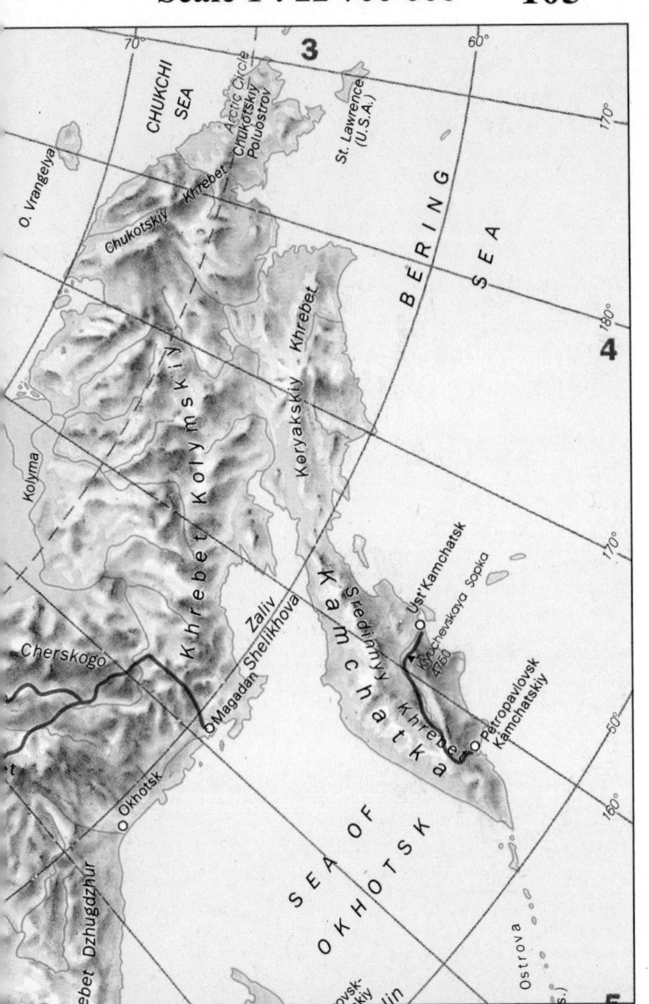

CHUKCHI SEA
O. Vrangelya
Arctic Circle
Chukotskiy Poluostrov
St. Lawrence (U.S.A.)
Chukotskiy Khrebet
BERING SEA
Koryakskiy Khrebet
Khrebet Kolymskiy
Kolyma
Cherskogo
Zaliv Shelikhova
Magadan
Okhotsk
Kamchatka
Sredinnyy Khrebet
Ust'Kamchatsk
Klyuchevskaya Sopka 4750
Petropavlovsk Kamchatskiy
SEA OF OKHOTSK
Khrebet Dzhugdzhur
Ostrova
70°
60°
50°
170°
180°
170°
160°
3
4

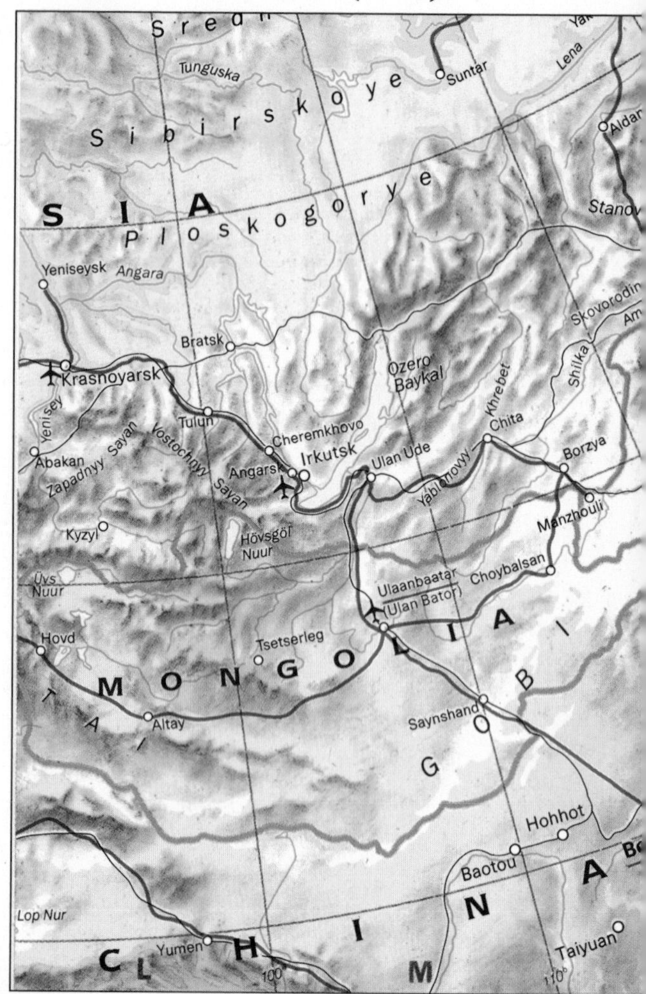

Sredn
Tunguska
Sibirskoye
Suntar
Lena
Aldan
SIA
Ploskogorye
Stanov
Yeniseysk
Angara
Skovorodin
Bratsk
Krasnoyarsk
Shilka
Ozero Baykal
Khrebet
Yenisey
Tulun
Chita
Abakan
Zapadnyy Sayan
Vostochnyy Sayan
Cheremkhovo
Irkutsk
Ulan Ude
Yablonovyy
Borzya
Angarsk
Manzhouli
Kyzyl
Hövsgöl Nuur
Üvs Nuur
Ulaanbaatar (Ulan Bator)
Choybalsan
Hovd
Tsetserleg
MONGOLIA
Altay
Saynshand
GOBI
Hohhot
Baotou
Lop Nur
Yumen
CHINA
Taiyuan
100°
110°

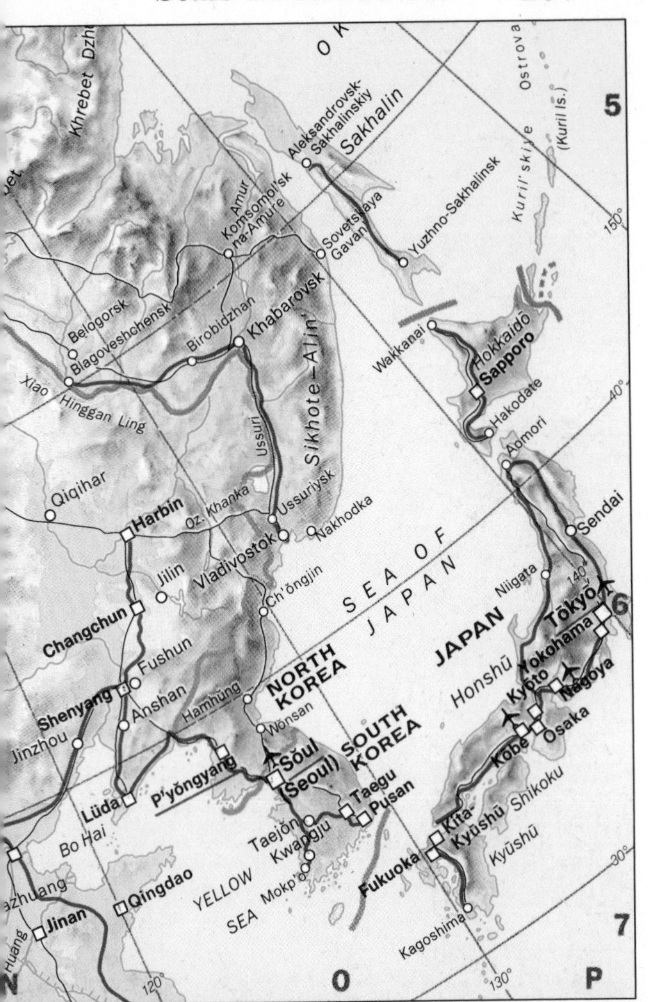
Khrebet Dzh
OK
Aleksandrovsk-Sakhalinskiy
Sakhalin
Ostrova
(Kuril Is.)
Kuril'skiye
5
Amur
Komsomol'sk na-Amure
Sovetskaya Gavan
Yuzhno-Sakhalinsk
150°
Belogorsk
Blagoveshchensk
Birobidzhan
Khabarovsk
Sikhote-Alin'
Wakkanai
Hokkaidō
Sapporo
Xiao
Hinggan Ling
Hakodate
40°
Aomori
Ussuri
Qiqihar
Oz. Khanka
Ussuriysk
Nakhodka
Harbin
Vladivostok
Sendai
SEA OF JAPAN
Jilin
Ch'ŏngjin
Niigata
140°
Tōkyō
6
Changchun
Yokohama
JAPAN
Fushun
NORTH KOREA
Honshū
Kyoto
Nagoya
Shenyang
Anshan
Hamhŭng
Wŏnsan
Osaka
Jinzhou
SOUTH KOREA
Kobe
Sŏul (Seoul)
P'yŏngyang
Lüda
Taegu
Pusan
Shikoku
Bo Hai
Taejŏn
Kwangju
Kita-Kyūshū
Kyūshū
Fukuoka
30°
YELLOW SEA
Mokp'o
Qingdao
Jinan
Huang
Kagoshima
7
120°
130°
O
P

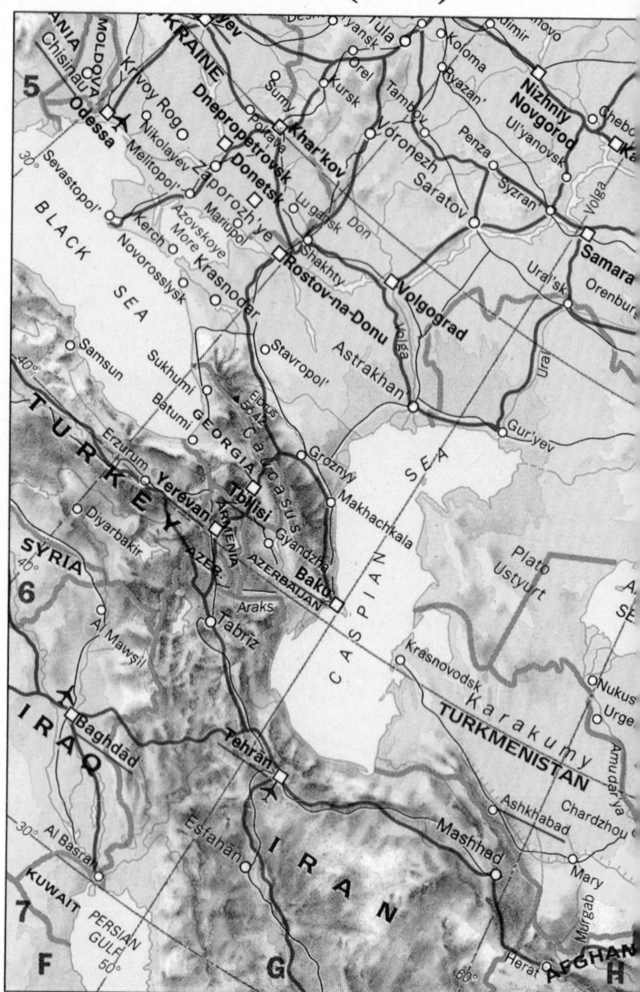

MOLDOVA
Chisinau
UKRAINE
Krivoy Rog
Odessa
Nikolayev
Melitopol'
Sevastopol'
Dnepropetrovsk
Donetsk
Zaporozh'ye
Mariupol
Azovskoye More
Kerch
Novorossiysk
Krasnodar
BLACK SEA
Sumy
Poltava
Khar'kov
Lugansk
Shakhty
Rostov-na-Donu
Don
Kursk
Orel
Tula
Koloma
Ryazan'
Tambov
Voronezh
Nizhniy Novgorod
Ul'yanovsk
Penza
Syzran'
Saratov
Samara
Volga
Volgograd
Ural'sk
Orenburg
Ural
Astrakhan
Stavropol'
Elbrus
Caucasus
Sukhumi
Batumi
GEORGIA
Tbilisi
Groznyy
Makhachkala
Gyandzha
Baku
AZERBAIJAN
ARMENIA
Yerevan
AZER.
Araks
Gur'yev
CASPIAN SEA
Plato Ustyurt
Samsun
Erzurum
TURKEY
Diyarbakir
SYRIA
Al Mawsil
Tabriz
Krasnovodsk
Nukus
Karakumy
TURKMENISTAN
Amudar'ya
Ashkhabad
Chardzhou
Mary
Murgab
Mashhad
Herat
Baghdād
IRAQ
Tehrān
Esfahān
IRAN
Al Basrah
KUWAIT
PERSIAN GULF
30°
40°
50°
60°
5
6
7
F
G
H

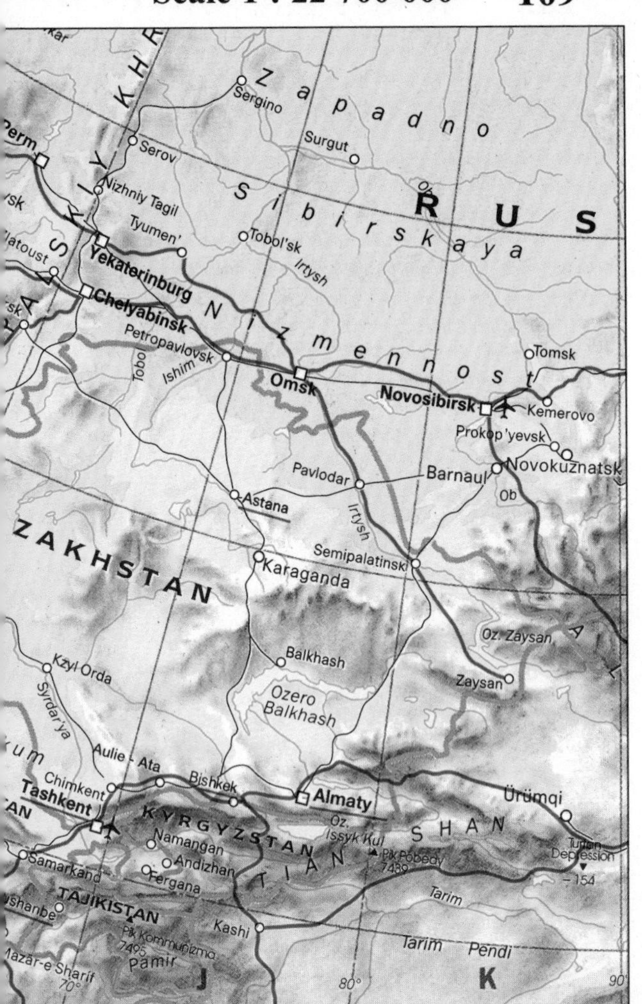
Zapadno Sibirskaya Nizmennost
RUS
ZAKHSTAN
Sergino
Surgut
Serov
Perm
Nizhniy Tagil
Ob
Tyumen'
Tobol'sk
Irtysh
Yekaterinburg
Chelyabinsk
Petropavlovsk
Tobol
Ishim
Omsk
Tomsk
Novosibirsk
Kemerovo
Prokop'yevsk
Novokuznatsk
Barnaul
Ob
Pavlodar
Astana
Irtysh
Semipalatinsk
Karaganda
Oz. Zaysan
Balkhash
Zaysan
Ozero Balkhash
Kzyl Orda
Syrdar'ya
Aulie - Ata
Chimkent
Bishkek
Almaty
Tashkent
Ürümqi
KYRGYZSTAN
Oz. Issyk Kul
SHAN
TIAN
Pik Pobedy 7439
Turfan Depression
– 154
Namangan
Andizhan
Fergana
Samarkand
TAJIKISTAN
Pik Kommunizma 7495
Kashi
Tarim
Tarim Pendi
Pamir
Mazār-e Sharīf
70°
80°
90°
J
K

A
B
2
1
3
70°
80°
50
40°
30°
Semipalatinsk
Irtysh
KAZAKHSTAN
Balkhash
Ozero Balkhash
Oz. Zaysan
Zaysan
Aulie - Ata
Bishkek
Almaty
Junggar Pendi
Namangan
KYRGYZSTAN
Andizhan
Fergana
Oz. Issyk Kul
7439
Ürümqi
TIAN SHAN
XINJIANG
Kashi
Tarim
Yarkant
Bosten Hu
Tarim Pendi
ZIZHIQU
U
Taklimakan Shamo
Hotan
Ruoqiang
Karakoram
Indus
Kunlun
Altun Shan
Xizang Gaoyuan
Dehra Dun
XIZAN

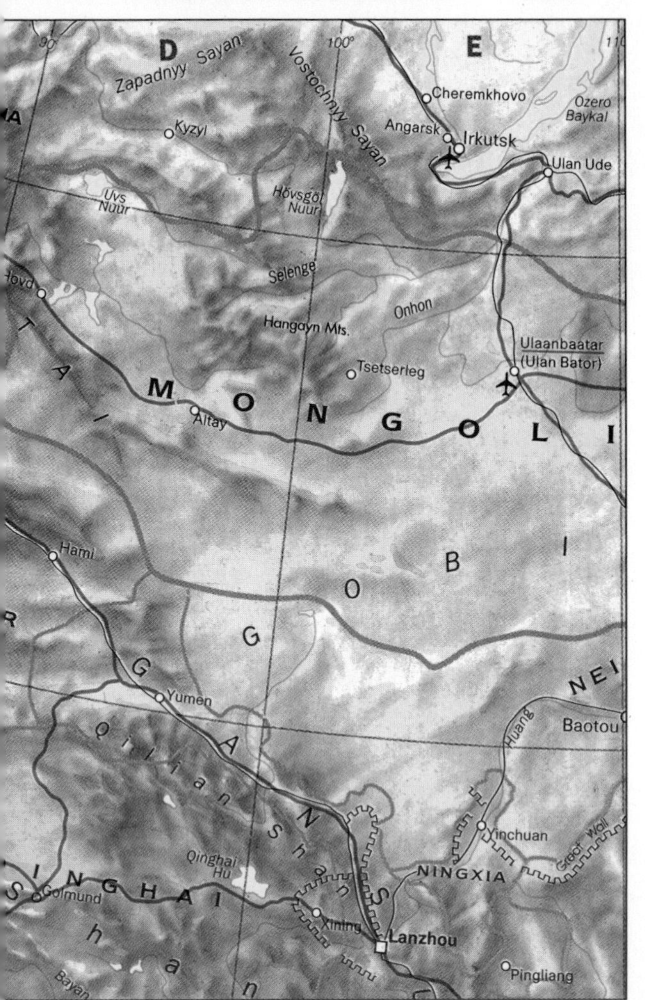

D
E
90°
100°
Zapadnyy Sayan
Vostochnyy Sayan
Cheremkhovo
Ozero Baykal
Angarsk
Irkutsk
Kyzyl
Ulan Ude
Uvs Nuur
Hövsgöl Nuur
Selenge
Hovd
Onhon
Hangayn Mts.
Ulaanbaatar (Ulan Bator)
Tsetserleg
M O N G O L I
Altay
Hami
G O B I
G
Yumen
NEI
Baotou
Huang
Qilian Shan
Yinchuan
Great Wall
Qinghai Hu
NINGXIA
Golmund
Xining
Lanzhou
Pingliang
Bayan

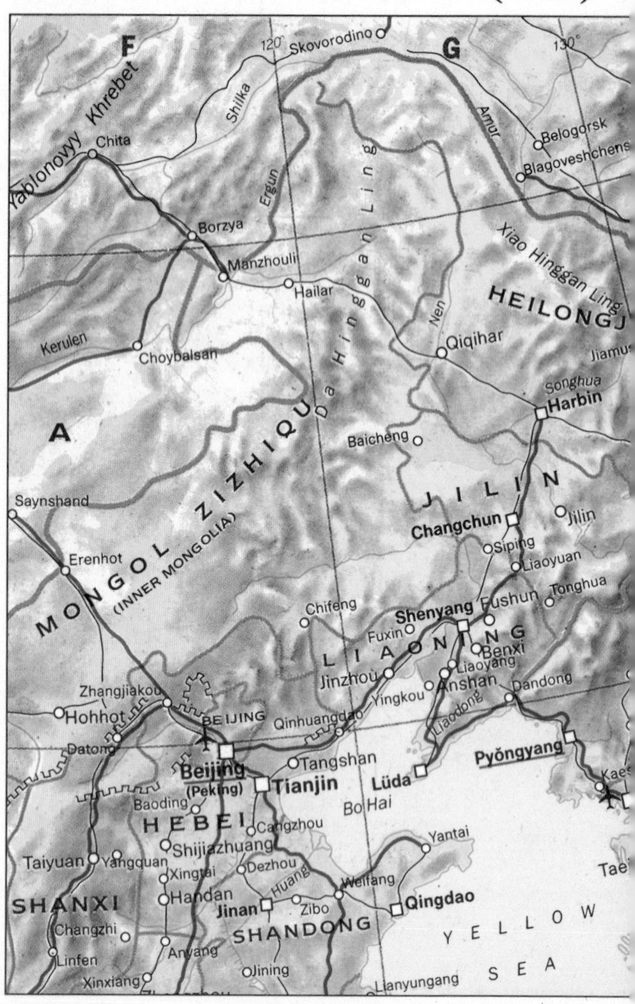

F
G
A
120°
130°
Skovorodino
Yablonovyy Khrebet
Chita
Shilka
Ergun
Amur
Belogorsk
Blagoveshchens
Da Hinggan Ling
Borzya
Manzhouli
Hailar
Xiao Hinggan Ling
HEILONGJ
Nen
Kerulen
Choybalsan
Qiqihar
Jiamus
Songhua
Harbin
Baicheng
MONGOL ZIZHIQU
(INNER MONGOLIA)
JILIN
Saynshand
Changchun
Jilin
Siping
Erenhot
Liaoyuan
Tonghua
Chifeng
Shenyang
Fushun
Fuxin
LIAONING
Benxi
Liaoyang
Jinzhou
Anshan
Yingkou
Dandong
Zhangjiakou
Hohhot
BEIJING
Qinhuangdao
Liaodong
Datong
Pyŏngyang
Tangshan
Beijing
(Peking)
Tianjin
Lüda
Kaes
Baoding
Bo Hai
HEBEI
Cangzhou
Yantai
Shijiazhuang
Taiyuan
Yangquan
Dezhou
Tae
Xingtai
Huang
Weifang
SHANXI
Handan
Jinan
Zibo
Qingdao
SHANDONG
YELLOW
Changzhi
Anyang
SEA
Linfen
Jining
Xinxiang
Lianyungang

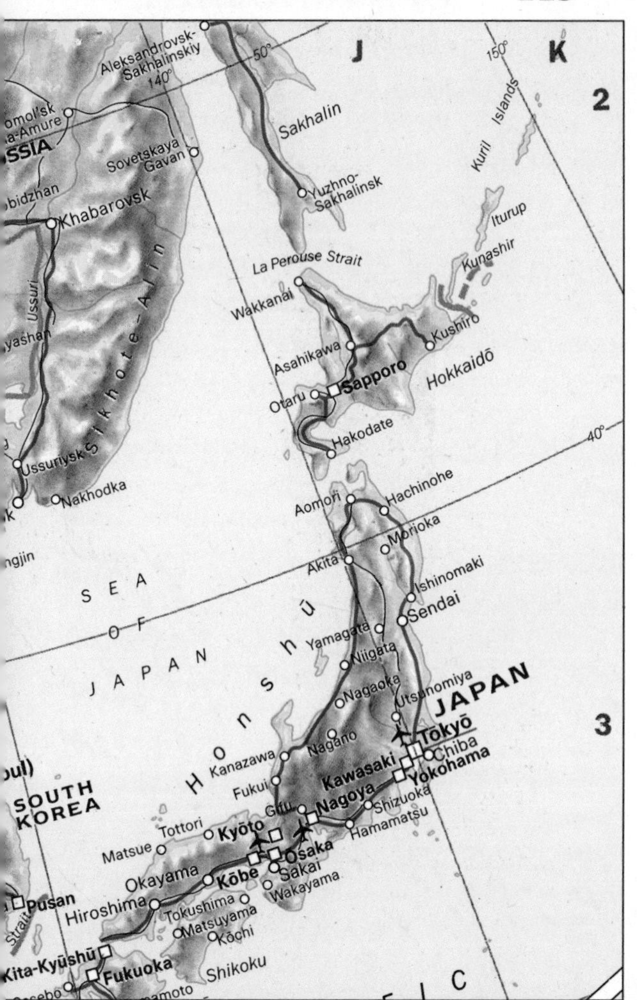
J
K
2
3
50°
140°
150°
40°
Aleksandrovsk-Sakhalinskiy
Sakhalin
Yuzhno-Sakhalinsk
Kuril Islands
Iturup
Kunashir
Sovetskaya Gavan
Khabarovsk
Ussuri
Sikhote-Alin
Ussuriysk
Nakhodka
La Perouse Strait
Wakkanai
Asahikawa
Kushiro
Sapporo
Hokkaidō
Otaru
Hakodate
Aomori
Hachinohe
Morioka
Akita
Ishinomaki
Sendai
SEA OF JAPAN
Honshū
Yamagata
Niigata
Nagaoka
Utsunomiya
JAPAN
Tokyō
Chiba
Yokohama
Kawasaki
Nagano
Kanazawa
Fukui
Gifu
Nagoya
Shizuoka
Hamamatsu
Tottori
Kyōto
Matsue
Ōsaka
Sakai
Kōbe
Okayama
Wakayama
Hiroshima
Tokushima
Matsuyama
Kōchi
Shikoku
SOUTH KOREA
Pusan
Kita-Kyūshū
Fukuoka
C

EASTERN ASIA (S.E.), CENTRAL JAPAN

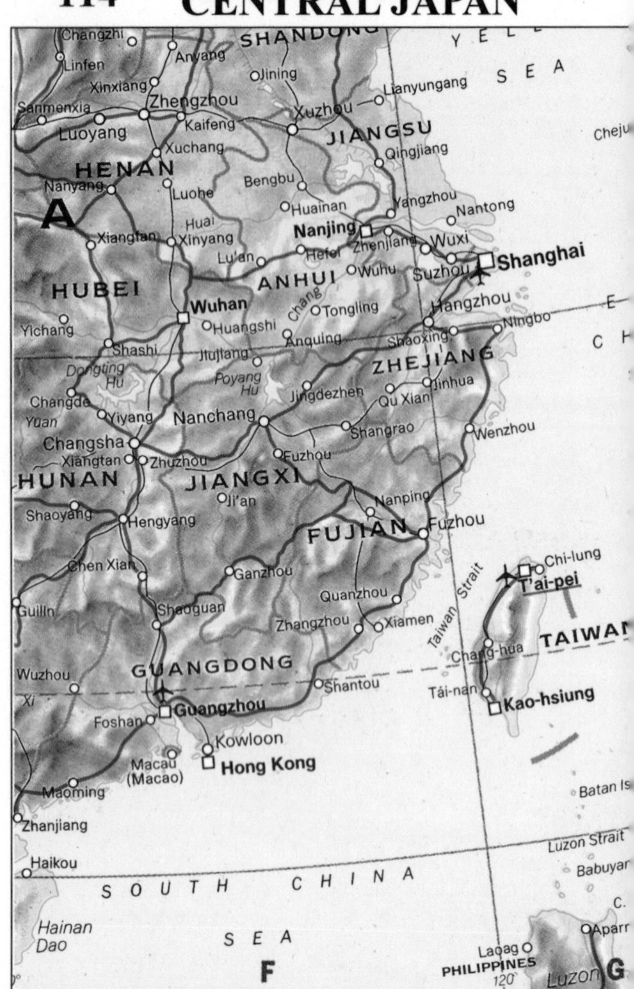

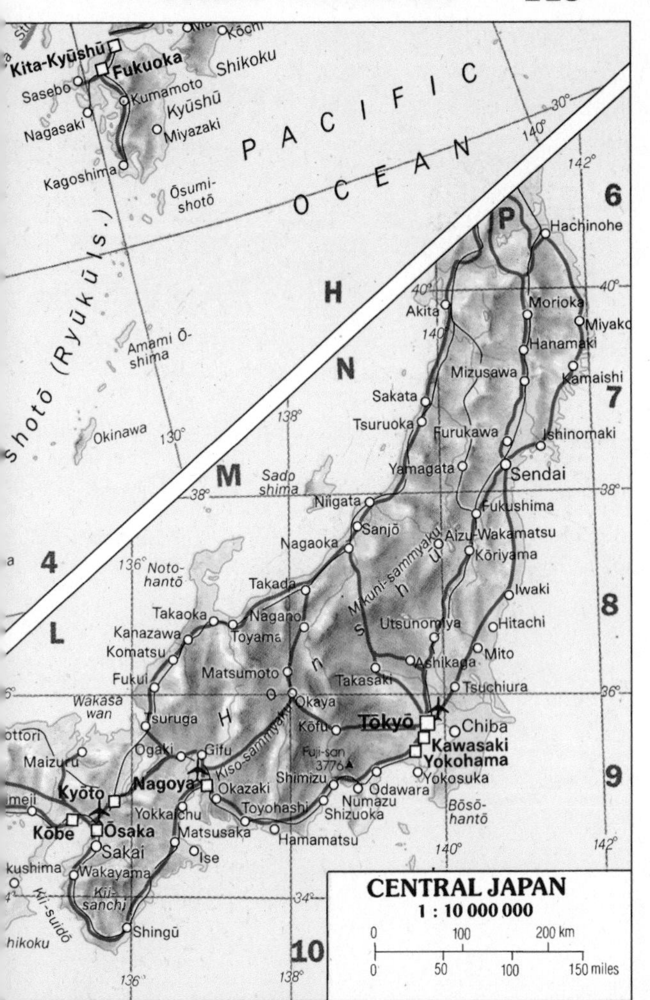
PACIFIC OCEAN
Kita-Kyūshū
Fukuoka
Sasebo
Nagasaki
Kumamoto
Kyūshū
Miyazaki
Kagoshima
Shikoku
Kōchi
Ōsumi-shotō
Amami Ō-shima
Okinawa
shotō (Ryūkyū Is.)
Hachinohe
Akita
Morioka
Miyako
Hanamaki
Mizusawa
Kamaishi
Sakata
Tsuruoka
Furukawa
Ishinomaki
Yamagata
Sendai
Sado shima
Niigata
Fukushima
Sanjō
Nagaoka
Aizu-Wakamatsu
Kōriyama
Noto-hantō
Takada
Iwaki
Mikuni-sammyaku
Takaoka
Nagano
Utsunomiya
Hitachi
Kanazawa
Toyama
Komatsu
Mito
Ashikaga
Matsumoto
Takasaki
Fukui
Tsuchiura
Wakasa wan
Okaya
Tsuruga
Kōfu
Tōkyō
Chiba
Kawasaki
Yokohama
Maizuru
Ogaki
Gifu
Fuji-san 3776
Kiso-sammyaku
Yokosuka
Kyōto
Nagoya
Okazaki
Shimizu
Odawara
Numazu
Bōsō-hantō
Toyohashi
Shizuoka
Kōbe
Ōsaka
Yokkaichi
Matsusaka
Hamamatsu
Sakai
Ise
Wakayama
Kii-sanchi
Kii-suidō
Shingū
H
N
M
L
4
6
7
8
9
10
CENTRAL JAPAN
1 : 10 000 000
0 100 200 km
0 50 100 150 miles

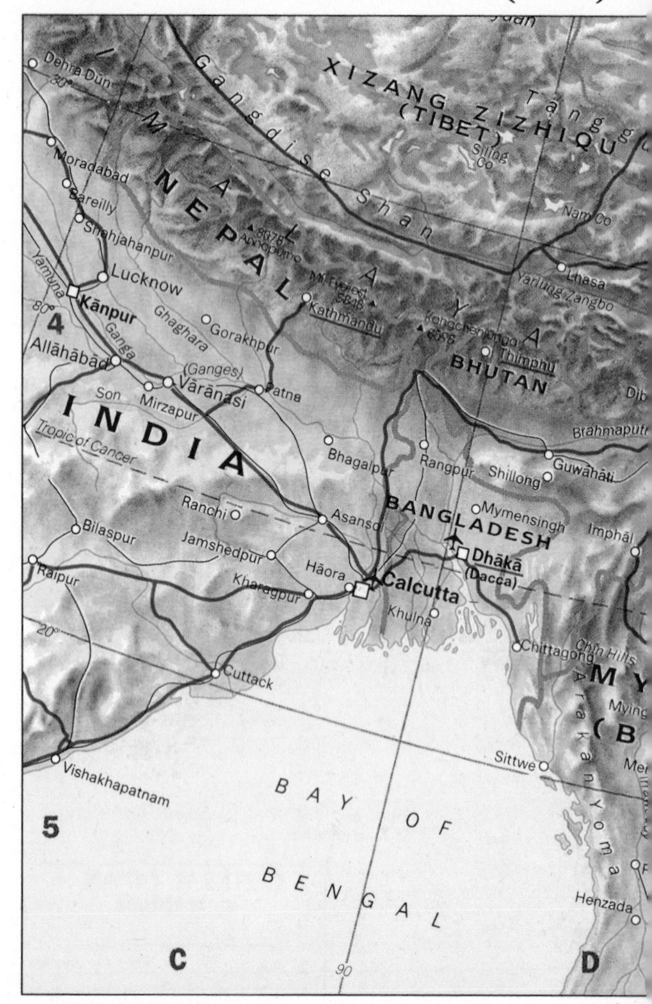
Dehra Dūn
30°
Gangdise Shan
XIZANG ZIZHIQU
(TIBET)
Siling Co
Nam Co
Lhasa
Yarlung Zangbo
Moradabad
Bareilly
Shahjahanpur
NEPAL
Lucknow
Yamuna
Kānpur
80°
4
Allāhābād
Ganga
Ghaghara
Gorakhpur
Kathmandu
Mt Everest
8848
Kangchenjunga
Thimphu
BHUTAN
(Ganges)
Vārānasi
Patna
Son
Mirzapur
INDIA
Tropic of Cancer
Bhagalpur
Rangpur
Shillong
Guwāhāti
Ranchi
Asansol
BANGLADESH
Mymensingh
Imphāl
Bilaspur
Jamshedpur
Hāora
Dhākā
(Dacca)
Raipur
Kharagpur
Calcutta
Khulna
20°
Chittagong
Chin Hills
Cuttack
Arakan Yoma
Sittwe
Vishakhapatnam
BAY OF BENGAL
5
Henzada
C
90
D

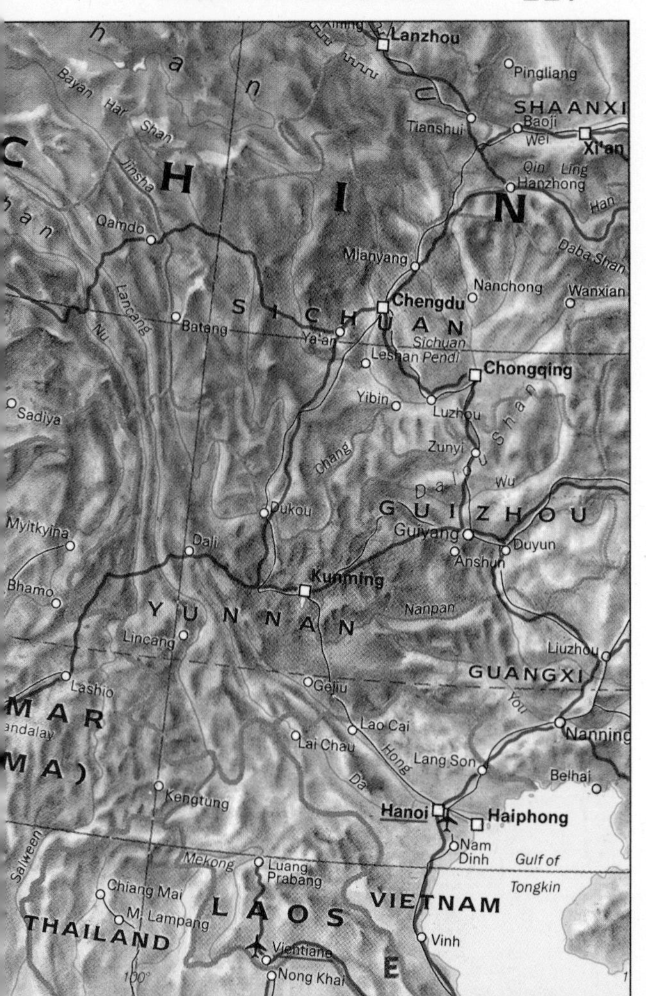

Lanzhou
Pingliang
SHAANXI
Tianshui
Baoji
Wei
Xi'an
Qin Ling
Hanzhong
Han
Bayan Har Shan
Jinsha
C H I N
Qamdo
Daba Shan
Mianyang
Nanchong
Wanxian
Chengdu
Lancang
Nu
Batang
S I C H U A N
Ya'an
Sichuan
Leshan Pendi
Chongqing
Yibin
Luzhou
Sadiya
Zunyi
Chang
Dalou Shan
Wu
Dukou
G U I Z H O U
Guiyang
Duyun
Anshun
Myitkyina
Dali
Bhamo
Kunming
Nanpan
Y U N N A N
Lincang
Liuzhou
GUANGXI
Lashio
Gejiu
You
Lao Cai
Nanning
Lai Chau
Hong
Lang Son
Da
Beihai
Kengtung
Hanoi
Haiphong
Nam Dinh
Gulf of Tongkin
Salween
Mekong
Luang Prabang
Chiang Mai
VIETNAM
L A O S
M. Lampang
THAILAND
Vinh
Vientiane
Nong Khai
100°

NEPAL
Thimphu
BHUTAN
A
B
1
2
20°
10°
90°
100°
Bhāgalpur
Rangpur
Brahmaputra
Sadiya
Dibrugarh
Guwāhāti
Shillong
Naga Hills
Nu
Jinsha
Lancang
Dukou
BANGLADESH
Ganga
INDIA
Myitkyina
Dali
Mymensingh
Imphāl
Dhākā
(Dacca)
Hāora
Khulna
Calcutta
Kunm
Bhamo
Chin Hills
Lincang
Chittagong
MYANMAR
(BURMA)
Lashio
Myingyan
Mandalay
Arakan
Irrawaddy
Kengtung
Sittwe
Meiktila
Pegu
Yoma
Mekong
Salween
BAY
OF
BENGAL
Prome
Chiang Mai
Henzada
M. Lampang
Ping
Nan
Dawna Ra.
Bassein
Pegu
Yangon
(Rangoon)
C. Negrais
M. Phitsanulok
Moulmein
THAILA
Ye
Nakhon Ratchasima
M. Nakhon Sawan
North Andaman
Tavoy
Thon Buri
Middle Andaman
ANDAMAN
SEA
Bangkok
(Krung Thep)
Andaman Islands
(India)
South Andaman
Batt
Mergui Archipelago
Little Andaman
Gulf
of
Thailand
Phnom
Ten Degree Channel
Isthmus of Kra
Chumphon
Kompong Som
Nicobar Islands
(India)
Nakhon Si Thammarat
Phuket
Great Nicobar

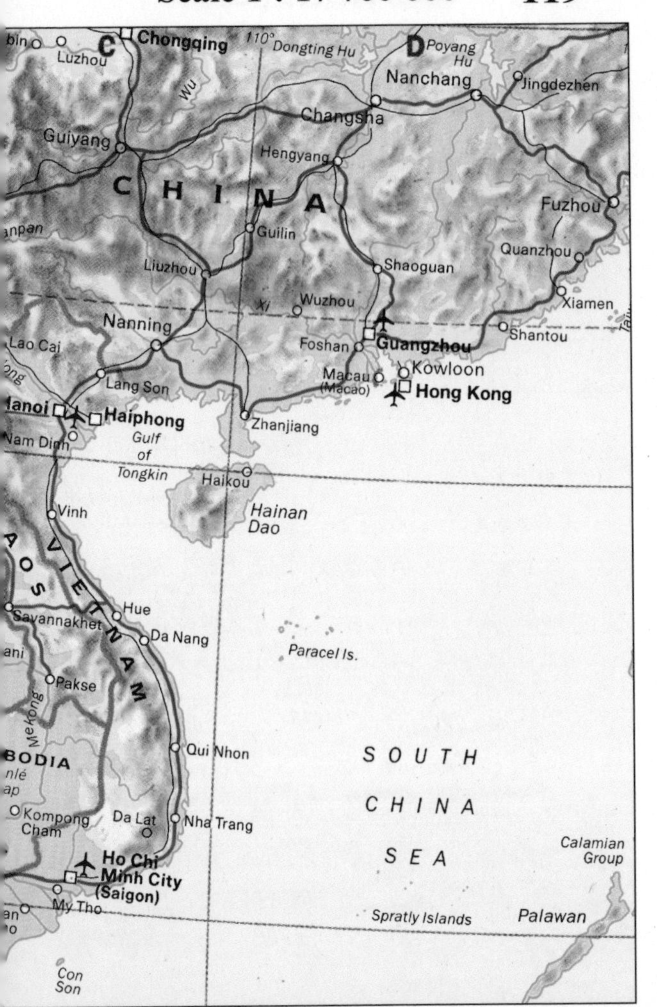
Chongqing
Luzhou
Dongting Hu
Poyang Hu
Nanchang
Jingdezhen
Changsha
Guiyang
Hengyang
CHINA
Fuzhou
Guilin
Quanzhou
Liuzhou
Shaoguan
Xiamen
Wuzhou
Xi
Nanning
Shantou
Lao Cai
Foshan
Guangzhou
Kowloon
Lang Son
Macau (Macao)
Hong Kong
Hanoi
Haiphong
Zhanjiang
Nam Dinh
Gulf of Tongkin
Haikou
Vinh
Hainan Dao
LAOS
VIETNAM
Hue
Savannakhet
Da Nang
Paracel Is.
Pakse
Mekong
Qui Nhon
SOUTH CHINA SEA
BODIA
Kompong Cham
Da Lat
Nha Trang
Calamian Group
Ho Chi Minh City (Saigon)
My Tho
Spratly Islands
Palawan
Con Son

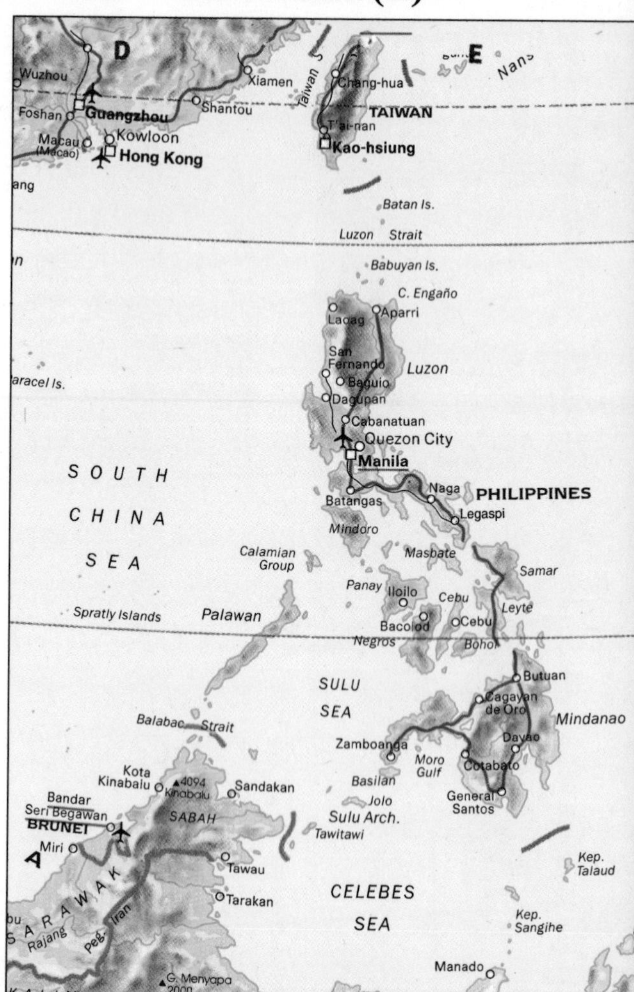
D
E
Wuzhou
Xiamen
Taiwan
Chang-hua
Nans
Shantou
Foshan
Guangzhou
TAIWAN
T'ai-nan
Kao-hsiung
Macau (Macao)
Kowloon
Hong Kong
Batan Is.
Luzon Strait
Babuyan Is.
C. Engaño
Laoag
Aparri
San Fernando
Luzon
Baguio
Dagupan
Paracel Is.
Cabanatuan
Quezon City
Manila
SOUTH CHINA SEA
Naga
PHILIPPINES
Batangas
Legaspi
Mindoro
Calamian Group
Masbate
Samar
Panay
Iloilo
Cebu
Leyte
Spratly Islands
Palawan
Bacolod
Cebu
Negros
Bohol
Butuan
SULU SEA
Cagayan de Oro
Mindanao
Balabac Strait
Davao
Zamboanga
Moro Gulf
Cotabato
Kota Kinabalu
4094 Kinabalu
Sandakan
Basilan
General Santos
Bandar Seri Begawan
Jolo
BRUNEI
SABAH
Sulu Arch.
Tawitawi
Miri
A
Tawau
Kep. Talaud
SARAWAK
Tarakan
CELEBES SEA
Kep. Sangihe
Rajang
Peg. Iran
Manado
G. Menyapa 2000

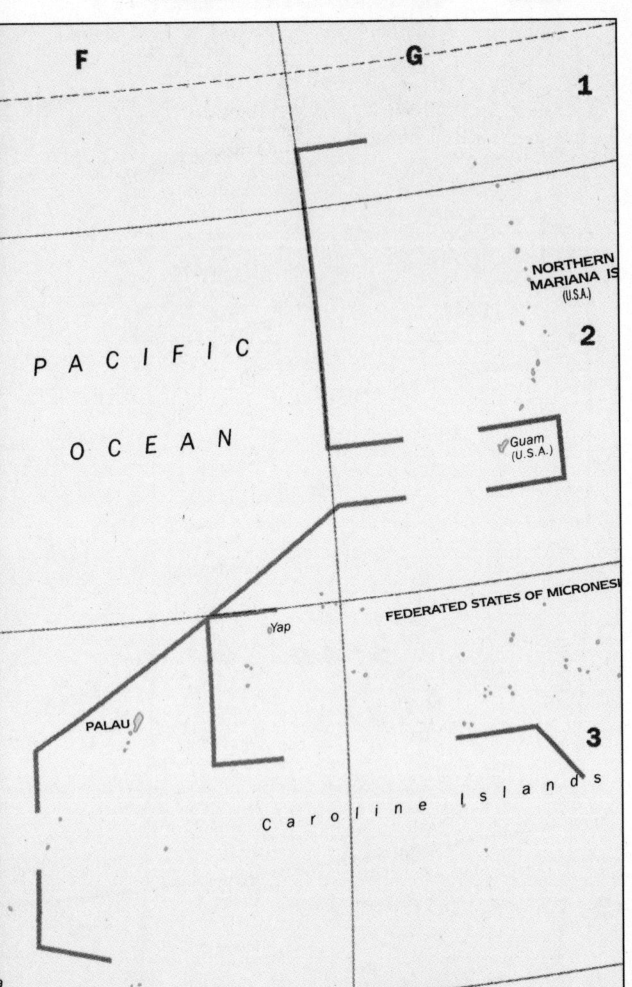
F
G
1
2
3
NORTHERN
MARIANA IS
(U.S.A.)
PACIFIC
OCEAN
Guam
(U.S.A.)
FEDERATED STATES OF MICRONESI
Yap
PALAU
Caroline Islands
ra

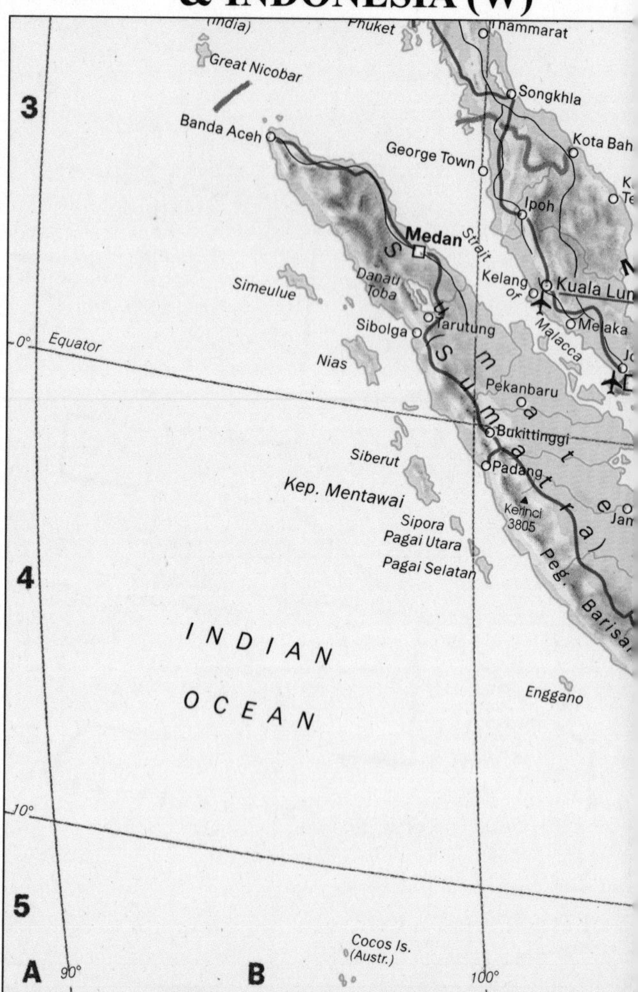
(India)
Phuket
Thammarat
Great Nicobar
Songkhla
Banda Aceh
Kota Bah
George Town
Ipoh
Medan
Strait
of
Malacca
Danau Toba
Simeulue
Kelang
Kuala Lum
Sibolga
Tarutung
Melaka
Equator
Nias
Pekanbaru
Sumatera (Sumatra)
Bukittinggi
Siberut
Padang
Kep. Mentawai
Kerinci 3805
Sipora
Pagai Utara
Pagai Selatan
Peg. Barisan
INDIAN OCEAN
Enggano
Cocos Is. (Austr.)
0°
10°
90°
100°
3
4
5
A
B

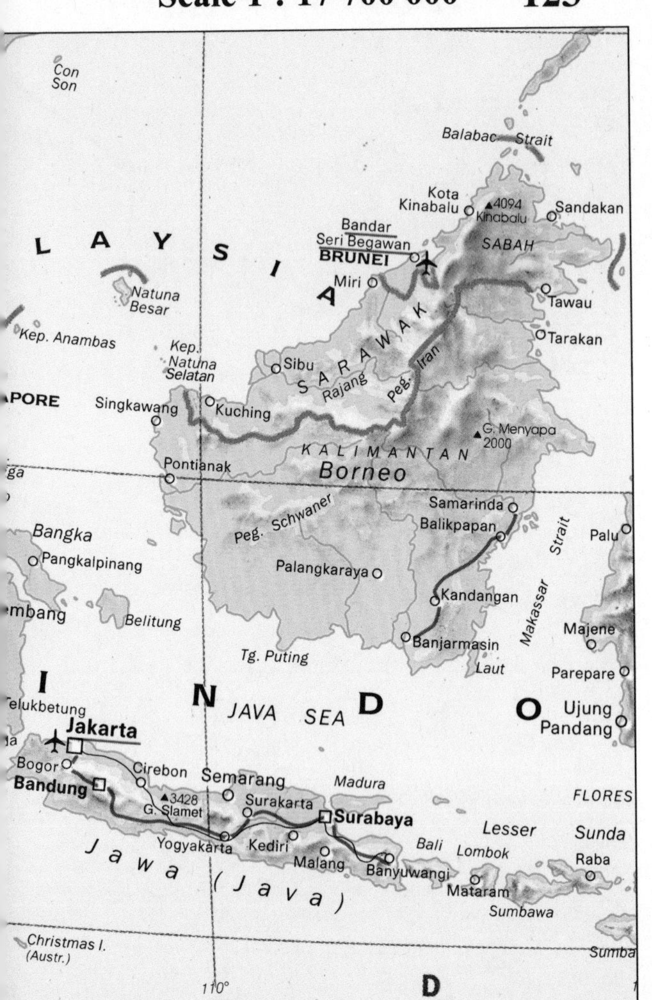
Con Son
L A Y S I A
Natuna Besar
Kep. Anambas
Kep. Natuna Selatan
PORE
Singkawang
Kuching
Sibu
SARAWAK
Rajang
Peg. Iran
Miri
BRUNEI
Bandar Seri Begawan
Kota Kinabalu
4094 Kinabalu
Sandakan
SABAH
Balabac Strait
Tawau
Tarakan
G. Menyapa 2000
KALIMANTAN
Borneo
Pontianak
Peg. Schwaner
Samarinda
Balikpapan
Palangkaraya
Kandangan
Banjarmasin
Makassar Strait
Palu
Majene
Parepare
Ujung Pandang
Laut
Tg. Puting
Bangka
Pangkalpinang
Belitung
I N D O
JAVA SEA
Telukbetung
Jakarta
Bogor
Bandung
Cirebon
Semarang
3428 G. Slamet
Surakarta
Madura
Surabaya
Yogyakarta
Kediri
Malang
Banyuwangi
Bali
Lombok
Mataram
Sumbawa
Lesser Sunda
FLORES
Raba
Jawa (Java)
Christmas I. (Austr.)
Sumba
110°
D

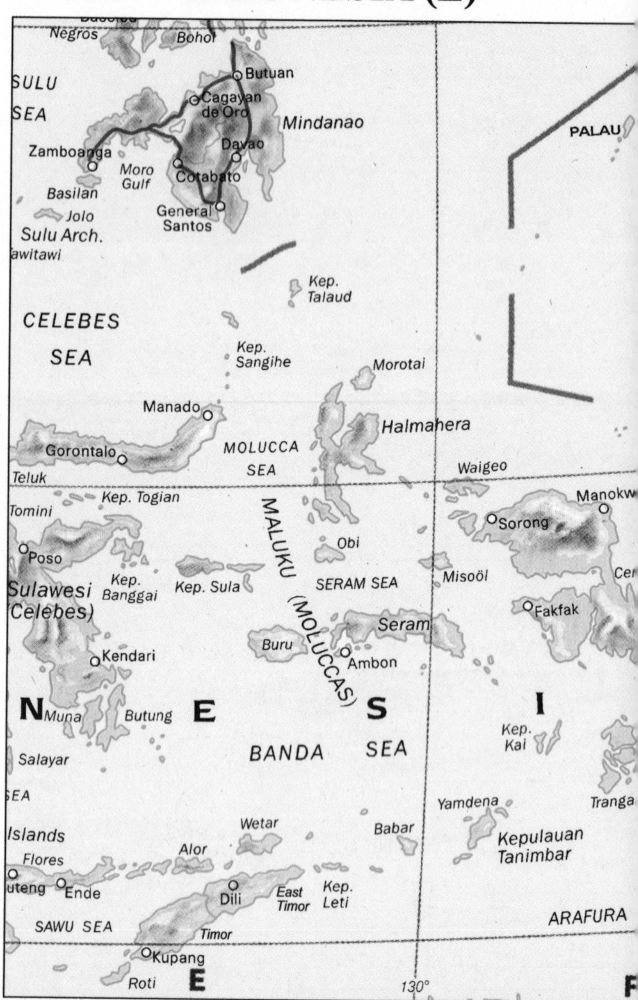
Negros
Bohol
SULU
SEA
Butuan
Cagayan de Oro
Mindanao
PALAU
Zamboanga
Davao
Moro Gulf
Cotabato
Basilan
Jolo
General Santos
Sulu Arch.
Kep. Talaud
CELEBES
SEA
Kep. Sangihe
Morotai
Manado
Halmahera
Gorontalo
MOLUCCA
SEA
Waigeo
Teluk
Tomini
Kep. Togian
MALUKU (MOLUCCAS)
Manokw
Sorong
Obi
Poso
Kep. Banggai
Kep. Sula
SERAM SEA
Misoöl
Sulawesi (Celebes)
Fakfak
Seram
Buru
Ambon
Kendari
N
E
S
I
Muna
Butung
Kep. Kai
Salayar
BANDA
SEA
EA
Yamdena
Tranga
Islands
Wetar
Babar
Kepulauan Tanimbar
Alor
Flores
Ende
Dili
East Timor
Kep. Leti
SAWU SEA
Timor
ARAFURA
Kupang
Roti
E
130°
F

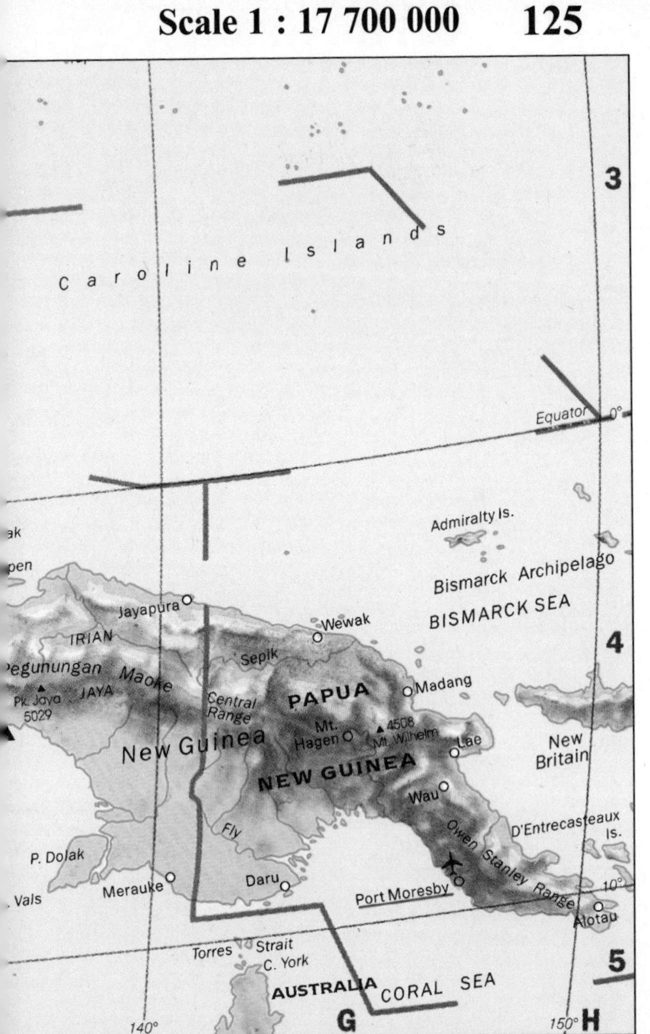
Caroline Islands
Equator
0°
Admiralty Is.
Bismarck Archipelago
BISMARCK SEA
Jayapura
Wewak
IRIAN
Sepik
Pegunungan Maoke
JAYA
Pk. Jaya
5029
Central Range
PAPUA
Madang
Mt. Hagen
4508
Mt. Wilhelm
Lae
New Guinea
NEW GUINEA
New Britain
Wau
Fly
D'Entrecasteaux Is.
Owen Stanley Range
P. Dolak
Merauke
Daru
Port Moresby
10°
Alotau
Vals
Torres Strait
C. York
AUSTRALIA
CORAL SEA
140°
150°
3
4
5
G
H

NORTHEN INDIA & THE HIMALAYAS

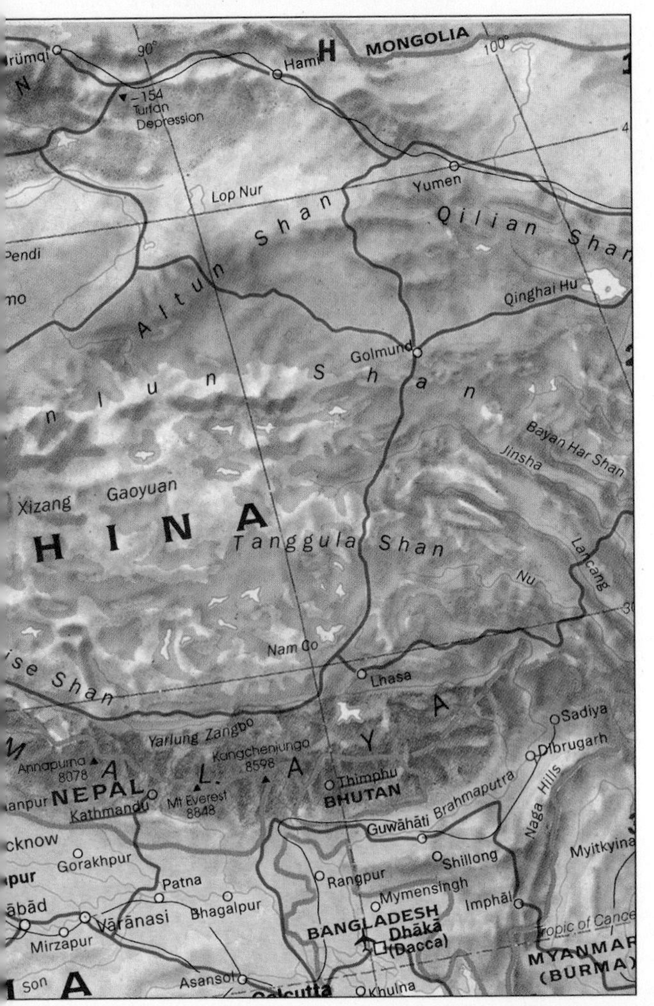
MONGOLIA
Hami
Turfan Depression
−154
Lop Nur
Yumen
Altun Shan
Qilian Shan
Qinghai Hu
Golmud
Kunlun Shan
Bayan Har Shan
Jinsha
Xizang Gaoyuan
CHINA
Tanggula Shan
Lancang
Nu
Nam Co
Lhasa
Yarlung Zangbo
Sadiya
Dibrugarh
Annapurna 8078
Kangchenjunga 8598
Mt Everest 8848
NEPAL
Kathmandu
Thimphu
BHUTAN
Brahmaputra
Naga Hills
Guwāhāti
Shillong
Myitkyina
Gorakhpur
Patna
Rangpur
Mymensingh
Imphāl
Bhagalpur
Vārānasi
Mirzapur
BANGLADESH
Dhākā (Dacca)
Tropic of Cancer
MYANMAR (BURMA)
Asansol
Son
Khulna
Calcutta

SOUTHERN INDIA

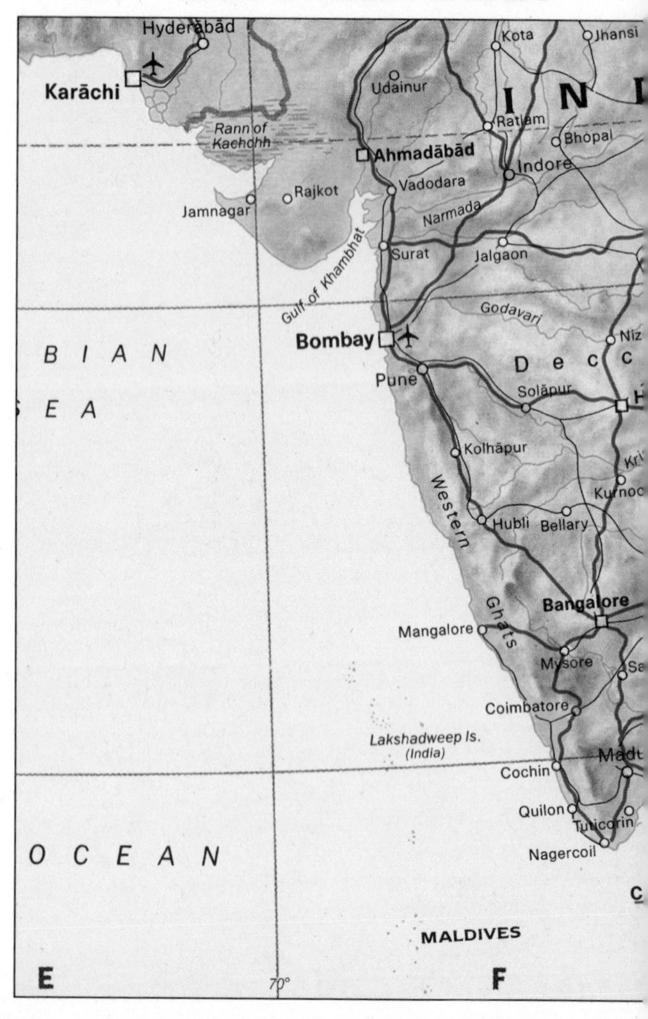

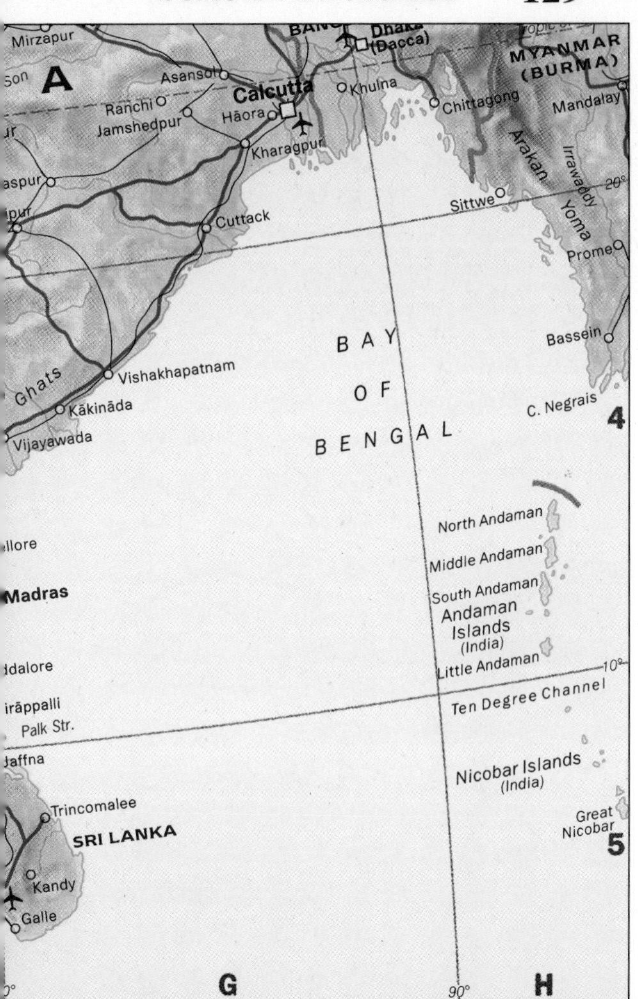
Mirzapur
Dhaka
(Dacca)
MYANMAR
(BURMA)
A
Asansol
Calcutta
Khulna
Ranchi
Jamshedpur
Hāora
Chittagong
Mandalay
Kharagpur
Arakan
Irrawaddy
Yoma
Sittwe
20°
Cuttack
Prome
BAY
OF
BENGAL
Bassein
Vishakhapatnam
Ghats
Kākināda
C. Negrais
4
Vijayawada
North Andaman
Middle Andaman
South Andaman
Andaman
Islands
(India)
Madras
Little Andaman
10°
Ten Degree Channel
Palk Str.
Nicobar Islands
(India)
Trincomalee
SRI LANKA
Great
Nicobar
5
Kandy
Galle
G
90°
H

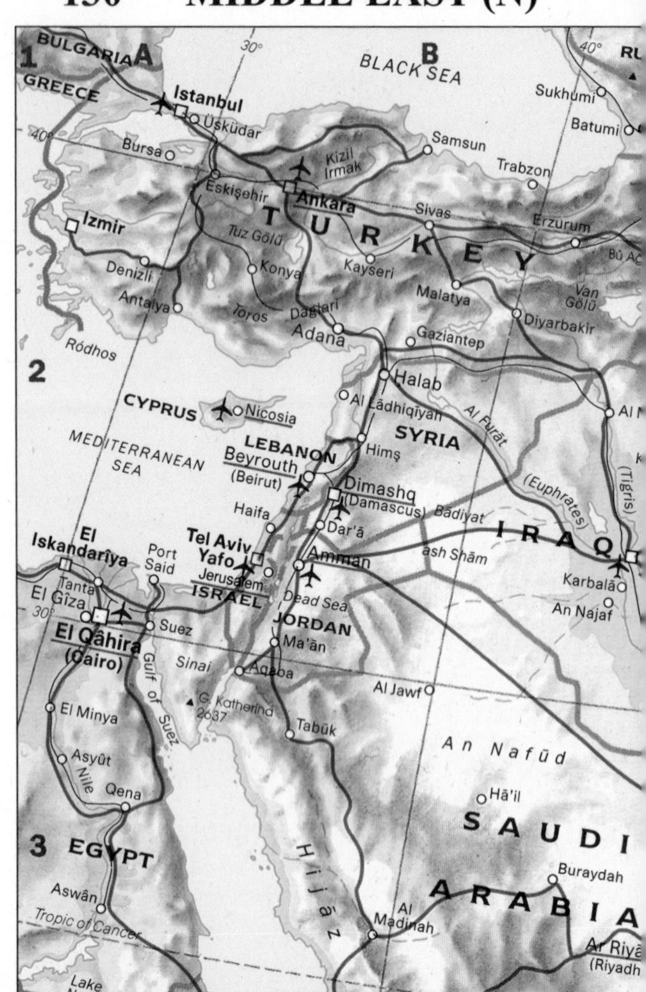

BULGARIA
GREECE
BLACK SEA
Istanbul
Üsküdar
Bursa
Samsun
Sukhumi
Batumi
Trabzon
Kizil Irmak
Eskişehir
Ankara
TURKEY
Izmir
Tuz Gölü
Konya
Sivas
Erzurum
Kayseri
Denizli
Malatya
Van Gölü
Antalya
Toros Dağlari
Adana
Diyarbakir
Gaziantep
Ródhos
Halab
CYPRUS
Nicosia
Al Lādhiqīyah
Al Furāt
SYRIA
LEBANON
Hims
MEDITERRANEAN SEA
Beyrouth (Beirut)
Dimashq (Damascus)
(Euphrates)
(Tigris)
Haifa
Bādiyat ash Shām
Dar'ā
IRAQ
El Iskandarîya
Port Said
Tel Aviv Yafo
Jerusalem
Amman
Tanta
ISRAEL
Karbalā
El Gîza
Dead Sea
An Najaf
El Qâhira (Cairo)
Suez
JORDAN
Ma'ān
Gulf of Suez
Sinai
Aqaba
Al Jawf
G. Katherina 2637
El Minya
Tabūk
An Nafūd
Asyût
Nile
Qena
Hā'il
SAUDI ARABIA
EGYPT
Hijāz
Buraydah
Aswân
Al Madīnah
Tropic of Cancer
Ar Riyā (Riyadh)
Lake Nasser

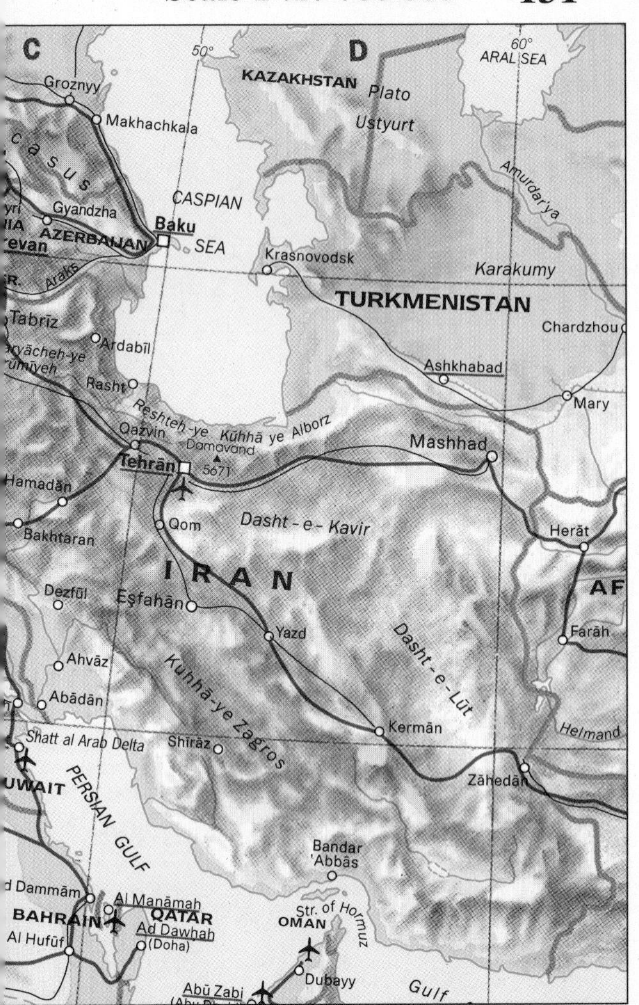
C
D
50°
60°
ARAL SEA
KAZAKHSTAN
Plato
Ustyurt
Groznyy
Makhachkala
casus
Amurdar'ya
CASPIAN
SEA
Gyandzha
Baku
AZERBAIJAN
Krasnovodsk
Karakumy
Araks
TURKMENISTAN
Tabrīz
Chardzhou
Ardabīl
Rasht
Ashkhabad
Mary
Reshteh-ye Kūhhā ye Alborz
Qazvīn
Damavand
5671
Mashhad
Tehrān
Hamadān
Qom
Dasht - e - Kavir
Bakhtaran
Herāt
IRAN
AF
Dezfūl
Eşfahān
Yazd
Dasht - e - Lūt
Farāh
Ahvāz
Kuhhā-ye Zagros
Abādān
Kermān
Helmand
Shatt al Arab Delta
Shīrāz
Zāhedān
KUWAIT
PERSIAN GULF
Bandar 'Abbās
Dammām
Al Manāmah
BAHRAIN
QATAR
Ad Dawhah
(Doha)
Str. of Hormuz
OMAN
Al Hufūf
Dubayy
Abū Zabi
Gulf

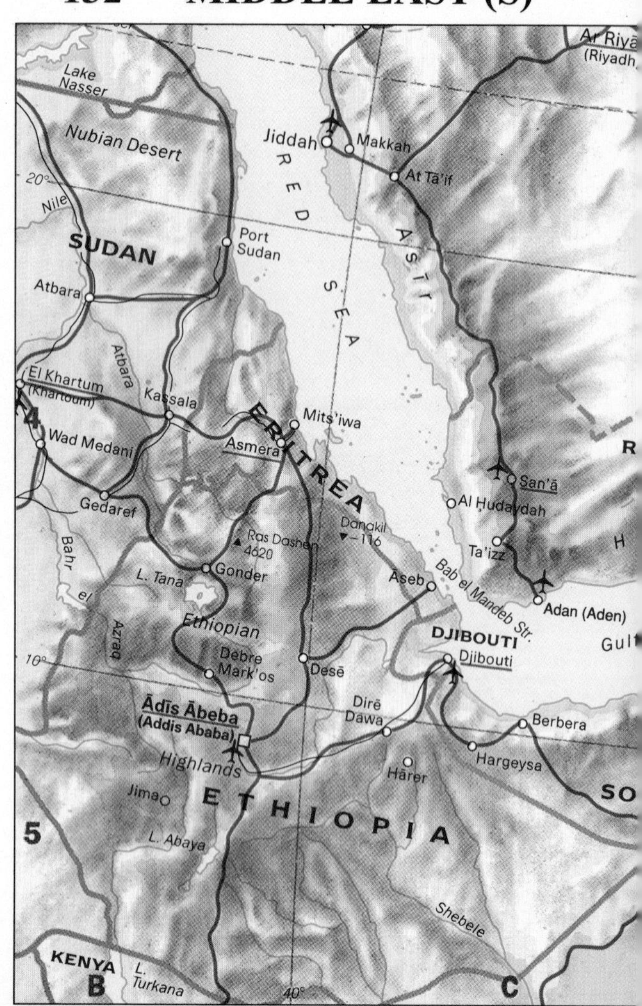

Ar Riyā
(Riyadh
Lake Nasser
Nubian Desert
Jiddah
Makkah
At Ta'if
20°
Nile
RED SEA
SUDAN
Port Sudan
Atbara
Atbara
El Khartum
(Khartoum)
Kassala
Mits'iwa
ERITREA
Asmera
Wad Medani
San'ā
Al Ḥudaydah
Gedaref
Ras Dashen 4620
Danakil −116
Ta'izz
Bahr el Azraq
L. Tana
Gonder
Āseb
Bab el Mandeb Str.
Adan (Aden)
Ethiopian Highlands
DJIBOUTI
Djibouti
10°
Debre Mark'os
Desē
Dirē Dawa
Berbera
Ādīs Ābeba
(Addis Ababa)
Hargeysa
Hārer
Jima
ETHIOPIA
L. Abaya
Shebele
KENYA
L. Turkana
40°
5
B
C

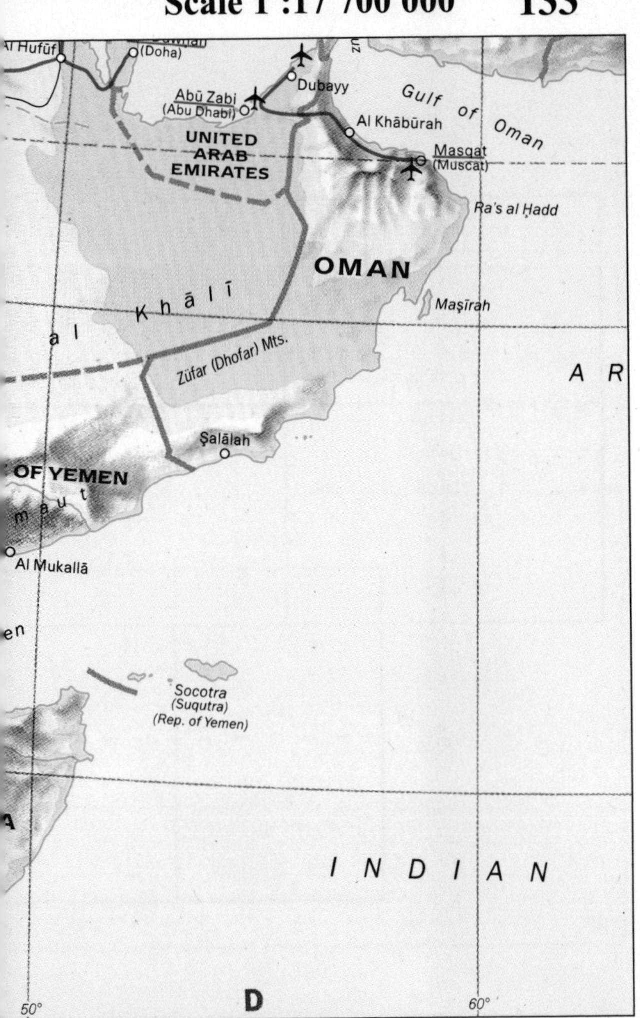

Al Hufūf
(Doha)
Dubayy
Abū Zabi
(Abu Dhabi)
Gulf of Oman
Al Khābūrah
UNITED
ARAB
EMIRATES
Masqat
(Muscat)
Ra's al Ḥadd
OMAN
Khālī
Maşīrah
Zūfar (Dhofar) Mts.
A R
Şalālah
OF YEMEN
Al Mukallā
Socotra
(Suqutra)
(Rep. of Yemen)
I N D I A N
D
50°
60°

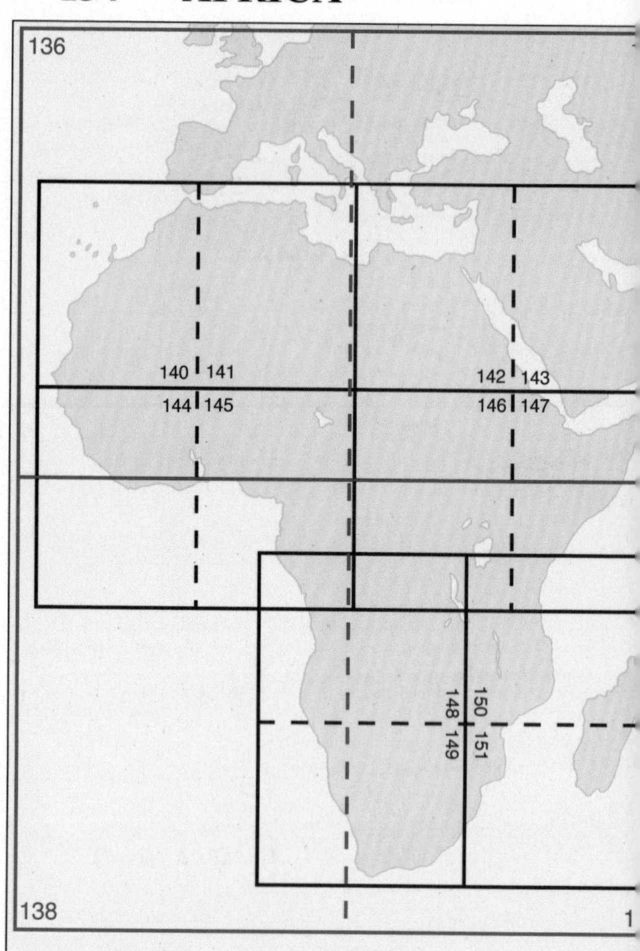
136
140
141
142
143
144
145
146
147
148
149
150
151
138

INDEX TO PAGES

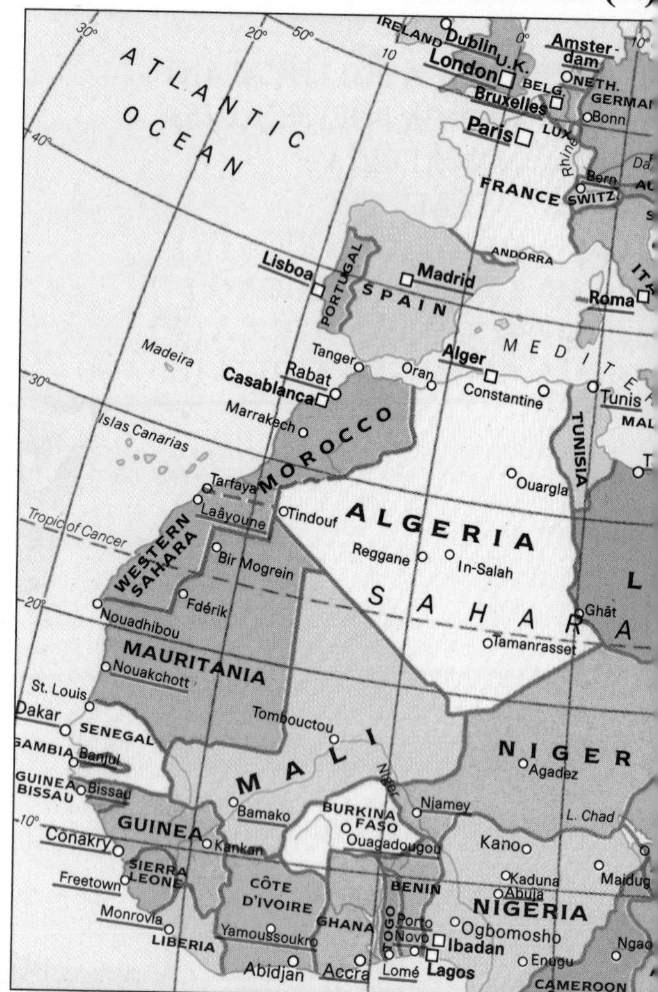
ATLANTIC OCEAN
IRELAND
Dublin
U.K.
London
Amster-dam
NETH.
BELG.
Bruxelles
GERMANY
Bonn
Paris
LUX.
Rhine
Bern
FRANCE
SWITZ.
ANDORRA
Lisboa
PORTUGAL
Madrid
SPAIN
Roma
Madeira
Tanger
Alger
MEDITE
Rabat
Casablanca
Oran
Constantine
Tunis
Marrakech
MOROCCO
TUNISIA
Islas Canarias
Tarfaya
Laâyoune
Tindouf
Ouargla
ALGERIA
Tropic of Cancer
WESTERN SAHARA
Bir Mogrein
Reggane
In-Salah
Fdérik
SAHARA
Ghât
Nouadhibou
Tamanrasset
MAURITANIA
Nouakchott
St. Louis
Dakar
SENEGAL
Tombouctou
MALI
Banjul
NIGER
Agadez
Niger
GUINEA BISSAU
Bissau
Bamako
BURKINA FASO
Niamey
L. Chad
GUINEA
Conakry
Kankan
Ouagadougou
Kano
Maidug
SIERRA LEONE
Freetown
CÔTE D'IVOIRE
BENIN
Kaduna
Abuja
NIGERIA
Monrovia
LIBERIA
Yamoussoukro
GHANA
TOGO
Porto Novo
Ogbomosho
Ibadan
Enugu
Abidjan
Accra
Lomé
Lagos
CAMEROON

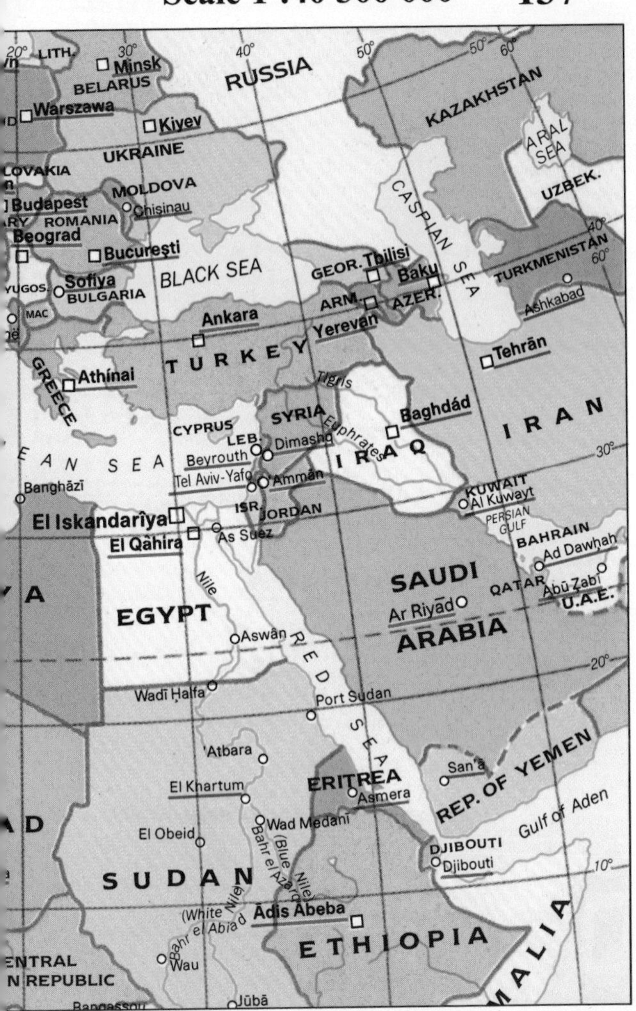
LITH.
Minsk
BELARUS
RUSSIA
KAZAKHSTAN
Warszawa
Kiyev
UKRAINE
ARAL SEA
LOVAKIA
MOLDOVA
Chişinau
UZBEK.
Budapest
ROMANIA
CASPIAN SEA
Beograd
Bucureşti
TURKMENISTAN
BLACK SEA
GEOR.
Tbilisi
Baku
Sofiya
BULGARIA
YUGOS.
ARM.
AZER.
Ashkabad
MAC
Ankara
Yerevan
Tehrān
TURKEY
GREECE
Athínai
Tigris
Baghdád
SYRIA
IRAN
CYPRUS
Euphrates
LEB.
Dimashq
IRAQ
Beyrouth
SEA
Tel Aviv-Yafo
'Ammān
Banghāzī
KUWAIT
Al Kuwayt
ISR.
JORDAN
PERSIAN GULF
El Iskandarîya
As Suez
BAHRAIN
El Qâhira
Ad Dawhah
Nile
SAUDI ARABIA
QATAR
Abū Zabī
U.A.E.
Ar Riyād
EGYPT
Aswân
RED SEA
Wadī Halfa
Port Sudan
'Atbara
San'ā
ERITREA
REP. OF YEMEN
El Khartum
Asmera
Gulf of Aden
Wad Medanī
El Obeid
Bahr el Azarq
(Blue Nile)
DJIBOUTI
Djibouti
SUDAN
(White Nile)
Bahr el Abiad
Ādis Ābeba
ETHIOPIA
Wau
ENTRAL
N REPUBLIC
Jūbā
MALIA
20°
30°
40°
50°
60°
10°

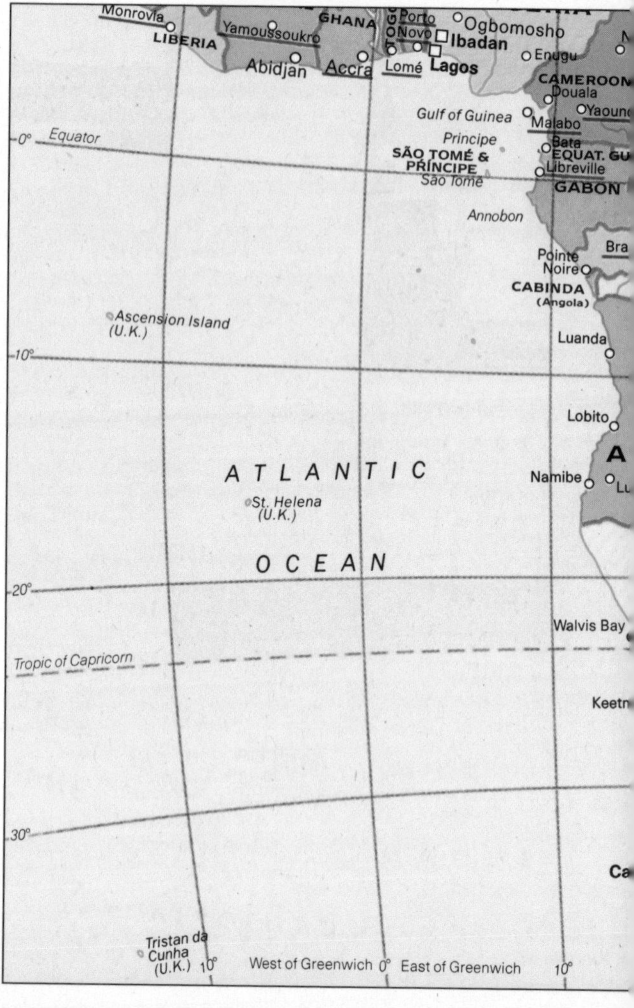

Monrovia
LIBERIA
Yamoussoukro
GHANA
TOGO
Porto
Novo
Ogbomosho
Ibadan
Enugu
Abidjan
Accra
Lomé
Lagos
CAMEROON
Douala
Yaoun
Gulf of Guinea
Malabo
0° Equator
Principe
SÃO TOMÉ & PRÍNCIPE
São Tomé
Bata
EQUAT. GU
Libreville
GABON
Annobon
Bra
Pointe Noire
CABINDA (Angola)
Ascension Island (U.K.)
Luanda
10°
Lobito
A
ATLANTIC
Namibe
Lu
St. Helena (U.K.)
OCEAN
20°
Walvis Bay
Tropic of Capricorn
Keetm
30°
Ca
Tristan da Cunha (U.K.)
10° West of Greenwich 0° East of Greenwich 10°

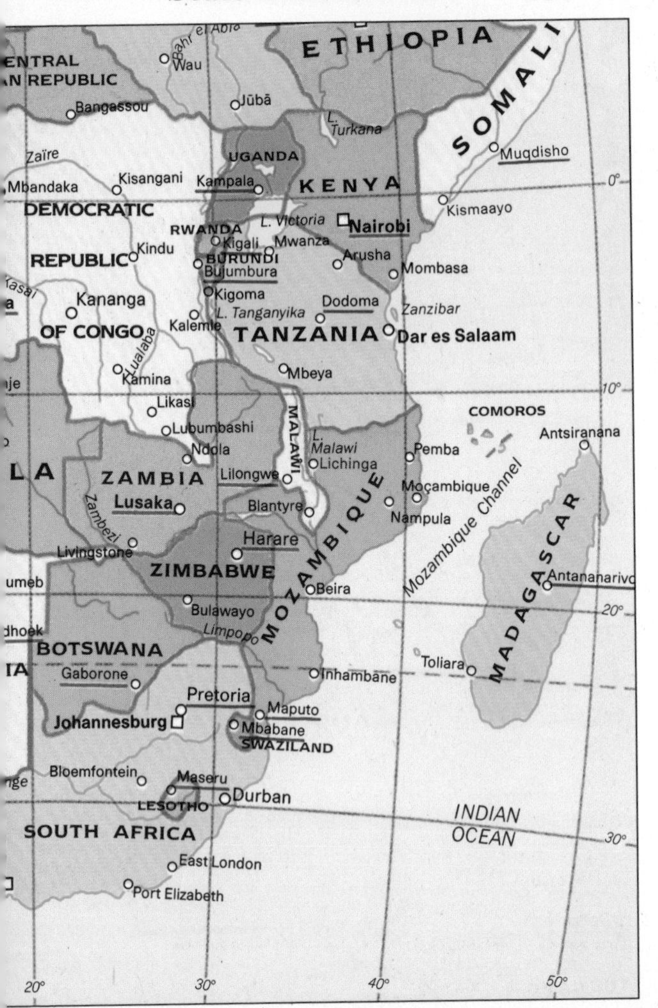

ETHIOPIA
SOMALI
ENTRAL
N REPUBLIC
Wau
Jūbā
Bangassou
L. Turkana
Zaïre
UGANDA
Muqdisho
Mbandaka
Kisangani
Kampala
KENYA
DEMOCRATIC
Kismaayo
RWANDA
L. Victoria
Nairobi
Kigali
Mwanza
REPUBLIC
Kindu
BURUNDI
Arusha
Bujumbura
Mombasa
Kigoma
Kananga
Dodoma
L. Tanganyika
Zanzibar
OF CONGO
Kalemie
TANZANIA
Dar es Salaam
Lualaba
Mbeya
Kamina
Likasi
MALAWI
COMOROS
Lubumbashi
L. Malawi
Antsiranana
Ndola
Pemba
Lichinga
ZAMBIA
Lilongwe
Moçambique
Mozambique Channel
Lusaka
Blantyre
Nampula
Zambezi
Livingstone
Harare
MOZAMBIQUE
ZIMBABWE
MADAGASCAR
Beira
Antananarivo
Bulawayo
Limpopo
BOTSWANA
Toliara
Gaborone
Inhambane
Pretoria
Maputo
Johannesburg
Mbabane
SWAZILAND
Bloemfontein
Maseru
Durban
LESOTHO
INDIAN OCEAN
SOUTH AFRICA
East London
Port Elizabeth
0°
10°
20°
30°
40°
50°

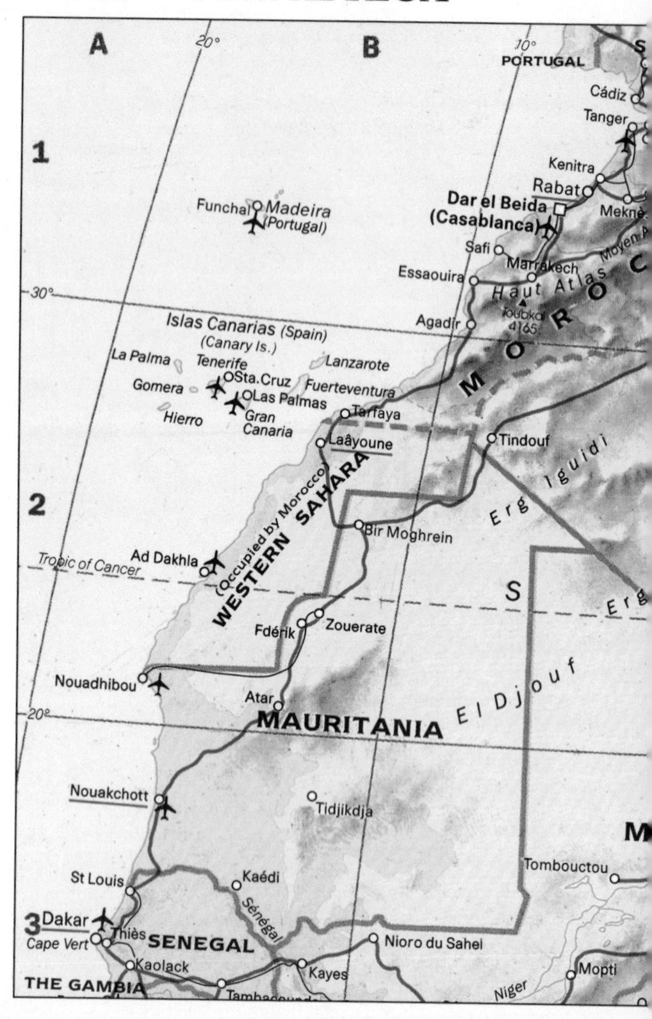

A
B
1
2
3
20°
10°
30°
20°
PORTUGAL
Cádiz
Tanger
Kenitra
Rabat
Dar el Beida
(Casablanca)
Safi
Marrakech
Essaouira
Haut Atlas
Agadir
Funchal
Madeira
(Portugal)
Islas Canarias (Spain)
(Canary Is.)
La Palma
Tenerife
Lanzarote
Sta.Cruz
Gomera
Fuerteventura
Las Palmas
Hierro
Gran
Canaria
Tarfaya
Laâyoune
Tindouf
Erg Iguidi
(Occupied by Morocco)
WESTERN SAHARA
Bir Moghrein
Ad Dakhla
Tropic of Cancer
Fdérik
Zouerate
Nouadhibou
Atar
MAURITANIA
El Djouf
Nouakchott
Tidjikdja
St Louis
Kaédi
Tombouctou
Dakar
Thiès
Cape Vert
SENEGAL
Sénégal
Nioro du Sahel
Kaolack
Kayes
Mopti
Niger
THE GAMBIA

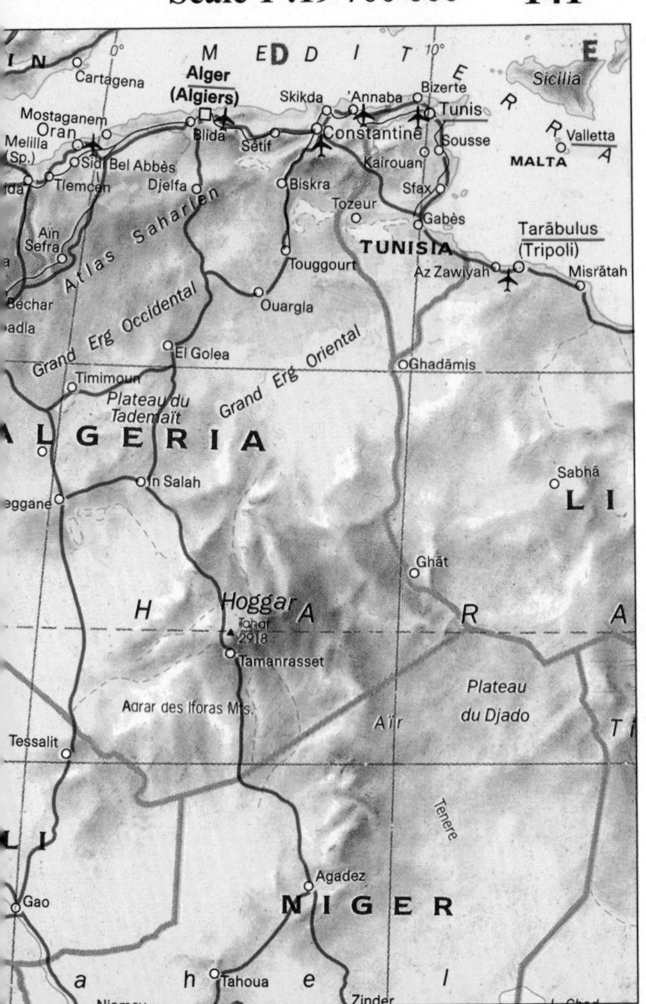

M E D I T E R R A
Cartagena
Alger
(Algiers)
Skikda
'Annaba
Bizerte
Tunis
Sicilia
Valletta
MALTA
Mostaganem
Oran
Melilla
(Sp.)
Blida
Sétif
Constantine
Sousse
Sidi Bel Abbès
Kairouan
Tlemcen
Djelfa
Biskra
Sfax
Tozeur
Gabès
Aïn
Sefra
Atlas Saharien
TUNISIA
Tarābulus
(Tripoli)
Touggourt
Az Zawiyah
Misrātah
Béchar
Ouargla
Grand Erg Occidental
El Golea
Grand Erg Oriental
Ghadāmis
Timimoun
Plateau du
Tademaït
ALGERIA
In Salah
Sabhā
LI
Ghāt
Hoggar
Tahat
2918
H A R A
Tamanrasset
Plateau
du Djado
Adrar des Iforas Mts.
Aïr
Tessalit
Tenere
Agadez
Gao
NIGER
Tahoua
Zinder

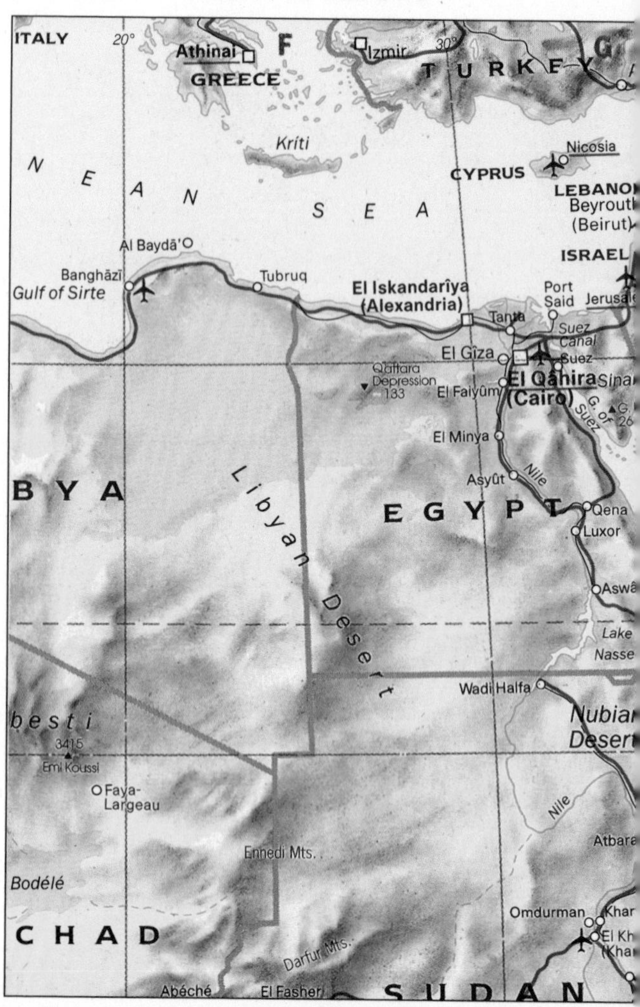
ITALY
20°
Athinai
F
Izmir
30°
G
TURKEY
GREECE
Kríti
Nicosia
CYPRUS
LEBANO
Beyrout
(Beirut)
N E A N S E A
Al Baydā'
ISRAEL
Banghāzī
Gulf of Sirte
Tubruq
El Iskandarîya
(Alexandria)
Port
Said
Jerusale
Tanta
Suez
Canal
El Gîza
Suez
Qattara
Depression
133
El Qâhira
(Cairo)
El Faiyûm
Sina
G. of
Suez
El Minya
Asyût
Nile
B Y A
Libyan Desert
E G Y P T
Qena
Luxor
Aswâ
Lake
Nasse
Wadi Halfa
Nubian
Desert
besti
3415
Emi Koussi
Faya-
Largeau
Nile
Atbara
Ennedi Mts.
Bodélé
Omdurman
Khar
C H A D
El Kh
(Kha
Darfur Mts.
Abéché
El Fasher
S U D A N

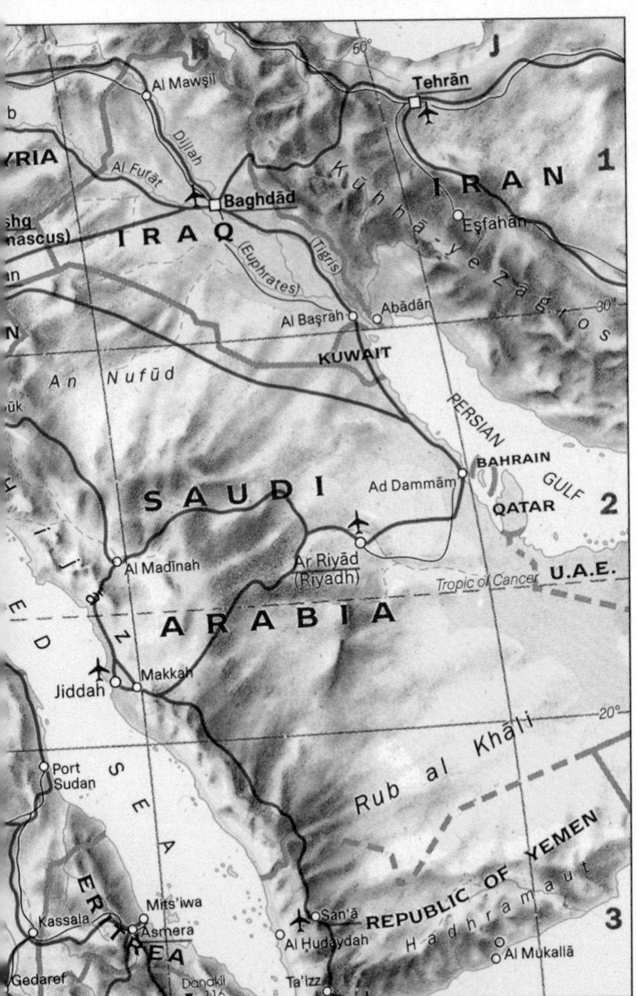

Al Mawşil
Tehrān
Dijlah
Al Furāt
IRAN
Baghdād
IRAQ
Eşfahān
(Euphrates)
(Tigris)
Kūhhā-ye Zāgros
Al Başrah
Abādān
KUWAIT
An Nufūd
PERSIAN GULF
BAHRAIN
Ad Dammām
QATAR
SAUDI ARABIA
Al Madīnah
Ar Riyād
(Riyadh)
Tropic of Cancer
U.A.E.
Makkah
Jiddah
RED SEA
Rub al Khāli
Port Sudan
REPUBLIC OF YEMEN
ERITREA
Mits'iwa
Kassala
Asmera
San'ā
Al Hudaydah
Hadhramaut
Al Mukallā
Gedaref
Ta'izz
30°
20°
50°

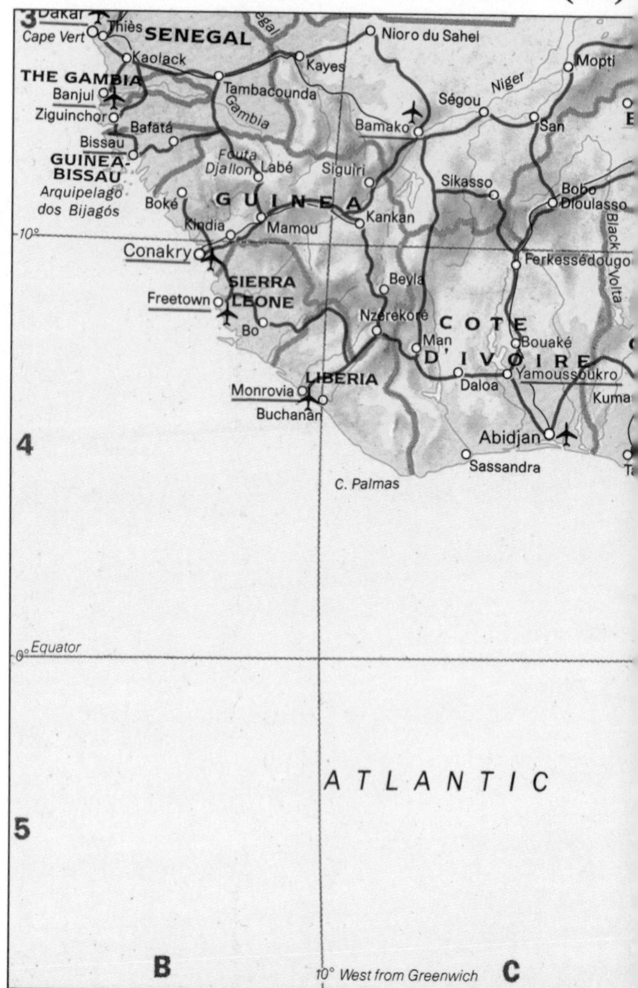

Dakar
Thiès
Cape Vert
SENEGAL
Nioro du Sahel
Kaolack
Kayes
Mopti
THE GAMBIA
Banjul
Tambacounda
Niger
Ségou
Gambia
Ziguinchor
Bafatá
Bamako
San
Bissau
GUINEA-BISSAU
Fouta Djallon
Labé
Siguiri
Sikasso
Bobo Dioulasso
Arquipelago dos Bijagós
Boké
GUINEA
Kankan
Kindia
Mamou
10°
Black Volta
Conakry
Ferkessédougo
SIERRA LEONE
Beyla
Freetown
Nzérekoré
COTE D'IVOIRE
Bo
Man
Bouaké
Yamoussoukro
LIBERIA
Daloa
Monrovia
Buchanan
Abidjan
4
Sassandra
C. Palmas
0° Equator
ATLANTIC
5
B
10° West from Greenwich
C

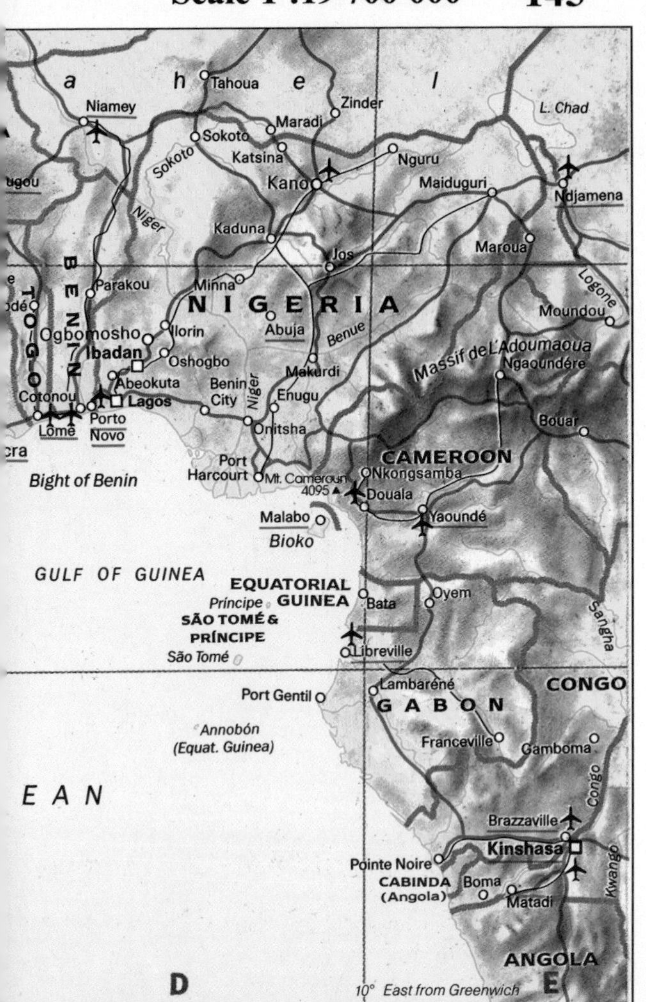
a h e l
Tahoua
Niamey
Zinder
L. Chad
Maradi
Sokoto
Katsina
Nguru
Sokoto
ugou
Kano
Maiduguri
Ndjamena
Niger
Kaduna
Maroua
Jos
BENIN
TOGO
Parakou
Minna
Logone
NIGERIA
Moundou
Abuja
Ogbomosho
Ilorin
Benue
Ibadan
Oshogbo
Massif de L'Adoumaoua
Ngaoundére
Makurdi
Abeokuta
Benin City
Niger
Cotonou
Lagos
Enugu
Lomé
Porto Novo
Bouar
Onitsha
cra
CAMEROON
Port Harcourt
Mt. Cameroun 4095
Nkongsamba
Bight of Benin
Douala
Malabo
Yaoundé
Bioko
GULF OF GUINEA
EQUATORIAL GUINEA
Príncipe
Bata
Oyem
SÃO TOMÉ & PRÍNCIPE
Sangha
São Tomé
Libreville
CONGO
Port Gentil
Lambaréné
GABON
Annobón (Equat. Guinea)
Franceville
Gamboma
E A N
Congo
Brazzaville
Kinshasa
Pointe Noire
Kwango
CABINDA (Angola)
Boma
Matadi
ANGOLA
D
10° East from Greenwich
E

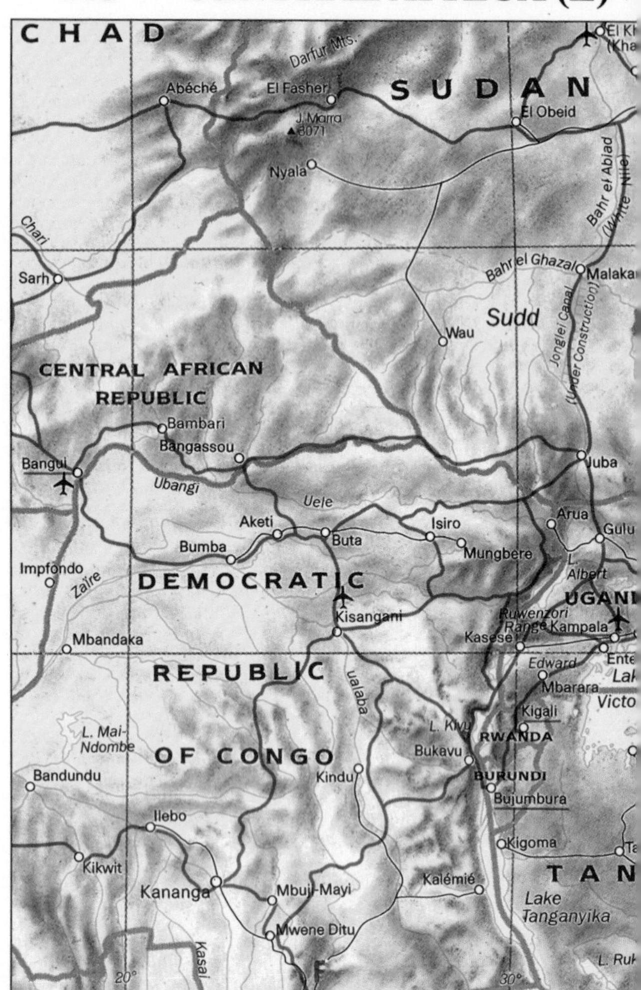
CHAD
Darfur Mts.
Abéché
El Fasher
J. Marra
3071
SUDAN
El Obeid
Nyala
Bahr el Abiad
(White Nile)
Chari
Sarh
Bahr el Ghazal
Sudd
Jonglei Canal
(Under Construction)
Wau
CENTRAL AFRICAN
REPUBLIC
Bambari
Bangassou
Bangui
Ubangi
Juba
Uele
Arua
Aketi
Isiro
Gulu
Buta
Bumba
Mungbere
L. Albert
Impfondo
Zaïre
DEMOCRATIC
Kisangani
Ruwenzori
Range
Kampala
Kasese
Mbandaka
Edward
REPUBLIC
ualaba
Mbarara
Kigali
L. Mai-
Ndombe
L. Kivu
RWANDA
OF CONGO
Bukavu
Kindu
BURUNDI
Bandundu
Bujumbura
Ilebo
Kigoma
Kikwit
Kalémié
Kananga
Mbuji-Mayi
Lake
Tanganyika
Mwene Ditu
Kasai
20°
30°

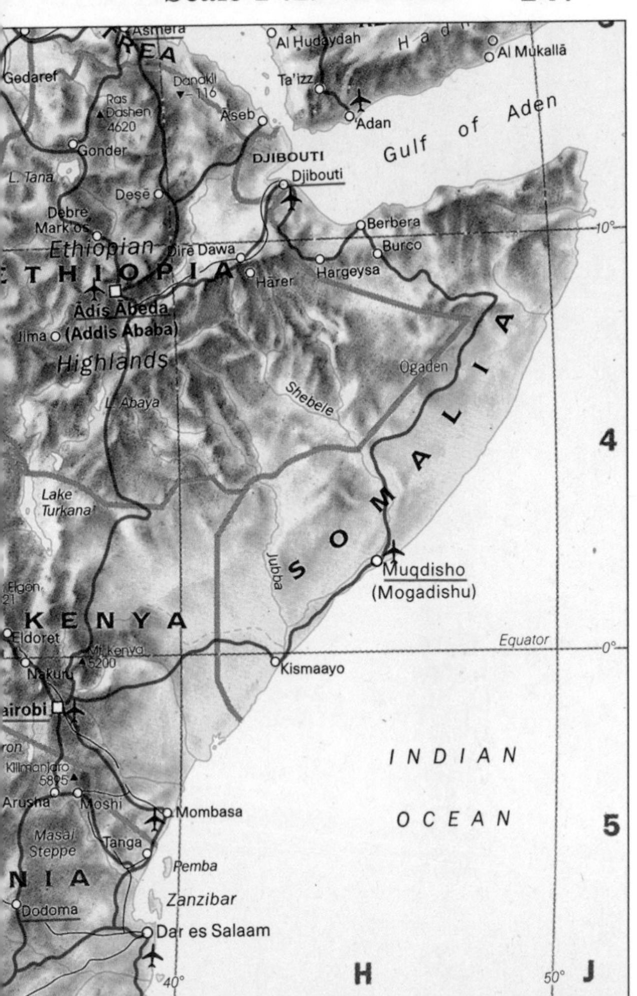
Asmera
ERITREA
Al Hudaydah
Hadramawt
Al Mukallā
Gedaref
Dankil
-116
Ras Dashen
4620
Ta'izz
Āseb
Adan
Gulf of Aden
Gonder
DJIBOUTI
Djibouti
L. Tana
Desē
Debre Markos
Berbera
10°
Ethiopian
Dire Dawa
Burco
ETHIOPIA
Härer
Hargeysa
Ādīs Ābeba
(Addis Ababa)
Jīma
Highlands
Ogaden
Shebele
L. Abaya
4
SOMALIA
Lake Turkana
Jubba
Muqdisho
(Mogadishu)
Elgon
KENYA
Eldoret
Mt. Kenya
5200
Equator
0°
Kismaayo
Nakuru
Nairobi
INDIAN
OCEAN
Kilimanjaro
5895
Arusha
Moshi
Mombasa
5
Masai Steppe
Tanga
Pemba
Zanzibar
Dodoma
Dar es Salaam
40°
H
50°
J

GABON
CONGO
DEMOCRATIC REPUBLIC OF CONGO
ANGOLA
ZAMBIA
RWANDA
BURUND
CABINDA (Angola)
Port Gentil
Franceville
Gamboma
Congo
L. Mai Ndombe
Bandundu
Brazzaville
Kinshasa
Pointe Noire
Boma
Matadi
Kwango
Kikwit
Ilebo
Kananga
Mbuji-Mayi
Mwene Ditu
Kasai
Kamina
Kindu
Lualaba
Bukavu
L. Kivu
Bujum
Kigo
Kalémié
L. Mweru
Luanda
Cuanza
Malanje
Kolwezi
Likasi
L. Bangweulu
Lubumbashi
Chingola
Mufulira
Kitwe
Ndola
Lobito
Benguela
Huambo
Bie Plateau
Menongue
Namibe
Lubango
Cuando
Mongu
Zambezi
Lusaka
A
B
C
1
2
10°
20°
30°

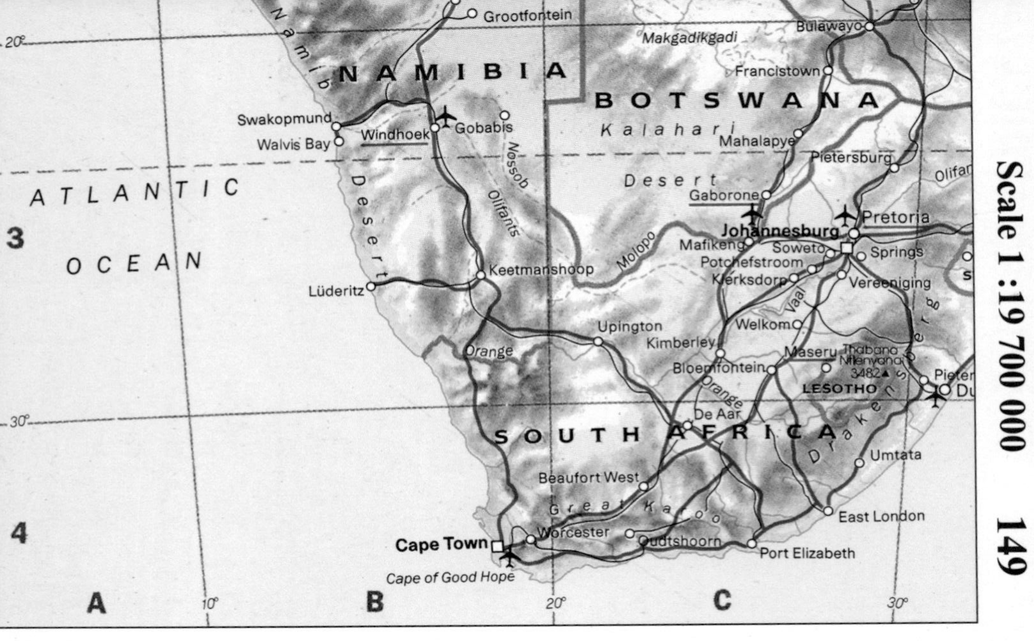
Grootfontein
Bulawayo
Makgadikgadi
NAMIBIA
Namib Desert
Francistown
BOTSWANA
Kalahari Desert
Swakopmund
Walvis Bay
Windhoek
Gobabis
Mahalapye
Nossob
Pietersburg
Olifants
ATLANTIC
OCEAN
Gaborone
Pretoria
Johannesburg
Mafikeng
Soweto
Springs
Molopo
Potchefstroom
Klerksdorp
Vereeniging
Keetmanshoop
Lüderitz
Vaal
Welkom
Upington
Kimberley
Orange
Maseru
Thabana Ntlenyana
3482
Bloemfontein
LESOTHO
De Aar
SOUTH AFRICA
Drakensberg
Umtata
Beaufort West
Great Karoo
East London
Worcester
Oudtshoorn
Cape Town
Port Elizabeth
Cape of Good Hope
3
4
A
B
C
10°
20°
30°

INDIAN OCEAN
SEYCHELLES
Amirante Is.
Farquhar Is.
COMOROS
Moroni
Mayotte (France)
Antsirañana
Massif du Tsaratanana
Mahajanga
KENYA
Nairobi
Mombasa
TANZANIA
Dar es Salaam
Dodoma
Zanzibar
Pemba
Mafia I
Rufiji
Kilimanjaro 5895
Moshi
Arusha
Masai Steppe
Mwanza
Lake Victoria
Tabora
Kigoma
Lake Tanganyika
L. Rukwa
Mbeya
Rungwe 2959
Iringa
Mtwara
Cape Delgado
Ruvuma
Pemba
Moçambique
Nampula
Lichinga
Lake Malawi
MALAWI
Lilongwe
Zomba
Blantyre
Shire
Zambezi
Tete
Cabora Bassa Dam
Kasama
Muchinga Mts.
Luangwa
RWANDA
Kigali
BURUNDI
Bujumbura
Ndola
50°
40°
30°
10°
D
E
F
1
2

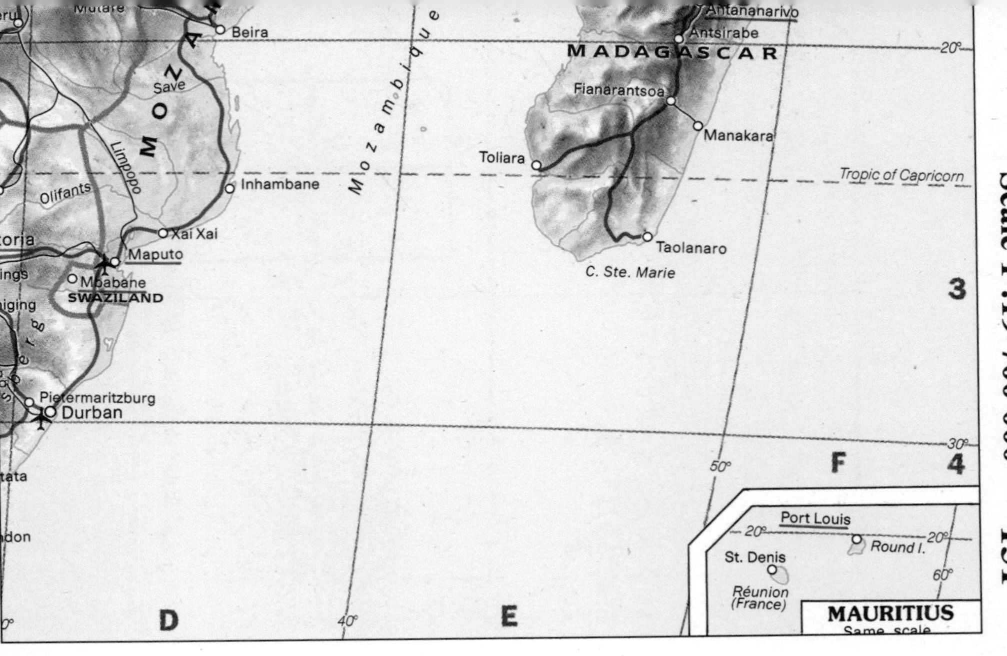
Beira
Antananarivo
Antsirabe
MADAGASCAR
Save
Fianarantsoa
Manakara
Mozambique
Limpopo
Toliara
Tropic of Capricorn
Olifants
Inhambane
Xai Xai
Taolanaro
Maputo
C. Ste. Marie
Mbabane
SWAZILAND
Pietermaritzburg
Durban
Port Louis
Round I.
St. Denis
Réunion
(France)
MAURITIUS
D
E
F
3
4
20°
30°
40°
50°
60°

AUSTRALASIA & OCEANIA

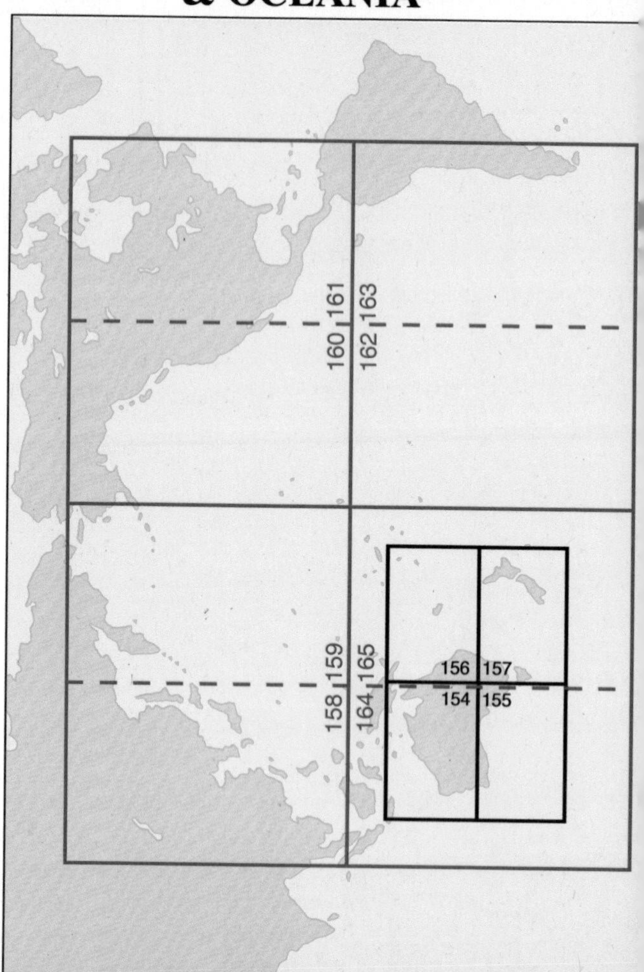

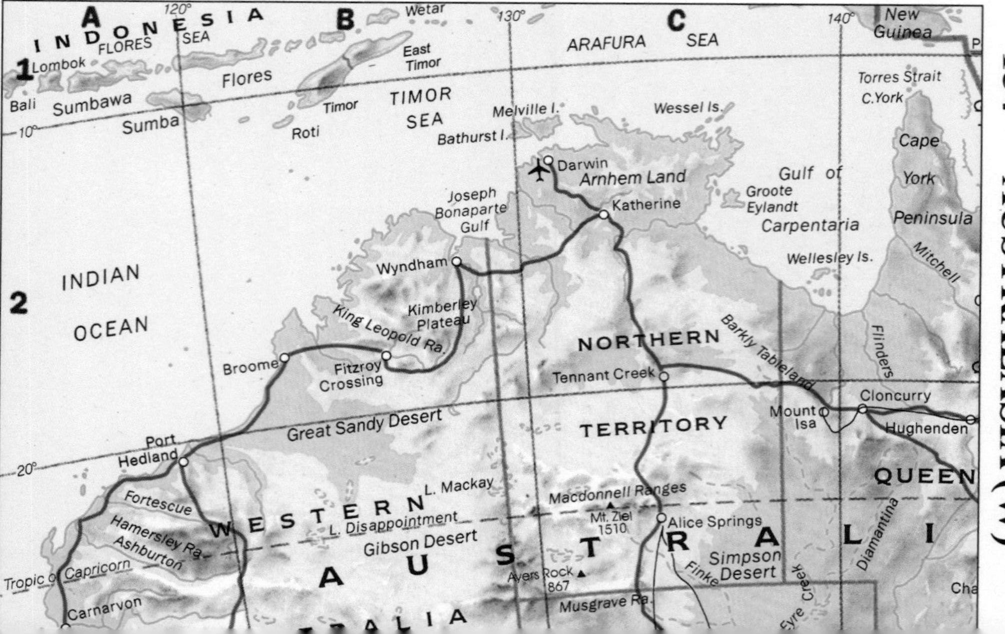

A
B
C
1
2
INDONESIA
FLORES SEA
Wetar
East Timor
ARAFURA SEA
New Guinea
Lombok
Bali
Sumbawa
Sumba
Flores
Timor
Roti
TIMOR SEA
Melville I.
Bathurst I.
Wessel Is.
Torres Strait
C.York
Cape York Peninsula
Darwin
Arnhem Land
Katherine
Joseph Bonaparte Gulf
Gulf of Carpentaria
Groote Eylandt
Wellesley Is.
Mitchell
INDIAN OCEAN
Wyndham
Kimberley Plateau
King Leopold Ra.
Broome
Fitzroy Crossing
NORTHERN
Barkly Tableland
Flinders
Tennant Creek
Cloncurry
Mount Isa
Hughenden
Great Sandy Desert
TERRITORY
Port Hedland
QUEEN
L. Mackay
Macdonnell Ranges
Mt. Ziel 1510
Alice Springs
Fortescue
WESTERN
L. Disappointment
Hamersley Ra.
Ashburton
Gibson Desert
Diamantina
AUSTRALIA
Simpson Desert
Finke
Eyre Creek
Ayers Rock 867
Tropic of Capricorn
Carnarvon
Musgrave Ra.
120°
130°
140°
10°
20°

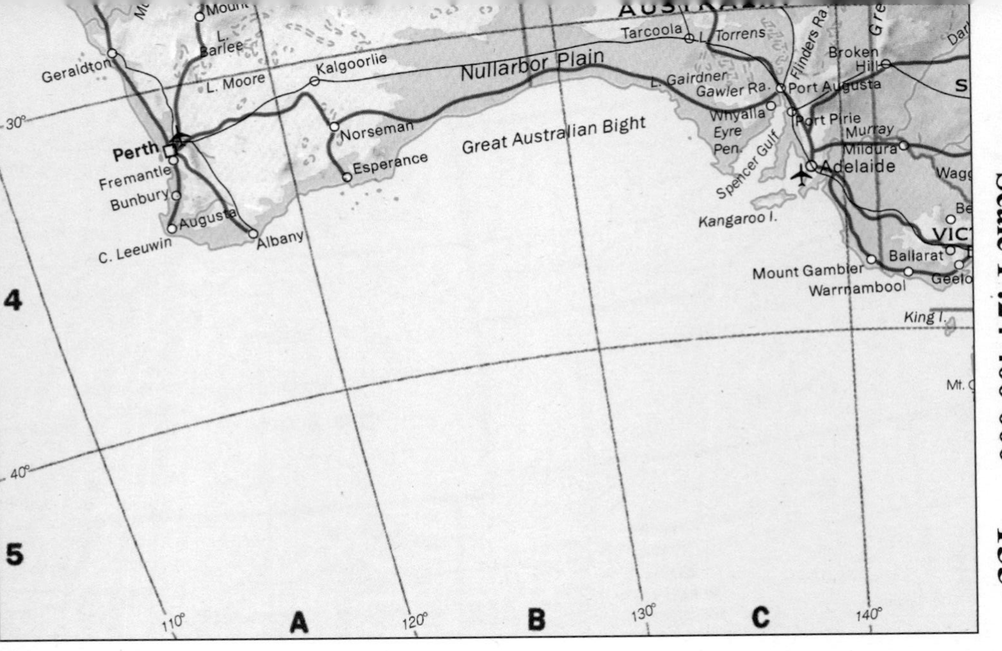
Geraldton
L. Barlee
L. Moore
Kalgoorlie
Perth
Fremantle
Bunbury
Augusta
C. Leeuwin
Albany
Norseman
Esperance
Nullarbor Plain
Great Australian Bight
Tarcoola
L. Torrens
L. Gairdner
Gawler Ra.
Flinders Ra.
Port Augusta
Whyalla
Eyre Pen.
Spencer Gulf
Port Pirie
Kangaroo I.
Broken Hill
Murray
Mildura
Adelaide
Ballarat
Mount Gambier
Warrnambool
King I.
30°
40°
110°
120°
130°
140°
A
B
C
4
5

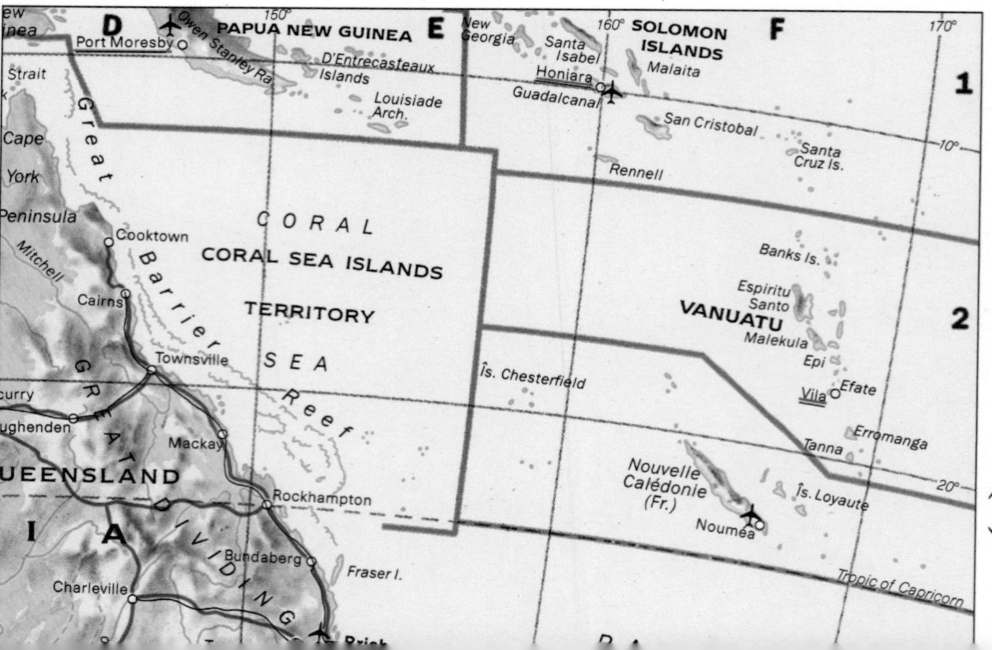

D
E
F
1
2
150°
160°
170°
10°
20°
PAPUA NEW GUINEA
Port Moresby
Owen Stanley Ra.
D'Entrecasteaux Islands
Louisiade Arch.
New Georgia
Santa Isabel
Honiara
Guadalcanal
SOLOMON ISLANDS
Malaita
San Cristobal
Santa Cruz Is.
Rennell
Strait
Cape
York
Peninsula
Great Barrier Reef
Cooktown
Cairns
Mitchell
CORAL
CORAL SEA ISLANDS
TERRITORY
SEA
Townsville
Mackay
QUEENSLAND
GREAT DIVIDING
Rockhampton
Bundaberg
Fraser I.
Charleville
Îs. Chesterfield
Banks Is.
Espiritu Santo
VANUATU
Malekula
Epi
Efate
Vila
Erromanga
Tanna
Nouvelle Calédonie (Fr.)
Îs. Loyauté
Nouméa
Tropic of Capricorn

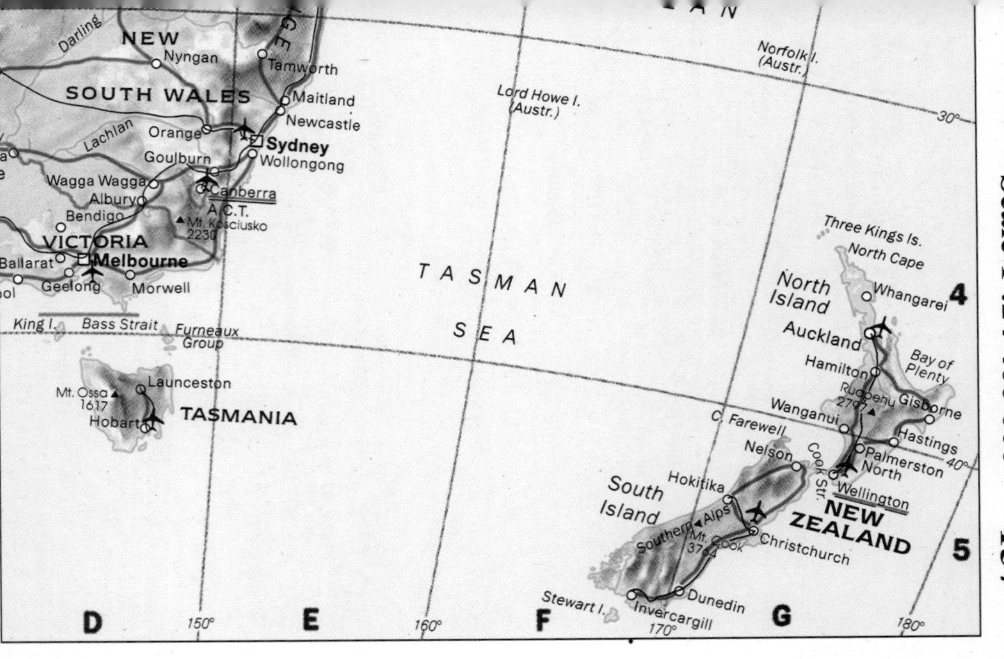

NEW SOUTH WALES
Darling
Nyngan
Tamworth
Maitland
Newcastle
Orange
Sydney
Wollongong
Lachlan
Goulburn
Wagga Wagga
Albury
Canberra
A.C.T.
Mt. Kosciusko
2230
Bendigo
VICTORIA
Ballarat
Melbourne
Geelong
Morwell
King I.
Bass Strait
Furneaux Group
Launceston
Mt. Ossa
1617
Hobart
TASMANIA
Lord Howe I. (Austr.)
Norfolk I. (Austr.)
TASMAN SEA
Three Kings Is.
North Cape
North Island
Whangarei
Auckland
Hamilton
Bay of Plenty
Ruapehu
2797
Gisborne
Wanganui
Hastings
C. Farewell
Nelson
Cook Str.
Palmerston North
Wellington
NEW ZEALAND
South Island
Hokitika
Southern Alps
Mt. Cook
3764
Christchurch
Dunedin
Stewart I.
Invercargill
30°
40°
150°
160°
170°
180°
D
E
F
G
4
5

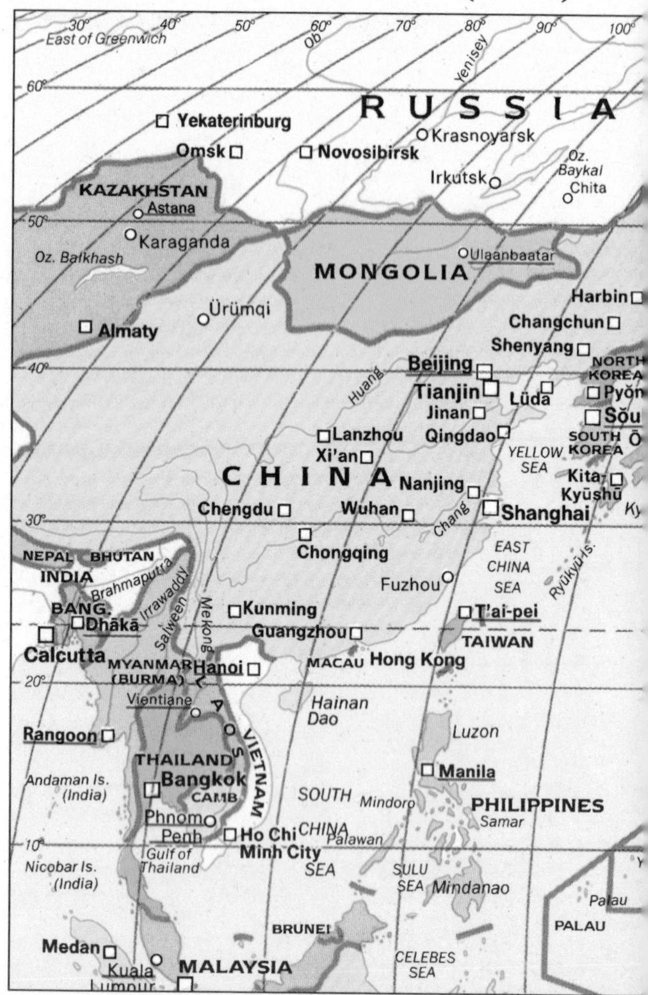
30°
40°
East of Greenwich
50°
60°
70°
80°
90°
100°
Ob
Yenisey
60°
RUSSIA
Yekaterinburg
Krasnoyarsk
Omsk
Novosibirsk
Oz. Baykal
Irkutsk
Chita
KAZAKHSTAN
Astana
50°
Karaganda
Oz. Balkhash
Ulaanbaatar
MONGOLIA
Harbin
Ürümqi
Changchun
Almaty
Shenyang
40°
Beijing
NORTH KOREA
Huang
Tianjin
Lüda
Pyŏn
Jinan
Sŏu
Lanzhou
Qingdao
SOUTH KOREA
Xi'an
YELLOW SEA
CHINA
Nanjing
Kita-Kyūshū
Chengdu
Wuhan
Shanghai
30°
Chang
Chongqing
EAST CHINA SEA
NEPAL
BHUTAN
INDIA
Brahmaputra
Ryūkyū Is.
Fuzhou
Irrawaddy
BANG.
Salween
Mekong
Kunming
T'ai-pei
Dhākā
Guangzhou
TAIWAN
Calcutta
MYANMAR (BURMA)
Hanoi
MACAU
Hong Kong
20°
Vientiane
Hainan Dao
LAOS
Rangoon
VIETNAM
Luzon
THAILAND
Manila
Andaman Is. (India)
Bangkok
CAMB.
SOUTH CHINA SEA
Mindoro
PHILIPPINES
Phnom Penh
Samar
Ho Chi Minh City
Palawan
10°
Gulf of Thailand
Nicobar Is. (India)
SULU SEA
Mindanao
Palau
BRUNEI
PALAU
Medan
Kuala Lumpur
MALAYSIA
CELEBES SEA

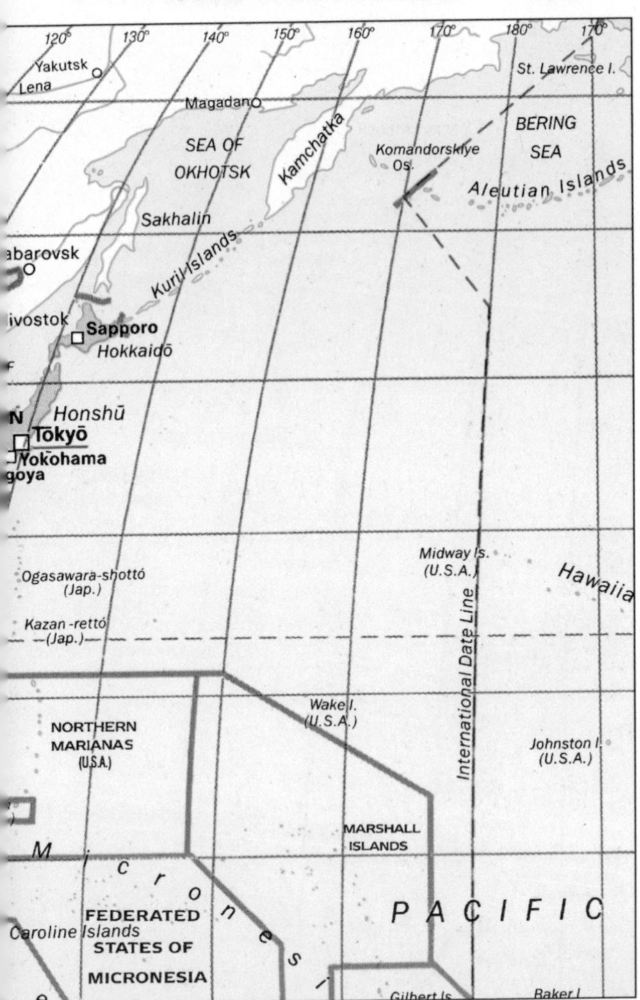
120°
130°
140°
150°
160°
170°
180°
170°
Yakutsk
Lena
St. Lawrence I.
Magadan
SEA OF
OKHOTSK
Kamchatka
Komandorskiye
Os.
BERING
SEA
Aleutian Islands
Sakhalin
Kuril Islands
abarovsk
ivostok
Sapporo
Hokkaidō
Honshū
Tōkyō
Yokohama
goya
Midway Is.
(U.S.A.)
Hawaiia
Ogasawara-shottó
(Jap.)
Kazan -rettó
(Jap.)
International Date Line
Wake I.
(U.S.A.)
NORTHERN
MARIANAS
(U.S.A.)
Johnston I.
(U.S.A.)
MARSHALL
ISLANDS
Micronesi
FEDERATED
STATES OF
MICRONESIA
Caroline Islands
PACIFIC
Gilbert Is.
Baker I.

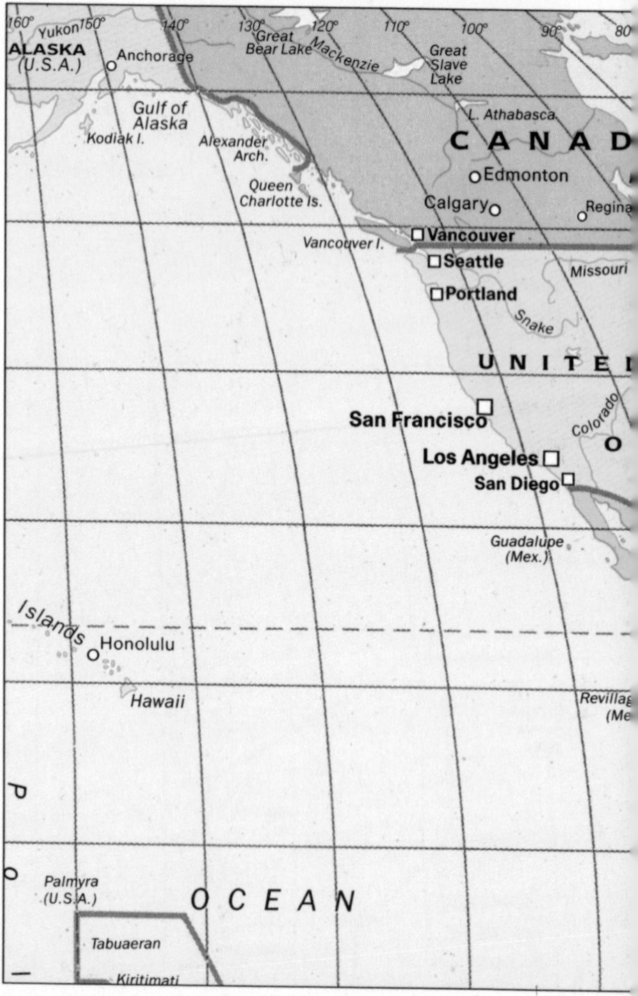

160°
Yukon
150°
140°
130°
120°
110°
100°
90°
80
ALASKA
(U.S.A.)
Anchorage
Great
Bear Lake
Mackenzie
Great
Slave
Lake
Gulf of
Alaska
L. Athabasca
Kodiak I.
Alexander
Arch.
CANAD
Edmonton
Queen
Charlotte Is.
Calgary
Regina
Vancouver I.
Vancouver
Seattle
Portland
Missouri
Snake
UNITE
San Francisco
Colorado
Los Angeles
San Diego
Guadalupe
(Mex.)
Islands
Honolulu
Hawaii
Revillag
(Me
P
O
Palmyra
(U.S.A.)
OCEAN
Tabuaeran
Kiritimati

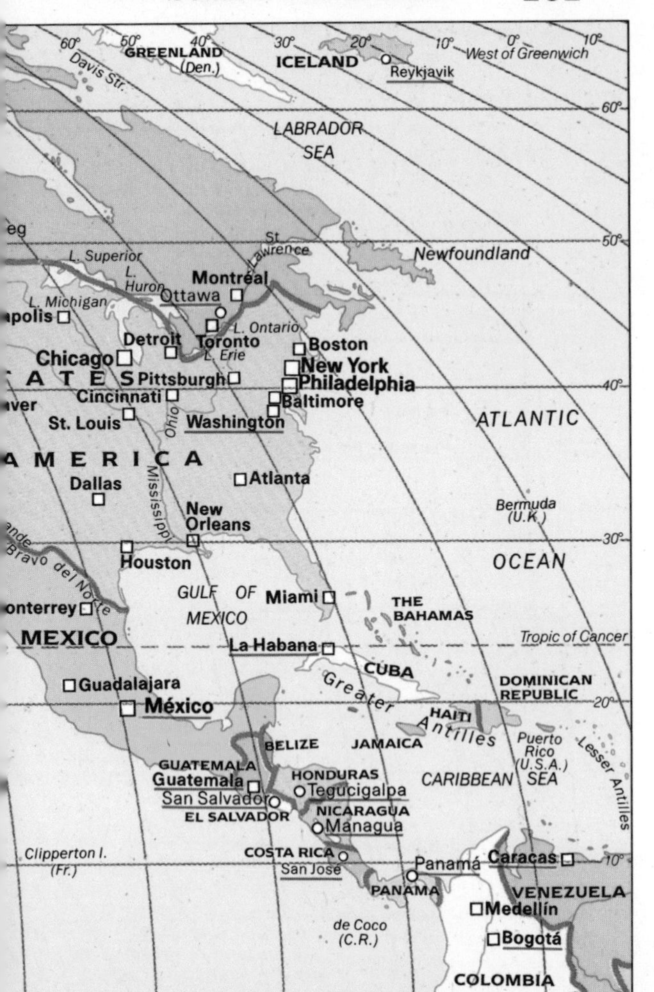

60°
50°
40°
30°
20°
10°
0°
10°
West of Greenwich
GREENLAND
(Den.)
Davis Str.
ICELAND
Reykjavik
60°
LABRADOR
SEA
St
Lawrence
Newfoundland
50°
L. Superior
L. Huron
L. Michigan
Montreal
Ottawa
L. Ontario
Detroit
Toronto
L. Erie
Boston
Chicago
New York
Pittsburgh
Philadelphia
Cincinnati
Baltimore
40°
St. Louis
Ohio
Washington
ATLANTIC
A M E R I C A
Dallas
Mississippi
Atlanta
New Orleans
Bermuda
(U.K.)
Houston
30°
Bravo del Norte
OCEAN
GULF OF
MEXICO
Miami
THE BAHAMAS
MEXICO
La Habana
Tropic of Cancer
CUBA
Guadalajara
Greater Antilles
DOMINICAN REPUBLIC
México
HAITI
20°
BELIZE
JAMAICA
Puerto Rico
(U.S.A.)
Lesser Antilles
GUATEMALA
Guatemala
HONDURAS
Tegucigalpa
CARIBBEAN SEA
San Salvador
EL SALVADOR
NICARAGUA
Managua
Clipperton I.
(Fr.)
COSTA RICA
San José
Panamá
Caracas
10°
PANAMA
VENEZUELA
Medellín
de Coco
(C.R.)
Bogotá
COLOMBIA

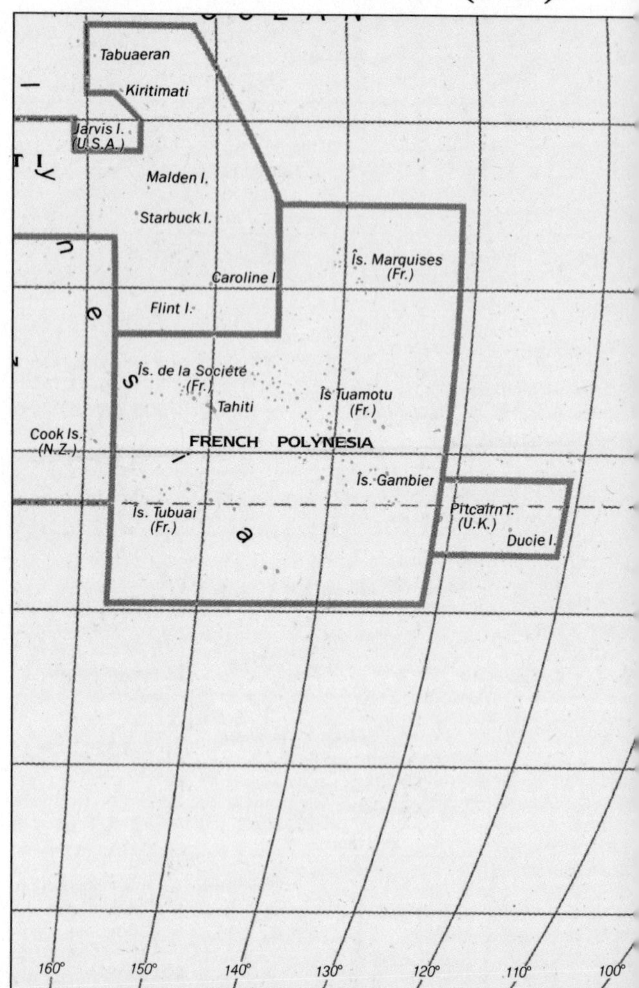

Tabuaeran
Kiritimati
Jarvis I.
(U.S.A.)
Malden I.
Starbuck I.
Caroline I.
Flint I.
Îs. Marquises
(Fr.)
Îs. de la Société
(Fr.)
Tahiti
Îs Tuamotu
(Fr.)
Cook Is.
(N.Z.)
FRENCH POLYNESIA
Îs. Gambier
Îs. Tubuai
(Fr.)
Pitcairn I.
(U.K.)
Ducie I.
160°
150°
140°
130°
120°
110°
100°

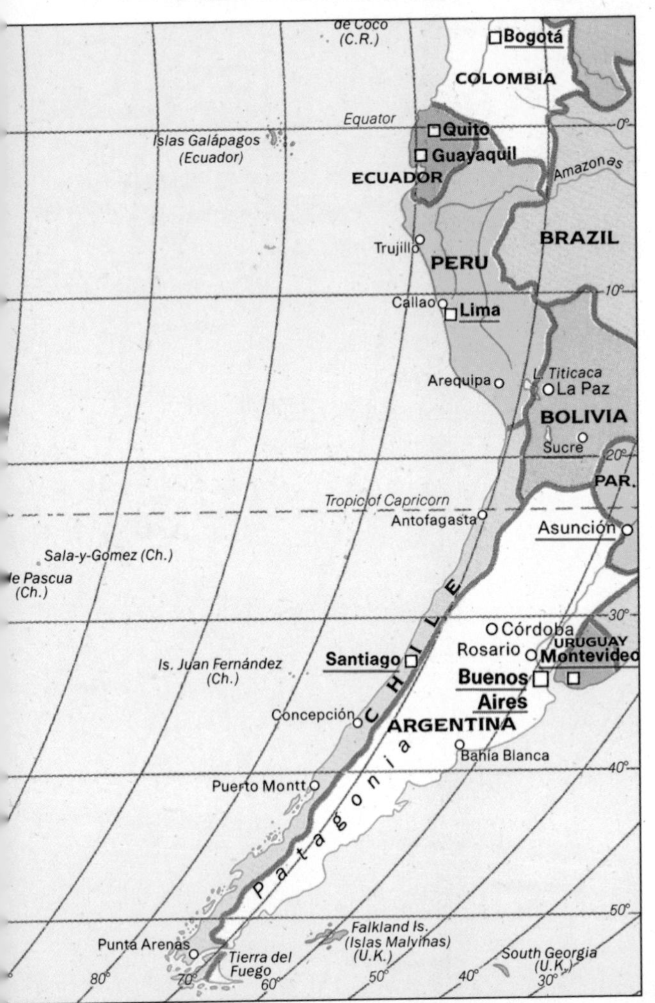
de Coco
(C.R.)
Bogotá
COLOMBIA
Equator
0°
Quito
Islas Galápagos
(Ecuador)
Guayaquil
ECUADOR
Amazonas
Trujillo
BRAZIL
PERU
10°
Callao
Lima
Arequipa
L. Titicaca
La Paz
BOLIVIA
Sucre
20°
PAR.
Tropic of Capricorn
Antofagasta
Asunción
Sala-y-Gomez (Ch.)
le Pascua
(Ch.)
30°
Córdoba
URUGUAY
Rosario
Montevideo
Santiago
Is. Juan Fernández
(Ch.)
Buenos
Aires
CHILE
Concepción
ARGENTINA
Bahía Blanca
40°
Puerto Montt
Patagonia
50°
Falkland Is.
(Islas Malvinas)
(U.K.)
Punta Arenas
Tierra del
Fuego
South Georgia
(U.K.)
80°
70°
60°
50°
40°
30°

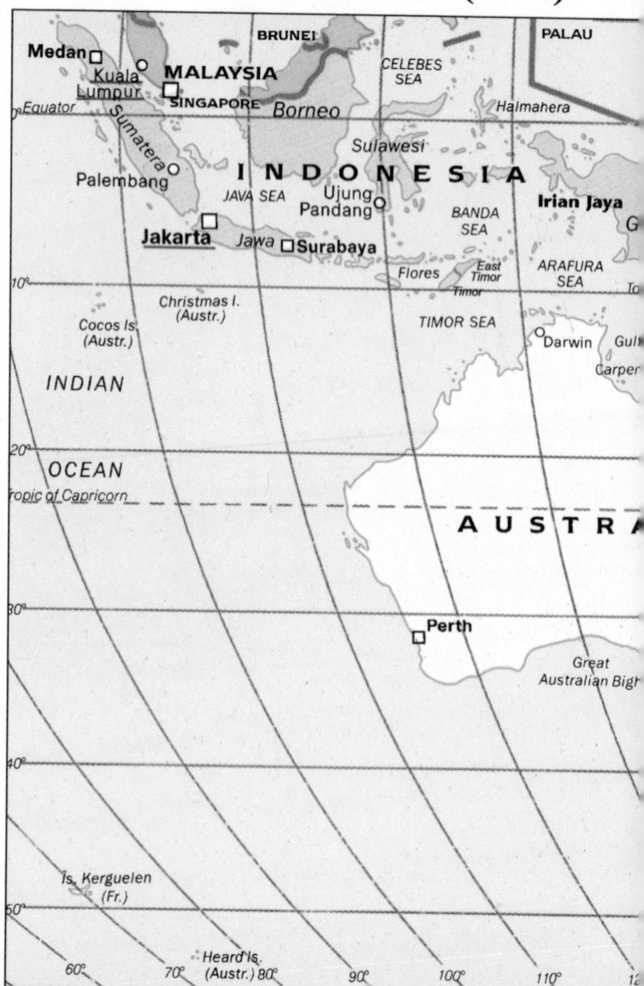
BRUNEI
PALAU
Medan
Kuala Lumpur
MALAYSIA
SINGAPORE
CELEBES SEA
Equator
Borneo
Halmahera
Sumatera
Sulawesi
Palembang
INDONESIA
JAVA SEA
Ujung Pandang
Irian Jaya
BANDA SEA
Jakarta
Jawa
Surabaya
Flores
East Timor
Timor
ARAFURA SEA
10°
Christmas I. (Austr.)
TIMOR SEA
Cocos Is. (Austr.)
Darwin
INDIAN
20°
OCEAN
Tropic of Capricorn
AUSTRA
30°
Perth
Great Australian Bight
40°
Is. Kerguelen (Fr.)
50°
Heard Is. (Austr.)
60°
70°
80°
90°
100°
110°

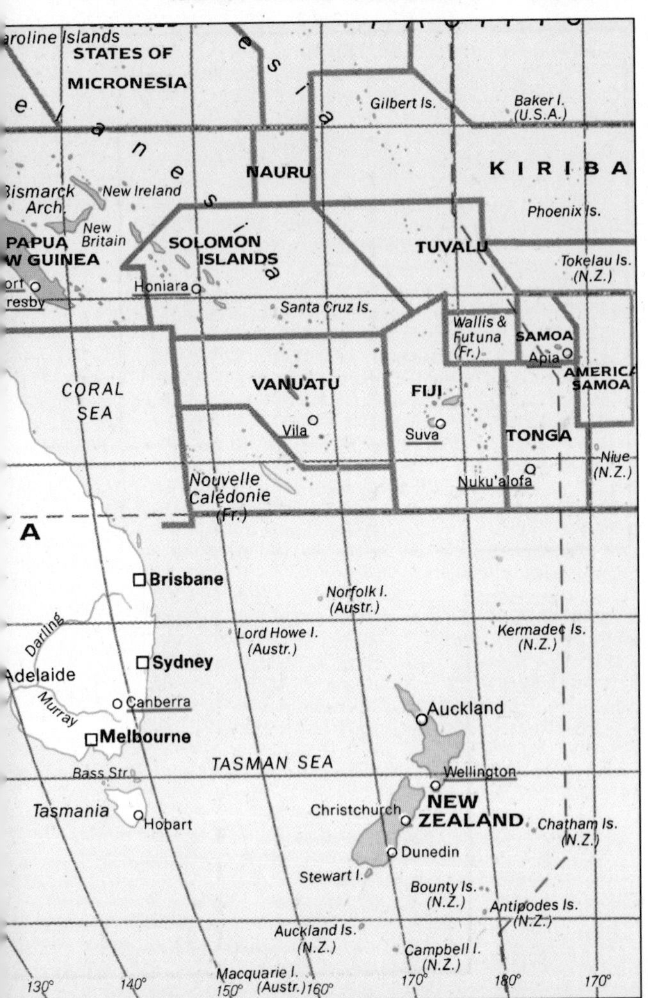

aroline Islands
STATES OF
MICRONESIA
Gilbert Is.
Baker I.
(U.S.A.)
NAURU
KIRIBA
Bismarck
Arch.
New Ireland
Phoenix Is.
New
Britain
PAPUA
W GUINEA
SOLOMON
ISLANDS
TUVALU
Tokelau Is.
(N.Z.)
ort
resby
Honiara
Santa Cruz Is.
Wallis &
Futuna
(Fr.)
SAMOA
Apia
AMERICA
SAMOA
CORAL
SEA
VANUATU
FIJI
Vila
Suva
TONGA
Niue
(N.Z.)
Nouvelle
Calédonie
(Fr.)
Nuku'alofa
A
Brisbane
Norfolk I.
(Austr.)
Darling
Lord Howe I.
(Austr.)
Kermadec Is.
(N.Z.)
Sydney
Adelaide
Murray
Canberra
Auckland
Melbourne
TASMAN SEA
Bass Str.
Wellington
Tasmania
Hobart
Christchurch
NEW
ZEALAND
Chatham Is.
(N.Z.)
Dunedin
Stewart I.
Bounty Is.
(N.Z.)
Antipodes Is.
(N.Z.)
Auckland Is.
(N.Z.)
Campbell I.
(N.Z.)
Macquarie I.
(Austr.)
130°
140°
150°
160°
170°
180°
170°

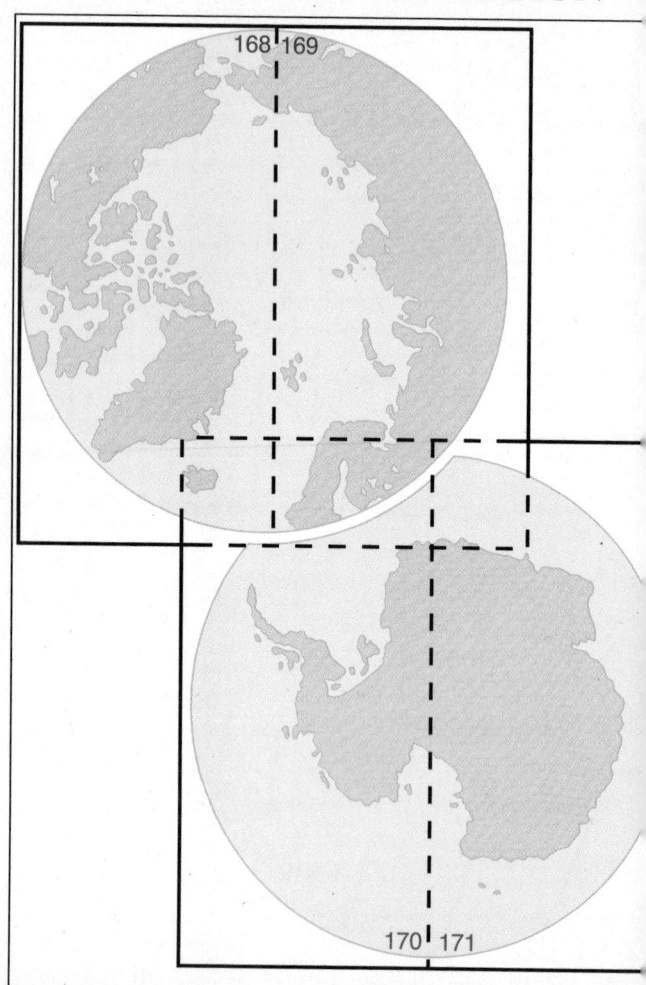
168
169
170
171

INDEX TO PAGES

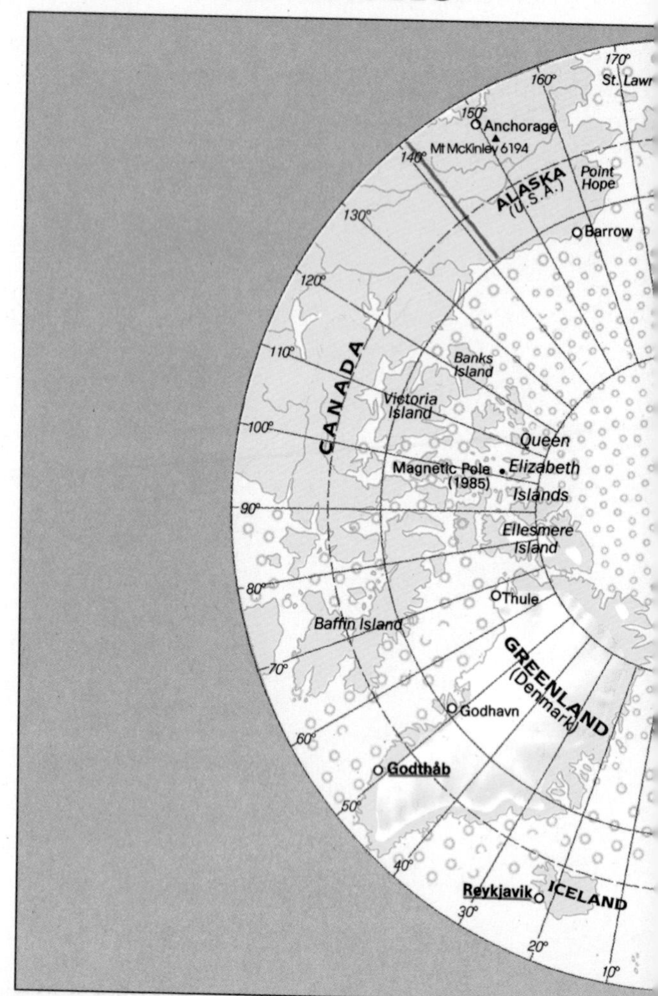
170°
160°
St. Lawr
150°
Anchorage
Mt McKinley 6194
140°
ALASKA
(U.S.A.)
Point
Hope
130°
Barrow
120°
110°
CANADA
Banks
Island
Victoria
Island
100°
Queen
Elizabeth
Islands
Magnetic Pole
(1985)
90°
Ellesmere
Island
80°
Thule
Baffin Island
70°
GREENLAND
(Denmark)
Godhavn
60°
Godthåb
50°
40°
Reykjavik
ICELAND
30°
20°
10°

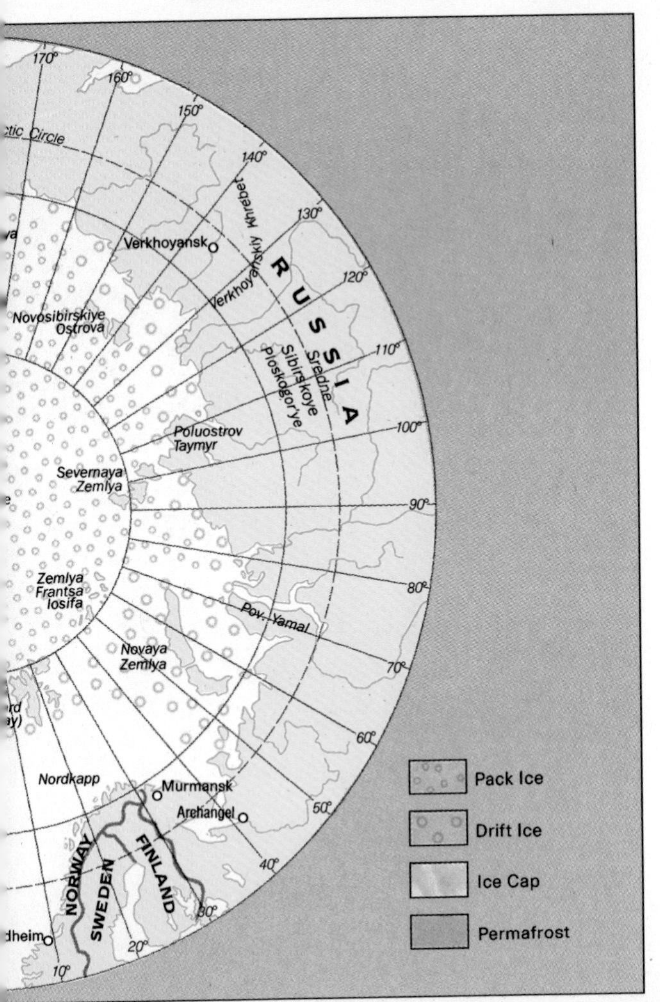
170°
160°
150°
140°
130°
120°
110°
100°
90°
80°
70°
60°
50°
40°
30°
20°
10°
Verkhoyansk
Verkhoyanskiy Khrebet
RUSSIA
Novosibirskiye Ostrova
Sredne Sibirskoye Ploskogor'ye
Poluostrov Taymyr
Severnaya Zemlya
Zemlya Frantsa Iosifa
Pov. Yamal
Novaya Zemlya
Nordkapp
Murmansk
Archangel
NORWAY
SWEDEN
FINLAND
Pack Ice
Drift Ice
Ice Cap
Permafrost

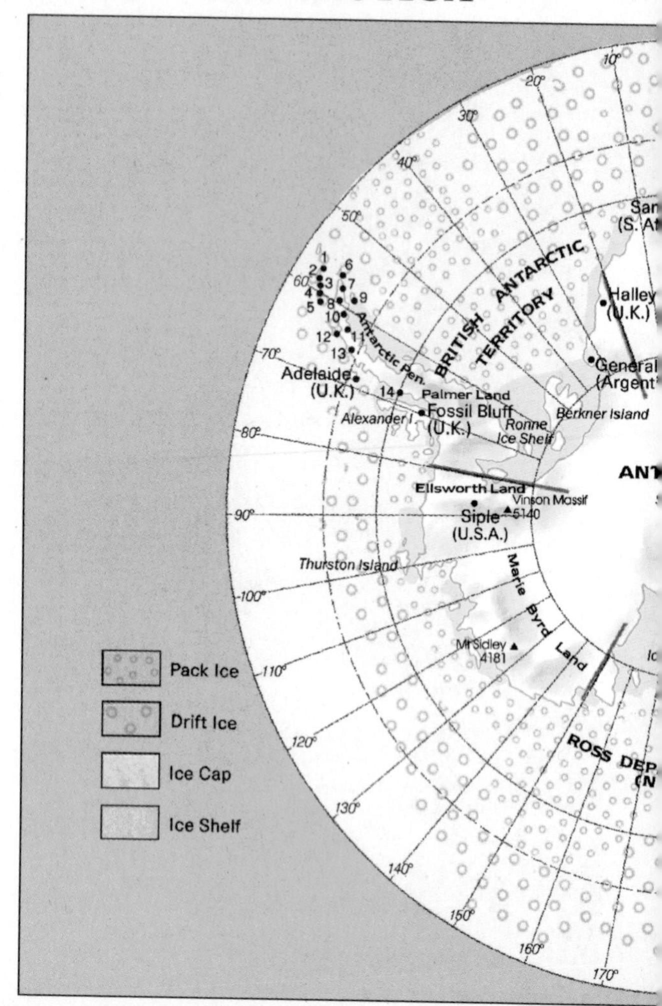

Pack Ice
Drift Ice
Ice Cap
Ice Shelf
BRITISH ANTARCTIC TERRITORY
Antarctic Pen.
Adelaide (U.K.)
Palmer Land
Fossil Bluff (U.K.)
Alexander I.
Ronne Ice Shelf
Berkner Island
Halley (U.K.)
General (Argent
San (S. Af
Ellsworth Land
Vinson Massif 5140
Siple (U.S.A.)
Thurston Island
Marie Byrd Land
Mt Sidley 4181
ROSS DEP (N
1
2
3
4
5
6
7
8
9
10
11
12
13
14
10°
20°
30°
40°
50°
60°
70°
80°
90°
100°
110°
120°
130°
140°
150°
160°
170°

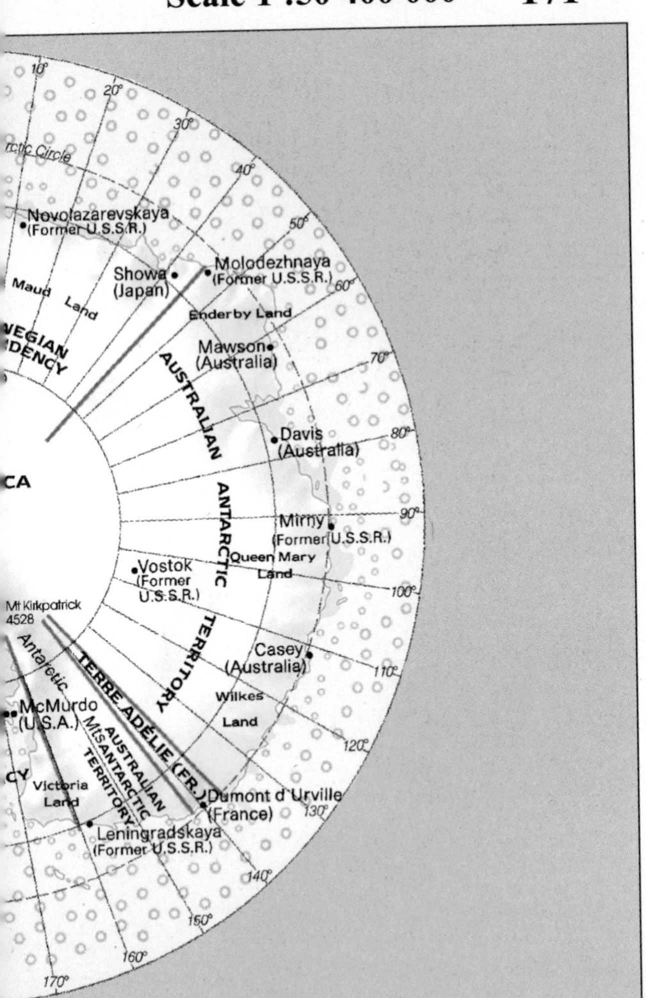

10°
20°
30°
40°
50°
60°
70°
80°
90°
100°
110°
120°
130°
140°
150°
160°
170°
rctic Circle
Novolazarevskaya
(Former U.S.S.R.)
Showa
(Japan)
Molodezhnaya
(Former U.S.S.R.)
Maud Land
Enderby Land
NEGIAN
DENCY
Mawson
(Australia)
AUSTRALIAN
ANTARCTIC
TERRITORY
Davis
(Australia)
CA
Mirny
(Former U.S.S.R.)
Queen Mary
Land
Vostok
(Former
U.S.S.R.)
Mt Kirkpatrick
4528
Antarctic
Mts
Casey
(Australia)
TERRE ADÉLIE (FR.)
Wilkes
Land
McMurdo
(U.S.A.)
AUSTRALIAN
ANTARCTIC
TERRITORY
CY
Victoria
Land
Dumont d'Urville
(France)
Leningradskaya
(Former U.S.S.R.)

Index

In the index, the first number refers to the page, and the following letter and number to the section of the map in which the index entry can be found. For example London 56G6 means that London can be found on page 56 where column G and row 6 meet.

Abbreviations used in the Index

Abbreviation	Meaning
Afghan	Afghanistan
Alb	Albania
Alg	Algeria
Arg	Argentina
Aust	Australia
Bang	Bangladesh
Belg	Belgium
Bol	Bolivia
Bos.Herz.	Bosnia Herzegovina
Bulg	Bulgaria
Camb	Cambodia
Can	Canada
CAR	Central African Republic
Cro.	Croatia
Czech.Rep.	Czech.Republic
Dem.Rep.of Congo	Democratic Republic of Congo
Den	Denmark
Dom Rep.	Dominican Republic
El Sal	El Salvador
Eng	England
Eq Guinea	Equatorial Guinea
Est	Estonia
Eth	Ethiopia
FRG	Federal Republic of Germany
Fin	Finland
Hung	Hungary
Indon.	Indonesia
Lat	Latvia
Leb	Lebanon
Lib	Liberia
Liech	Leichtenstein
Lith	Lithuania
Lux	Luxembourg
Madag	Madagascar
Malay	Malaysia
Maur	Mauritania
Mor	Morocco
Mozam	Mozambique
N.Ire	Northern Ireland
N.Korea	North Korea
NZ	New Zealand
Neth	Netherlands
Nic	Nicaragua
Nig	Nigeria
Nor	Norway
PNG	Papua New Guinea
Pak	Pakistan
Par	Paraguay
Phil	Phillipines
Pol	Poland
Port	Portugal
Rep.Yemen	Republic of Yemen
Rom	Romania
S.Africa	South Africa
S.Arabia	Saudi Arabia
S.Korea	South Korea
Scot	Scotland
Sen	Senegal
Slo	Slovenia
Switz	Switzerland
Tanz	Tanzania
Thai	Thailand
Turk	Turkey
UAE	United Arab Emirates
UK	United Kingdom
USA	United States of America
Urug	Uruguay
Ven	Venezuela
Viet	Vietnam
Yugos	Yugoslavia
Zim	Zimbabwe

A

Aachen *FRG* 90B2
Äänekoski *Fin* 93F3
Abādān *Iran* 131C2
Abadla *Alg.* 141C3
Abakan *Rus.* 106L4
Abbeville *France* 68C1
Abéché *Chad* 146F3
Abeokuta *Nig.* 145D2
Aberdeen *Scot* 61F3
Aberfeldy *Scot* 63E4
Abergavenney *Wales* 58D6
Abersoch *Wales* 53C5
Aberystwyth *Wales* 58C5
Abidjan *Côte d'Ivoire* 144B2
Aboyne *Scot* 61F3
Abrantes *Port.* 72A2
Abū Zabī *UAE* 133D3
Abuja *Nig.* 145D2
Acapulco *Mexico* 23D4
Accra *Ghana* 145C4
Achill I. *Ireland* 64A3
Acklins I. *The Bahamas* 26E2
Acre State *Brazil* 35B3
Adan *Rep.Yemen* 132C4
Adana *Turk.* 130B2
Ad Dakhla *Mor.* 140B4
Ad Dammām *S.Arabia* 131D3
Ad Dawhah *Qatar* 131D3
Adelaide *Aust.* 155C4
Admiralty Is. *Pacific O.* 125G4
Agadez *Niger* 141D5
Agadir *Mor.* 140C3
Agen *France* 69C3
Agra *India* 126F3
Agrigento *Italy* 79C3
Agropoli *Italy* 79C2
Aguascalientes *Mexico* 23C3
Ahmadābād *India* 128F3
Ahvāz *Iran* 131C2
Aïn Sefra *Alg.* 141C3
Aizu-Wakamatsu *Japan* 115N8
Ajaccio *Corse* 76B2
Ajmer *India* 126F3
Aketi *Dem. Rep. of Congo* 146F4
Akita *Japan* 115P7
Akmola *Kazakhstan* 109J4
Akron *USA* 18E1
Aksu *China* 126G1
Akureyri *Iceland* 92B1
Alabama State *USA* 20E2
Alagoas State *Brazil* 37F3
Alagoinhas *Brazil* 37F4
Alajuela *Costa Rica* 25C5
Åland Is. *Fin* 95E3
Alaska Pen. *USA* 12C4
Alaska State. *USA* 22J
Albacete *Spain* 75B2
Albany *Aust.* 155A4
Albany *USA* 19F1
Al Basrah *Iraq* 131C2
Al Baydā' *Libya* 142F1
Alberta State *Canada* 13G4
Ålborg *Den.* 94C4
Albuquerque *USA* 17C2
Albury *Aust.* 157D4
Alcalá de Henares *Spain* 72B1
Alcañiz *Spain* 74B1
Alcàzar de San Juan *Spain* 73B2
Alcoy *Spain* 75B2
Aldan *Russia* 106O4
Alderney I. *UK* 59E8
Aldershot *Eng.* 56G6
Aleksandrovsk-Sakhalinskly *Russia* 107Q4
Alessandria *Italy* 76B2
Ålesund *Nor.* 92B3
Aleutian Is. *USA* 22J
Alexander Arch. *USA* 23J
Alexander I. *Ant.* P170
Alexandria *Egypt* 142F1
Alexandroúpolis *Greece* 81F2
Algeciras *Spain* 73A2
Alger *Alg.* 141D3
Alicante *Spain* 75B2
Alice Springs *Aust.* 154C3
Allhābād *India* 127G3

Al Hudaydah *Rep.Yemen* 132C4
Al Hufūf *S.Arabia* 131C3
Al Jawf *S.Arabia* 130B3
Al Khābūrah *Oman* 133D3
Al Kuwayt *Kuwait* 131C3
Al Lādhiqiyah *Syria* 130B2
Al Madinah *S.Arabia* 130B3
Almada *Port.* 73A2
Almaty *Kazakhstan* 109J5
Al Manāmah *Bahrain* 131D3
Al Mawsil *Iraq* 130C2
Al Mukallā *Rep. Yemen* 133C4
Almeria *Spain* 75B2
Alnwick *Eng* 54F2
Alorl. *Indon.* 124E4
Alotau *PNG* 125H5
Alta *Nor.* 93E2
Altay *Mongolia* 111D2
Amami Ō-shima I. *Japan* 115G4
Amapá State *Brazil* 36D2
Amarillo *USA* 17C2
Amazonas State *Brazil* 35C3
Ambon *Indon.* 124E4
Amfilokhía *Greece* 80E3
Amiens *France* 68C2
Amirante Is. *Indian O.* 150F1
Amman *Jordan* 130B2
Amorgós I. *Greece* 81F3
Ampia *Western Samoa* 165
Amposta *Spain* 74C1
Amritsar *India* 126F2
Amsterdam *Neth.* 84A2
An Najaf *Iraq* 130C2
An Uaimh *Ireland* 67E3
Anáfi I. *Greece* 81F3
Anápolis *Brazil* 37E4
Anchorage *USA* 12D3
Ancona *Italy* 77C2
Andalucia Region *Spain* 73A2
Andaman Islands *India* 129H4
Andizhan *Uzbekistan* 109J5
Andorra la Vella *Andorra* 74C1
Andorra, Principality *SW Europe* 74C1
Andros I. *Bahamas* 24D2
Ándros *Greece* 81E3
Angarsk *Rus* 106M4
Angers *France* 68B2
Anglesey I. *Wales* 53C4
Angoulême *France* 69C2
Anguilla I. *Caribbean Sea* 26G3
Anhui Province *China* 114F3
Anjou Province *France* 68B2
Ankara *Turk.* 130B2
'Annaba *Alg.* 141D3
Annapolis *USA* 18F2
Annecy *France* 71D2
Annobón I. *Eq.Guinea* 145D3
Anqing *China* 114F3
Anshan *China* 112G2
Anshun *China* 117E4
Antalya *Turk.* 130B2
Antananarivo *Madag.* 151E2
Antarctic Circle *Ant.* P170
Antequera *Spain* 73B2
Anticosti I. *Canada* 15M5
Antigua I. *Leeward Is.* 26G3
Antipodes Is. *NZ* 165
Antofagasta *Chile* 40B5
Antrim *N.Ire.* 65E2
Antsirabe *Madag.* 151E2
Antsiranana *Madag.* 150E2
Antwerpen *Belg.* 70C1
Anyang *China* 112F3
Aomori *Japan* 113J2
Aosta *Italy* 76B1
Aparri *Phil.* 120E2
Apatity *Rus* 93G2
Apeldoorn *Neth.* 84B2
Appleby-in-Westmorland *Eng* 53E3
Aqaba *Jordan* 130B3
Ar Riyād *S.Arabia* 130C3
Aracaju *Brazil* 37F4
Aracena *Spain* 73A2
Arad *Rom.* 88E3
Aran I. *Ireland* 64C1
Aran Is. *Ireland* 66B3
Aranda de Duero *Spain* 72B1
Arbatax *Sardegna* 78B3
Arbroath *Scot* 63F4
Arcachon *France* 69B3
Arch de los Chonos *Chile* 41B7
Archangel *Rus* 102F3
Ardabīl *Iran* 131C2
Ardara *Ireland* 64C2
Arendal *Nor.* 94B4
Arequipa *Peru* 35B4
Arezzo *Italy* 77C2
Argenton-S-Creuse *France* 69C2
Argos *Greece* 80E3
Århus *Den.* 94C4
Arica *Chile* 35B4
Arisaig *Scot* 62C4
Arizona State *USA* 16B2
Arkansas State *USA* 18D2
Arklow *Ireland* 67E4
Arles *France* 71C3
Armagh *N.Ire.* 65E2
Arnhem *Neth.* 84B2
Arran I. *Scot* 62C5
Arrochar *Scot* 62D4
Árta *Greece* 80E3
Artois Province *France* 68C1
Arua *Uganda* 146G4
Aruba I. *Caribbean Sea* 27F4
Arusha *Tanz.* 147G5
Arvida *Canada* 15L5
Arvika *Sweden* 94C4
Asahikawa *Japan* 113J2
Asansol *India* 129G3
Åseb *Eth.* 147H3
Ashford *Eng* 56H6
Ashikaga *Japan* 115N8
Ashington *Eng* 54F2
Ashkhabad *Turkmenistan* 108G6
Asmera *Eritrea.* 143G3
Astípálaia I. *Greece* 81F3
Astrakhan' *Rus* 108F5
Asturias Region *Spain* 72A1
Asunción *Par.* 38E5
Aswân *Egypt* 142G2
Asyût *Egypt* 142G2
At. Martin's *Isles of Scilly* 59A8
At Tā'if *S.Arabia* 132C3
Atar *Maur.* 140B4
Atbara *Sudan* 142G3
Athenry *Ireland* 66C3
Athens *Greece* 81E3
Athínai *Greece* 81E3
Athlone *Ireland* 66D3
Atlanta *USA* 18E2
Atyrau *Kazakhstan* 108G5
Auckland *NZ* 157G4
Auckland Is. *NZ* 165
Augsburg *FRG* 91C3
Augusta *Aust.* 155A4
Augusta Georgia *USA* 18E2
Augusta Maine *USA* 19G1
Augustow *Pol.* 86E2
Aulie-Ata *Kazakhstan* 109J5
Austin *USA* 23D2
Auvergne Province *France* 71C2
Auxerre *France* 70C2
Aveiro *Port.* 72A1
Avellino *Italy* 79C2
Avesta *Sweden* 94D3
Avezzano *Italy* 77C2
Aviemore *Scot* 61E3
Avignon *France* 71C3
Avila *Spain* 74B1
Avilés *Spain* 72A1
Axel Heiberg I. *Canada* 14J2
Axminster *Eng* 59E7
Áyios Evstrátios I. *Greece* 81F3
Aylesbury *Eng* 56G6
Ayr *Scot* 62D5
Az Zawiyah *Libya* 141E3

B

Babar I. *Indon.* 124E4
Babuyan I. *Phil.* 120E2
Bacau *Rom.* 89F3
Bacolod *Phil.* 120E2
Badajoz *Spain* 73A2
Badalona *Spain* 74C1
Bafatá *Guinea-Bissau* 144A1
Baffin Island *Canada* 14K2
Bagé *Brazil* 38E6
Baghdād *Iraq* 130C2
Baghlān *Afghan.* 126E2
Baguio *Phil.* 120E2
Bahamas Is.,The, *Caribbean* 26E1
Bahawalpur *Pak.* 126F3
Bahía Blanca *Arg.* 40C6
Bahia State *Brazil* 37E4
Baia Mare *Rom.* 88E3
Baicheng *China* 112K2
Baker I. *Pacific O.* 165
Bakhtaran *Iran* 131C2
Baku *Azerbaijan* 108F5
Bala *Wales* 53D5
Balbriggan *Ireland* 67E3
Balearic Is. *Spain* 74C2
Bali I. *Indon.* 123D4
Balikpapan *Indon.* 123D4
Balkhash *Kazakhstan* 109J5
Ballachulish *Scot* 62C4
Ballantrae *Scot* 62D5
Ballarat *Aust.* 157D4

Ballina *Ireland* **64B2**
Ballinasloe *Ireland* **66C3**
Ballygawley *N.Ire.* **65D2**
Ballymena *N.Ire.* **65E2**
Baltimore *USA* **19F2**
Bamako *Mali* **144B1**
Bambari *CAR* **146F4**
Bamberg *FRG* **91C3**
Banbury *Eng* **56F5**
Banda Aceh *Indon.* **122B3**
Bandar 'Abbās *Iran* **131D3**
Bandar Seri Begawan *Brunei* **123D3**
Bandon *Ireland* **66C5**
Bandundu *Dem. Rep. of Congo* **146E5**
Bandung *Indon.* **123C4**
Banff *Scot* **61F3**
Bangalore *India* **128F4**
Bangassou *CAR* **146F4**
Banghāzi *Libya* **142F1**
Bangka I. *Indon.* **123C4**
Bangkok *Thai.* **118C2**
Bangor *N.Ire.* **65F2**
Bangor *Wales* **53C4**
Bangui *CAR* **146E4**
Banja Luka *Bos. Herz.* **77D2**
Banjarmasin *Indon.* **123D4**
Banjul *The Gambia* **140B5**
Bank Is. *Vanuatu* **156F2**
Banks I. *Canada* **12F2**
Bantry *Ireland* **66B5**
Banyuwangi *Indon.* **123D4**
Baoding *China* **112F3**
Baoji *China* **117E3**
Baotou *China* **111E2**
Baracaldo *Spain* **72B1**
Barbados I. *Caribbean Sea* **27H4**
Barbuda I. *Leeward Is.* **26G3**
Barcelona *Spain* **74C1**
Barcelona *Ven.* **34C1**
Bareilly *India* **126F3**
Bari *Italy* **79D2**
Barletta *Italy* **79D2**
Barnaul *Russia* **109K4**
Barnstable *Eng* **58C6**
Barquisimeto *Ven.* **34C1**
Barra I. *Scot* **60A3**
Barranquilla *Colombia* **34B1**
Barrow *USA* **12C2**
Barrow-in-Furness *Eng* **53D3**
Barry *Wales* **58D6**
Basel *Switz.* **70D2**
Basilan I. *Phil.* **120E3**
Basildon *Eng* **56H6**
Basingstoke *Eng* **56F6**
Bassein *Myanmar* **118B2**
Bastia *Corse* **76B2**
Bata *Eq. Guinea* **145D2**
Batan I. *Phil.* **120E1**
Batang *China* **117D3**
Batangas *Phil.* **120E2**
Bath *Eng* **58E6**
Bathurst I. *Aust.* **154B2**
Bathurst I. *Canada* **12H2**
Batley *Eng* **55F4**
Battambang *Camb.* **118C2**
Batumi *Georgia* **108F5**
Bayeaux *France* **68B2**
Bayonne *France* **69B3**
Bayreuth *FRG* **91C3**
Baza *Spain* **73B2**
Beaufort West *S.Africa* **149C4**
Beauly *Scot* **60D3**
Beauvais *France* **68C2**
Béchar *Alg.* **141C3**
Bedford *Eng* **56G5**
Beijing *China* **112F3**
Beijing Province *China* **112F3**
Beira *Mozam.* **151D2**
Beja *Port.* **73A2**
Béjar *Spain* **72A1**
Belcher Is. *Canada* **15K4**
Belcoo *N.Ire.* **64D2**
Belém *Brazil* **36E2**
Belfast *N.Ire.* **65F2**
Belfort *France* **70D2**
Belgrade *Yugos.* **82E2**
Belhai *China* **117E4**
Belitung *Indon.* **123C4**
Belize *Belize* **24B3**
Bellary *India* **128F4**
Belle Île *France* **68B2**
Bello *Colombia* **34B2**
Belmullet *Ireland* **64A2**
Belo Horizonte *Brazil* **37E4**
Belogorsk *Rus* **107O4**
Belopan *Guatemala* **24B3**
Benavente *Spain* **72A1**
Benbecula I. *Scot* **60A3**
Bendigo *Aust.* **157D4**
Benevento *Italy* **79C2**
Bengbu *China* **114F3**
Benguela *Angola* **148B2**
Benicarló *Spain* **74C1**
Benidorm *Spain* **75B2**
Benin City *Nig.* **145D2**
Benxi *China* **112G2**
Berat *Alb.* **80D2**
Berbera *Somalia* **147H3**
Bergamo *Italy* **76B1**
Bergen *Nor.* **94B3**
Berkner I. *Ant.* **P170**
Berlin *FRG* **85C2**
Bermuda I. *Atlantic O.* **19G2**
Bern *Switz.* **70D2**
Berry Province *France* **68C2**
Berwick-upon-Tweed *Eng* **54F2**
Besançon *France* **70D2**
Betanzos *Spain* **72A1**
Beverley *Eng* **55G4**
Beyla *Guinea* **144B2**
Beyrouth *Leb.* **130B2**
Béziers *France* **71C3**
Bhagalpur *India* **127G3**
Bhamo *Myanmar* **118B1**
Bhopal *India* **128F3**
Biak I. *Indon.* **125F4**
Bialystok *Pol.* **86E2**
Bideford *Eng* **58C6**
Biel *Switz.* **70D2**
Bikaner *India* **126F3**
Bilaspur *India* **129G3**
Bilbao *Spain* **72B1**
Billings *USA* **17C1**
Bioko I. *Atlantic O.* **145D2**
Bir Moghrein *Maur.* **140B4**
Birkenhead *Eng* **53D4**
Bîrlad *Rom.* **89F3**
Birmingham *Eng* **56F5**
Birmingham *USA* **18E2**
Birobidzhan *Russia* **107P5**
Birr *Ireland* **66D3**
Bishkek *Kyrgyztan* **109J5**
Bishop Auckland *Eng* **54F3**
Biskra *Alg.* **141D3**
Bismarck *USA* **17C1**
Bismarck Arch. *Pacific O.* **125H4**
Bissau *Guinea-Bissau* **144A1**
Bitola *Yugos.* **80E2**
Bizerte *Tunisia* **141D3**
Blace *Cro.* **82D2**
Blackburn *Eng* **53E4**
Blackpool *Eng* **53D4**
Blagævgrad *Bulg.* **82E2**
Blagoveshchensk *Russia* **107O4**
Blair Atholl *Scot* **62E4**
Blantyre *Malawi* **150D2**
Blida *Alg.* **141D3**
Bloemfontein *S.Africa* **149C3**
Blönduós *Iceland* **92A1**
Bluefields *Nic.* **25C4**
Blyth *Eng* **54F2**
Bo *Sierra Leone* **144A2**
Boa Vista *Brazil* **34C2**
Bobo Dioulasso *Burkina Faso* **144B1**
Bocas del Toro *Panama* **25C5**
Boden *Sweden* **93E2**
Bodmin *Eng* **59C7**
Bodō *Nor.* **92C2**
Bodrum *Turkey* **81F3**
Bognor Regis *Eng* **57G7**
Bogor *Indon.* **123C4**
Bogotá *Colombia* **34B2**
Bohol *Phil.* **120E3**
Boise *USA* **16B1**
Boké *Guinea* **144A1**
Bollnäs *Sweden* **94D3**
Bologna *Italy* **77C2**
Bolton *Eng* **53E4**
Boma *Dem. Rep. of Congo* **145E3**
Bombay (Mumbai) *India* **124E4**
Bonaire *Caribbean Sea* **27F4**
Bonn *FRG* **90B2**
Boothia Pen. *Canada* **14J2**
Borås *Sweden* **94C4**
Bordeaux *France* **69B3**
Borneo *Indon./Malay.* **123D3**
Bornholm I. *Den.* **94C4**
Borzya *Russia* **106N4**
Bosanski Brod *Cro.* **82D1**
Boston *Eng* **55G5**
Boston *USA* **19F1**
Bouaké *Côte d'Ivoire* **144B2**
Bouar *CAR* **145E2**
Bouârfa *Mor.* **141C3**
Boulogne *France* **68C1**
Bounty Is. *NZ* **165**
Bourg-en-Bresse *France* **71D2**
Bourges *France* **68C2**
Bourgogne Province *France* **70C2**
Bournemouth *Eng* **57F7**
Boyle *Ireland* **64C3**
Brac I. *Yugos.* **77D2**
Bräcke *Sweden* **92D3**

Bradford *Eng* **55F4**
Braga *Port.* **72A1**
Braila *Rom.* **89F3**
Brasília *Brazil* **37E4**
Brasov *Rom.* **89F3**
Bratislava *Slovakia* **88D3**
Bratsk *Russia* **106M4**
Braunschweig *FRG* **85C2**
Bray *Ireland* **67E3**
Brazzaville *Congo* **145E3**
Breda *Neth.* **84A2**
Bremen *FRG* **84B2**
Bremerhaven *FRG* **84B2**
Brescia *Italy* **76C1**
Bressay *Scot* **61J7**
Bressuire *France* **68B2**
Brest *Belarus* **102D4**
Brest *France* **68B2**
Bretagne Province *France* **68B2**
Briançon *France* **71D3**
Briare *France* **70C2**
Bridgetown *Barbados* **27H4**
Bridgwater *Eng* **58D6**
Bridlington *Eng* **55G3**
Brighton *Eng* **57G7**
Brindisi *Italy* **79D2**
Brisbane *Aust.* **156E3**
Bristol *Eng* **58E6**
British Columbia State *Canada* **13F4**
Brive-la-Gaillarde *France* **69C2**
Brno *Czech.* **91D3**
Broken Hill *Aust.* **155E4**
Broome *Aust.* **154B2**
Brora *Scot* **61E2**
Brownsville *USA* **23D3**
Bruck an der Mur *Aust.* **91D3**
Brunei, Sultanate *SE Asia* **123D3**
Brussels *Belg.* **70C1**
Bruxelles *Belg.* **70C1**
Bryansk *Russia* **102E4**
Bucaramanga *Colombia* **34B2**
Buchanan *Lib.* **144A2**
Bucharest *Rom.* **83F2**
Buckie *Scot* **61F3**
Buckingham *Eng* **56F6**
Budapest *Hung.* **88D3**
Bude *Eng* **59C7**
Buenaventura *Colombia* **34B2**
Buenos Aires *Arg.* **40D6**
Buenos Aires State *Arg.* **38D6**
Buffalo *USA* **17C1**
Buffalo *USA* **18F1**
Builth Wells *Wales* **58D5**
Bujumbura *Burundi* **146F5**
Bukavu *Dem.Rep.of Congo* **146F5**
Bukhara *Uzbekistan* **108H6**
Bukittinggi *Indon.* **122C4**
Bulawayo *Zim.* **149C3**
Bumba *Dem.Rep. of Congo* **146F4**
Bunbury *Aust.* **155A4**
Bundaberg *Aust.* **156E3**
Bundoran *Ireland* **64C2**
Buraydah *S.Arabia* **130C3**
Burco *Somalia* **147H4**
Burgas *Bulg.* **83F2**
Burgos *Spain* **72B1**
Burley *USA* **17B1**
Bursa *Turk.* **130A1**
Buru I. *Indon.* **124E4**
Bury St. Edmunds *Eng* **56H5**
Buta *Dem.Rep. of Congo* **146F4**
Bute *Scot* **62C5**
Butte *USA* **17B1**
Butuan *Phil.* **120E3**
Butung I. *Indon.* **124E4**
Buzau *Rom.* **89F3**
Byala *Bulg.* **83F2**
Bydgoszcz *Pol.* **86D2**
Bylot I. *Canada* **14L2**
Bytom *Pol.* **88D2**

C

Cabanatuan *Phil.* **120E2**
Cabimas *Ven.* **34B1**
Cabinda *Angola* **145E3**
Cacak *Yugos.* **82E2**
Cáceres *Spain* **73A2**
Cádiz *Spain* **73A2**
Caen *France* **68B2**
Caernarfon *Wales* **53C4**
Cagayan de Oro *Phil.* **120E3**
Cagliari *Sardegna* **78B3**
Caher *Ireland* **66D4**
Cahors *France* **69C3**
Caicos Is. *Caribbean Sea* **26E2**
Cairns *Aust.* **156D2**
Cairo *Egypt* **142G1**
Calahorra *Spain* **74B1**
Calais *France* **68C1**
Calama *Chile* **40B5**
Calamian Group *Phil.* **120D2**
Calatayud *Spain* **74B1**
Calcutta *India* **129G3**
Calgary *Canada* **13G4**
Cali *Colombia* **34B2**
California State *USA* **16A2**
Callao *Peru* **35B4**
Calvi *Corse* **76B2**
Camagüey *Cuba* **24D2**
Cambeltown *Scot* **62C5**
Cambridge *Eng* **56H5**
Camden *USA* **19F2**
Campbell I. *NZ* **165**
Campinas *Brazil* **38F5**
Campo Grande *Brazil* **37D5**
Campos *Brazil* **38F5**
Can Tho *Viet.* **119C2**
Canberra *Aust.* **157D4**
Cangzjou *China* **112F3**
Cannes *France* **71D3**
Canterbury *Eng* **56J6**
Cap-Haïtien *Haiti* **26E3**
Cape Breton I. *Canada* **15M5**
Cape Town *S.Africa* **149B4**
Capri I. *Italy* **79C2**
Caracal *Rom.* **83E2**
Caracaraí *Brazil* **34C2**
Caracas *Ven.* **34C1**
Caransebes *Rom.* **88E3**
Carbonia *Sardegna* **78B3**
Carcassonne *France* **69C3**
Cardiff *Wales* **58D6**
Cardigan *Wales* **58C5**
Carlisle *Eng* **52E3**
Carlow *Ireland* **67E4**
Carmarthen *Wales* **58C6**
Carnarvon *Aust.* **154A3**
Carolina *Brazil* **37E3**
Caroline I. *Kiribati* **162**
Caroline Is. *Pacific O.* **125G3**
Carrick on Shannon *Ireland* **64C3**
Carrickmacross *Ireland* **65E3**
Carson City *USA* **16B2**
Cartagena *Colombia* **34B1**
Cartagena *Spain* **75B2**
Cartago *Costa Rica* **25C5**
Caserta *Italy* **79C2**
Cashel *Ireland* **67D4**
Casper *USA* **17C1**
Cassino *Italy* **79C2**
Castellón de la Plana *Spain* **74B2**
Castilla La Mancha Region *Spain* **73B2**
Castilla y León Region *Spain* **72A1**
Castlebar *Ireland* **64B3**
Castleford *Eng* **55F4**
Castries *St. Lucia* **27G4**
Castrovillari *Italy* **79D3**
Cat Island *The Bahamas* **26D1**
Cataluña Region *Spain* **74C1**
Catamarca State *Arg.* **40C5**
Catania *Italy* **79D3**
Catanzaro *Italy* **79D3**
Cateraggio *Corse* **76B2**
Cavan *Ireland* **65D3**
Cayenne *French Guiana* **36D2**
Cayman Islands *Caribbean Sea* **24C3**
Ceará State *Brazil* **37F3**
Cebu I. *Phil.* **120E2**
Cebu *Phil.* **120E2**
Cecina *Italy* **76C2**
Cefalû *Italy* **79C3**
Cerignola *Italy* **79D2**
Ceské Budejovice *Czech. Rep* **91C3**
Ceuta *Spain* **73A2**
Ch'ongjin *N.Korea* **113G2**
Chaco State *Arg.* **40C5**
Chalon-sur-Saône *France* **71D2**
Châlons-sur-Marne *France* **70C2**
Chambéry *France* **71D2**
Champagne Province *France* **70C2**
Chañaral *Chile* **40B5**
Chandigarh *India* **126F2**
Chang-hua *Taiwan* **120E1**
Changchun *China* **112G2**
Changde *China* **114F4**
Changsha *China* **114F4**
Changzhi *China* **112F3**
Channel Is. *UK* **59E8**
Channel Port-aux-Basques *Canada* **15N5**
Chardzhou *Turkmenistan* **108H6**
Charleroi *Belg.* **70C1**
Charleston *USA* **18F2**
Charleville *Aust.* **156D3**
Charlotte *USA* **18E2**
Charlottetown *Canada* **15M5**
Chartres *France* **68C2**
Châteauroux *France* **69C2**
Chatham Is. *NZ* **165**
Chattanooga *USA* **18E2**
Chaumont *France* **70D2**
Chaves *Port.* **72A1**

Cheboksary *Russia* 108F4
Cheju do I. *S.Korea* 114G3
Chelmsford *Eng* 56H6
Cheltenham *Eng* 59E6
Chelyabinsk *Russia* 109H4
Chemnitz *FRG* 91C2
Chen Xian *China* 114F4
Chengdu *China* 117E3
Chennai (Madras) *India* 129G4
Cherbourg *France* 68B2
Cheremkhovo *Russia* 106M4
Cherepovets *Russia* 102E4
Chernigor *Ukraine* 102E4
Chernovtsy *Ukraine* 102D5
Chesham *Eng* 56G6
Chester *Eng* 53E4
Chesterfield Inlet *Canada* 14J3
Chetumal *Mexico* 24B3
Cheyenne *USA* 17C1
Chiang Mai *Thai.* 118B2
Chiba *Japan* 115P9
Chicago *USA* 18E1
Chichester *Eng* 57G7
Chiclayo *Peru* 35B3
Chifeng *China* 112F2
Chihuahua *Mexico* 23C3
Chi-lung *Taiwan* 120E1
Chimbote *Peru* 35B3
Chimkent *Kazakhstan* 109H5
Chingola *Zambia* 148C2
Chippenham *Eng* 56E6
Chisinau *Moldova* 108D5
Chita *Russia* 106N4
Chittagong *Bang.* 129H3
Chojnice *Pol.* 85D2
Chongqing *China* 117E4
Chorley *Eng* 53E4
Choybalsan *Mongolia* 112F2
Christchurch *NZ* 157G5
Christmas I. *Indian O.* 123C5
Chubut State *Arg.* 41C7
Chumphon *Thai.* 118B2
Church Stretton *Eng* 58E5
Churchill *Canada* 15J4
Cienfuegos *Cuba* 24C2
Cieza *Spain* 75B2
Cîmpina *Rom.* 89F3
Cincinnati *USA* 18E2
Cirebon *Indon.* 123C4
Citta di Castello *Italy* 77C2
Ciudad Bolivar *Ven.* 34C2
Ciudad Guayana *Ven.* 34C2
Ciudad Juárez *Mexico* 23C2
Ciudad Real *Spain* 73B2
Ciudad Rodrigo *Spain* 72A1
Civitanova Marche *Italy* 77C2
Civitavecchia *Italy* 77C2
Clacton-on-Sea *Eng* 56J6
Clare I. *Ireland* 64A3
Claremorris *Ireland* 66B3
Clermont Ferrand *France* 71C2
Cleveland *USA* 18E1
Clifden *Ireland* 66A3
Cloghan *Ireland* 66D3
Cloncurry *Aust.* 154D2
Clonmel *Ireland* 67D4
Cluj-Napoca *Rom.* 88E3
Coatbridge *Scot* 63D5
Cobán *Guatemala* 25A3
Cobh *Ireland* 66C5
Cochabamba *Bolivia* 35C4
Cochin *India* 128F5
Cocos I. *Indian O.* 122B5
Codó *Brazil* 37E3
Coimbatore *India* 128F4
Coimbra *Port.* 72A1
Colchester *Eng* 56H6
Coleraine *N.Ire.* 65E1
Coll I. *Scot* 62B4
Collooney *Ireland* 64C2
Colmar *France* 70D2
Colombo *Sri Lanka* 129F5
Colombus *USA* 18E2
Colón *Panama* 25D5
Colonsay I. *Scot* 62B4
Colorado Springs *USA* 17C2
Colorado State *USA* 17C2
Columbia *USA* 18E2
Columbus *USA* 20E2
Como *Italy* 76B1
Comodoro Rivadavia *Arg.* 41C7
Comoros Is. *Indian O.* 150E2
Compiégne *France* 70C2
Conakry *Guinea* 144A2
Concepción *Chile* 40B6
Concepción *Par.* 38E5
Concord *USA* 19F1
Concordia *Arg.* 38E6
Connecticut State *USA* 19F1
Consett *Eng* 54F3
Constanta *Rom.* 83F2
Constantine *Alg.* 141D3
Contonou *Benin* 145D2
Cook Is. *Pacific O.* 162
Cooktown *Aust.* 156D2
Copenhagen *Den.* 94C4
Corby *Eng* 56G5
Corcubíon *Spain* 72A1
Córdoba *Arg.* 40C6
Córdoba *Spain* 73B2
Cordoba State *Arg.* 40C6
Corfu I. *Greece* 80D3
Corigliano *Italy* 79D3
Corinto *Nic.* 25B4
Cork *Ireland* 66C5
Coro *Ven.* 34C1
Corpus Christi *USA* 23D3
Corrientes *Arg.* 40D5
Corrientes State *Arg.* 38E5
Corse I. *France* 76B2
Corumbá *Brazil* 37D4
Cosenza *Italy* 79D3
Cospic *Cro.* 77D2
Cotabato *Phil.* 120E3
Cottbus *FRG* 85C2
Coventry *Eng* 56F5
Cowes *Isle of Wight* 57F7
Craiova *Rom.* 82E2
Crawley *Eng* 56G6
Cres I. *Cro.* 77C2
Crete I. *Greece* 81E3
Crewe *Eng* 53E4
Crianlarich *Scot* 62D4
Crieff *Scot* 62E4
Cromer *Eng* 55J5
Crotone *Italy* 79D3
Cruzeiro do Sul *Brazil* 35B3
Cucuí *Brazil* 34C2
Cúcuta *Colombia* 34B2
Cuddalore *India* 129F4
Cuenca *Ecuador* 35B3
Cuenca *Spain* 74B1
Cuiabá *Brazil* 37D4
Culiacán *Mexico* 23C3
Cumbernauld *Scot* 63D5
Cumnock *Scot* 62D5
Cuneo *Italy* 76B2
Cupar *Scot* 63E4
Curaçao *Caribbean Sea* 27F4
Curitiba *Brazil* 38F5
Cuttack *India* 129G3
Cuxhaven *FRG* 84B2
Cuzco *Peru* 35B4
Cwmbran *Wales* 58D6
Cyprus *Med.Sea* 130B2
Czestochowa *Pol.* 88D2

D

Dagupan *Phil.* 120E2
Dakar *Sen.* 140B5
Da Lat *Viet.* 119C2
Dali *China* 117E4
Dallas *USA* 23D2
Dalmally *Scot* 62D4
Daloa *Côte d'Ivoire* 144B2
Da Nang *Viet.* 119C2
Dandong *China* 112G2
Dar'ā *Syria* 130B2
Dar el Beida *Mor.* 140C3
Dar es Salaam *Tanz.* 147G5
Darlington *Eng* 55F3
Darmstadt *FRG* 90B3
Daroca *Spain* 74B1
Daru *PNG* 125G4
Darwin *Aust.* 154C2
Datong *China* 112F2
Daugavpils *Latvia* 102D4
Dauphine Province *France* 71D3
Davao *Phil.* 120E3
David *Panama* 25C5
Dawson Creek *Canada* 13F4
Dax *France* 69B3
Dayton *USA* 18E2
Daytona Beach *USA* 20E3
D'Entrecasteaux I. *PNG* 125H4
De Aar *S.Africa* 149C4
Debre Mark'os *Eth.* 147G3
Debrecen *Hung.* 88E3
Dehra Dun *India* 126F2
Delaware State *USA* 19F2
Delhi *India* 126F3
Den Helder *Neth.* 84A2
Denbigh *Wales* 53D4
Denizli *Turk.* 130A2
Denver *USA* 17C2
Derby *Eng* 55F5
Des Moines *USA* 18D1
Desé *Eth.* 147G3
Dessau *FRG* 85C2
Detroit *USA* 18E1
Deva *Rom.* 88E3
Devon I. *Canada* 14K2
Dezfūl *Iran* 131C2
Dezhou *China* 112F3
Dhāka *Bang.* 127H3
Ídhra *Greece* 81E3
Dibrugarh *India* 127H3

Didcot *Eng* 56F6
Dieppe *France* 68C2
Dijon *France* 70C2
Dili *Indon.* 124E4
Dimashq *Syria* 130B2
Dimitrovgrad *Bulg.* 83F2
Dingle *Ireland* 66A4
Dingwall *Scot* 60D3
Diré Dawa *Eth.* 147H4
Ådîs Âbeba *Eth.* 147G4
Disko I. *Greenland* 14N3
Dist. Fed. State *Brazil* 37E4
Diyarbakir *Turk.* 130B2
Djelfa *Alg.* 141D3
Djibouti *Djibouti* 147H3
Dnepropetrovsk *Ukraine* 108E5
Dobreta-Turnu-Severin *Rom.* 82E2
Dodoma *Tanz.* 147G5
Dôle *France* 70D2
Dolgellau *Wales* 58D5
Dombås *Nor.* 92B3
Dominica I. *Caribbean* 27G3
Domodossola *Italy* 76B1
Doncaster *Eng* 55F4
Donegal *Ireland* 64C2
Donetsk *Russia* 108E5
Dorchester *Eng* 59E7
Dornie *Scot* 60C3
Dortmund *FRG* 84B2
Douala *Cameroon* 145D2
Douglas *Isle of Man* 53C3
Dourados *Brazil* 38E5
Dover *Eng* 56J6
Dover *USA* 19F2
Dráma *Greece* 81E2
Drammen *Nor.* 94C4
Dresden *FRG* 91C2
Drogheda *Ireland* 67E3
Dubayy *UAE* 133D3
Dublin *Ireland* 67E3
Dubrovnik *Cro.* 82D2
Ducie I. *Pacific O.* 162
Dudley *Eng* 58E5
Dugi I. *Cro.* 77C2
Duisburg *FRG* 84B2
Dukou *China* 117E4
Duluth *USA* 18D1
Dumbarton *Scot* 62D5
Dumfries *Scot* 63E5
Dun Laoghaire *Ireland* 67E3
Dunbar *Scot* 63F5
Dundalk *Ireland* 65E2
Dundee *Scot* 63F4
Dundrum *N.Ire.* 65F2
Dunedin *NZ* 157G5
Dunfermline *Scot* 63E4
Dungarvan *Ireland* 67D4
Dungiven *N.Ire.* 65E2
Dunkeld *Scot* 62E4
Dunkerque *France* 68C1
Dunleer *Ireland* 65E3
Durban *S.Africa* 151D3
Durham *Eng* 54F3
Durham *USA* 18F2
Durness *Scot* 60D2
Durrës *Alb.* 80D2
Durrow *Ireland* 67D4
Dushanbe *Tajikistan* 109H6
Dusseldorf *FRG* 84B2
Duyun *China* 117E4

E

Eastbourne *Eng* 57H7
East Falkland I. *South Atlantic O.* 39D8
East Kilbride *Scot* 63D5
East London *S.Africa* 149C4
Eboli *Italy* 79D2
Ecija *Spain* 73A2
Eday I. *Scot* 61F1
Edgeworthstown *Ireland* 67D3
Edinburgh *Scot* 63E5
Edmonton *Canada* 13G4
Efate I. *Vanuatu* 156F2
Egadi I. *Italy* 78C3
Egersund *Nor.* 94B4
Eigg I. *Scot* 62B4
Eindhoven *Neth.* 84B2
Eisenach *FRG* 91C2
Elba I. *Italy* 76C2
Elblag *Pol.* 86D2
Elche *Spain* 75B2
El Djouf *Maur* 140C4
El Dorado *Ven.* 34C2
Eldoret *Kenya* 147G4
Eleuthera I. *The Bahamas* 24D1
El Faiyûm *Egypt* 142G2
El Fasher *Sudan* 146F3
El Ferrol *Spain* 72A1
Elgin *Scot* 61E3
El Gîza *Egypt* 142G1
El Golea *Alg.* 141D3
El Iskandarîya *Egypt* 142F1
El Khartum *Sudan* 142G3
Ellesmere I. *Canada* 14K2
Ellesmere Port *Eng* 53E4
Ellon *Scot* 61F3
El Minya *Egypt* 142G2
El Obeid *Sudan* 146G3
El Paso *USA* 23C2
El Qâhira *Egypt* 142G1
Elvas *Port.* 73A2
Ely *Eng* 56H5
Enarración *Par.* 38E5
Ende *Indon.* 124E4
Enggano I. *Indon.* 122C4
Enna *Italy* 79C3
Ennis *Ireland* 66B4
Enniscorthy *Ireland* 67E4
Enniskillen *N.Ire.* 65D2
Ennistymon *Ireland* 66B4
Enschede *Neth.* 84B2
Entebbe *Uganda* 146G4
Enugu *Nig.* 145D2
Epi I. *Vanuatu* 156F2
Erenhot *China* 112F2
Erfurt *FRG* 91C2
Eriskay I. *Scot* 60A3
Erlangen *FRG* 91C3
Erromanga I. *Vanuatu* 156F2
Erzurum *Turk.* 130C2
Esbjerg *Den.* 94B4
Esfahān *Iran* 131D2
Eskisehir *Turk.* 130B2
Esperance *Aust.* 155B4
Espírito Santo *Brazil* 37E4
Espíritu Santo I. *Vanuatu* 156F2
Espoo *Fin* 95E3
Essaouira *Mor.* 140C3
Essen *FRG* 84B2
Estremoz *Port.* 73A2
Evansville *USA* 18E2
Evvoia I. *Greece* 81E3
Exeter *Eng* 59D7
Extremadura Region *Spain* 73A2

F

Faeroes I. *Den.* 92A2
Fair I. *Scot* 61J8
Fairbanks *USA* 12D3
Faisalābād *Pak.* 126F4
Fakfak *Indon.* 124F4
Falcarragh *Ireland* 64C1
Falkirk *Scot* 63E4
Falkland Islands *South Atlantic O.* 39D8
Falmouth *Eng* 59B7
Falster I. *Den.* 94C5
Falun *Sweden* 94D3
Fano *Italy* 77C2
Farāh *Afghan.* 131E2
Fareham *Eng* 57F7
Fargo *USA* 17D1
Faro *Port.* 73A2
Faroe I. *Den.* 92A2
Farquhar Is. *Indian O.* 150F1
Fauske *Nor.* 92D2
Faya-Largeau *Chad* 142E3
Fdérik *Maur.* 140B4
Felixstowe *Eng* 56J6
Fergana *Uzbekistan* 109J5
Ferkessédougou *Côte d'Ivoire* 144B2
Fermoy *Ireland* 66C4
Ferrara *Italy* 77C2
Fés *Mor.* 140C3
Fetlar I. *Scot* 61K7
Feyzābād *Afghan.* 126F2
Fianarantsoa *Madag.* 151E3
Figueras *Spain* 74C1
Fiji Is. *Pacific O.* 165
Filiasi *Rom.* 82E2
Firenze *Italy* 77C2
Fishguard *Wales* 58C6
Fitzroy Crossing *Aust.* 154B2
Fleetwood *Eng* 53D4
Flensburg *FRG* 84B2
Flint I. *Kiribati* 162
Flores I. *Indon.* 124E4
Flores *Guatemala* 24B3
Florianópolis *Brazil* 38F5
Florida State *USA* 20E3
Focsani *Rom* 89F3
Foggia *Italy* 79D2
Foligno *Italy* 77C2
Follonica *Italy* 76C2
Forfar *Scot* 63F4
Forli *Italy* 77C2
Formentera *Spain* 75C2
Formia *Italy* 79C2
Formosa State *Arg.* 40C5
Fortaleza *Brazil* 37F3
Fort Augustus *Scot* 60D3
Fort-de-France *Martinique* 27G4
Fort Lauderdale *USA* 21E3
Fort Simpson *Canada* 12F3

Fort William *Scot* 62C4
Fort Yukon *USA* 12D3
Fort Worth *USA* 23D2
Foshan *China* 114F4
Foula I. *Scot* 61H7
Fougéres *France* 68B2
Foz do Iguacu *Brazil* 38E5
Fraga *Spain* 74C1
Franca *Brazil* 37E5
Franceville *Gabon* 145E3
Franche-Comte Province *France* 71D2
Francistown *Botswana* 149C3
Frankfort *USA* 18E2
Frankfurt *FRG* 90B2
Fraser I. *Aust.* 156E3
Fraserburgh *Scot* 61F3
Frederikshåb *Greenland* 14O3
Frederikshavn *Den.* 94C4
Frederikstad *Nor.* 94C4
Freetown *Sierra Leone* 144A2
Freiburg *FRG* 90B3
Fremantle *Aust.* 155A4
Fresno *USA* 16B2
Frosinone *Italy* 77C2
Ft. Wayne *USA* 18E1
Fuerteventura I. *Canary Is.* 140B4
Fujian Province *China* 114F4
Fukui *Japan* 115M8
Fukuoka *Japan* 115H3
Fukushima *Japan* 115P8
Funchal *Madeira* 140B3
Furneaux Group I. *Aust.* 157D5
Fürth *FRG* 91C3
Furukawa *Japan* 115P7
Fushun *China* 112G2
Fuxin *China* 112G2
Fuzhou *China* 114F4
Fyn I. *Den.* 94C4

G

Gabès *Tunisia* 141D3
Gaborone *Botswana* 149C3
Gainsborough *Eng* 55G4
Gairloch *Scot* 60C3
Galashiels *Scot* 63F5
Galati *Rom.* 89F3
Galicia Region *Spain* 72A1
Galle *Sri Lanka* 129G5
Gallipoli *Italy* 79D2
Gällivare *Sweden* 93E2
Galveston *USA* 20D3
Galway *Ireland* 66B3
Gambier Is. *Pacific O.* 162
Gamboma *Congo* 145E3
Gandia *Spain* 75B2
Ganzhou *China* 114F4
Gao *Mali* 141C3
Garve *Scot* 60D3
Gascogne Province *France* 69B3
Gateshead *Eng* 54F3
Gauhati *India* 127H3
Gävle *Sweden* 94D3
Gaziantep *Turk.* 130B2
Gdansk *Pol.* 86D2
Gdynia *Pol.* 86D2
Gedaref *Sudan* 147G3
Geelong *Aust.* 157D4
Gejiu *China* 117E4
Gela *Italy* 79C3
Gelati *Rom.* 89F3
General Santos *Phil.* 120E3
Genéve *Switz.* 71D2
Genova *Italy* 76B2
Gent *Belg.* 70C1
George Town *Malay.* 122C3
Georgetown *Guyana* 34D2
Georgetown *St. Vincent* 27G4
Georgia State *USA* 20E2
Gera *FRG* 91C2
Geraldton *Aust.* 155A3
Gerona *Spain* 74C1
Getafe *Spain* 72B1
Gevgelija *Yugos.* 80E2
Ghadāmis *Libya* 141D3
Ghāt *Libya* 141E4
Gibraltar Colony *SW Europe* 73A2
Gifu *Japan* 115M9
Giglio I. *Italy* 76C2
Gijón *Spain* 72A1
Gilbert Is. *Kiribati* 165
Gilgit *Pak.* 126F2
Girvan *Scot* 62D5
Gisborne *NZ* 157G4
Giurgiu *Rom.* 83F2
Glasgow *Scot* 63D5
Glenrothes *Scot* 63E4
Gliwice *Pol.* 88D2
Gloucester *Eng* 58E6
Gniezno *Pol.* 85D2
Gobabis *Namibia* 149B3
Godthåb *Greenland* 14N3
Goiânia *Brazil* 37E4
Goiás State *Brazil* 37E4
Gol *Nor.* 94B3
Golmund *China* 111D3
Gomel' *Belarus* 102E4
Gomera *Canary Is.* 140B4
Gonaïves *Haiti* 26E3
Gonder *Eth.* 147G3
Goole *Eng* 55G4
Gorontalo *Indon.* 124E3
Gort *Ireland* 66C3
Gorzów Wielkopolski *Pol.* 85D2
Göteborg *Sweden* 94C4
Gotland I. *Sweden* 95D4
Gottingen *FRG* 84B2
Goulburn *Aust.* 157D4
Gran Canaria *Canary Is.* 140B4
Granada *Nic.* 25B4
Granada *Spain* 73B2
Grand Bahama I. *The Bahamas* 24D1
Grand Rapids *USA* 18E1
Grandola *Port.* 73A2
Graz *Aust.* 91D3
Great Abaco I. *The Bahamas* 24D1
Great Exuma I. *The Bahamas* 24D2
Great Inagua I. *The Bahamas* 26E2
Great Nicobar I. *India* 129H5
Great Yarmouth *Eng* 56J5
Greater Antilles Is. *Car* 24D3
Greenland Dependency *N.A.* 14O2
Greenock *Scot* 62D5
Greensboro *USA* 18F2
Grenada *Caribbean Sea* 27G4
Grenada, I. *Caribbean* 27G4
Grenadines Is.,The. *Caribbean* 27G4
Grenoble *France* 71D2
Gretna *Scot* 63E5
Grimsby *Eng* 55G4
Grong *Nor.* 92C3
Groningen *Neth.* 84B2
Groote Eylandt I. *Aust.* 154C2
Grootfontein *Namibia* 149B2
Grosseto *Italy* 77C2
Groznyy *Russia* 108F5
Grudziadz *Pol.* 86D2
Guadalajara *Mexico* 23C3
Guadalajara *Spain* 72B1
Guadalcanal I. *Solomon Is.* 156E2
Guadalupe I. *Mexico* 22B3
Guadeloupe I. *Caribbean Sea* 26G3
Guam *Pacific O.* 121G2
Guangdong Province *China* 114F4
Guangxi Province *China* 117E4
Guangzhou *China* 114F4
Guantánamo *Cuba* 26D2
Guarda *Port.* 72A1
Guatemala *Guatemala* 25A4
Guayaquil *Ecuador* 35B3
Guernsey I. *UK* 59E8
Guildford *Eng* 56G6
Guilin *China* 114F4
Guiria *Ven.* 34C1
Guiyang *China* 117E4
Guizhou Province *China* 117E4
Gulu *Uganda* 146G4
Guyenne Province *France* 69B3
Gwalior *India* 126F3
Gweru *Zim.* 149C2
Gyor *Hung.* 88D3

H

Hā'il *S.Arabia* 130C3
Haarlem *Neth.* 84A2
Hachinohe *Japan* 115P6
Hagen *FRG* 84B2
Haifa *Israel* 130B2
Haikou *China* 114F4
Hailar *China* 112F2
Hainan Dao I. *China* 114F5
Haiphong *Viet.* 119C1
Hakodate *Japan* 113J2
Halab *Syria* 130B2
Halden *Nor.* 94C4
Halifax *Canada* 15M5
Halifax *Eng* 55F4
Halle *FRG* 85C2
Halmahera I. *Indon.* 124E3
Halmstad *Sweden* 94C4
Hamadān *Iran* 131C2
Hamamatsu *Japan* 115M9
Hamar *Nor.* 94C3
Hamburg *FRG* 85C2
Hamhung *N.Korea* 112G2
Hami *China* 111D2
Hamilton *Canada* 15K5
Hamilton *NZ* 157G4
Hamm *FRG* 84B2
Hammerfest *Nor.* 93E1

Hanamaki *Japan* **115P7**
Handan *China* **112F3**
Hangzhou *China* **114G3**
Hannover *FRG* **84B2**
Hanoi *Viet.* **119C1**
Hanzhong *China* **117E3**
Hāora *India* **129G3**
Harare *Zim.* **150D2**
Harbin *China* **112G2**
Hārer *Eth.* **147H4**
Hargeysa *Somalia* **147H4**
Harlow *Eng* **56H6**
Harris I. *Scot* **60B3**
Harrisburg *USA* **18F1**
Harrogate *Eng* **55F4**
Hartford *USA* **19F1**
Hartlepool *Eng* **54F3**
Harwich *Eng* **56J6**
Hässleholm *Sweden* **94C4**
Hastings *Eng* **57H7**
Hastings *NZ* **157G4**
Haugesund *Nor.* **94B4**
Havana (La Habana)*Cuba* **24C2**
Havant *Eng* **57G7**
Hawaii *Hawaiian Is.* **22H**
Hawaiian Is. *Pacific O.* **22H**
Hawick *Scot* **63F5**
Hay River *Canada* **13G3**
Heanor *Eng* **55F4**
Heard Is. *Indian O.* **164**
Hebei *China* **112F3**
Hefei *China* **114F3**
Hegang *China* **112H2**
Heidelberg *FRG* **90B3**
Heilongjiang Province *China* **112G2**
Helena *USA* **17B1**
Hella *Iceland* **92A2**
Hellín *Spain* **75B2**
Helmsdale *Scot* **61E2**
Helsinborg *Sweden* **94C4**
Helsingfors *Fin* **95F3**
Helsinki *Fin* **95F3**
Henan Province *China* **114F3**
Hengyang *China* **114F4**
Henzada *Myanmar* **118B2**
Herāt *Afghan.* **131E2**
Hereford *Eng* **58E5**
Hermosillo *USA* **23B3**
Hexham *Eng* **52E3**
Hierro *Canary Is.* **140B4**
Hiiumaa I. *Estonia* **95E4**
Himeji *Japan* **115L9**
Hims *Syria* **130B2**
Hinckley *Eng* **56F5**
Hinnöy I. *Nor.* **92D2**
Hiroshima *Japan* **113H3**
Hîrsova *Rom.* **83F2**
Hispaniola I. *Caribbean Sea* **26E3**
Hitachi *Japan* **115P8**
Ho Chi Minh City *Viet.* **119C2**
Hobart *Tasmania* **157D5**
Höfn *Iceland* **92B2**
Hohhot *China* **112F2**
Hokitika *NZ* **157G5**
Hokkaidó I. *Japan* **113J2**
Holguín *Cuba* **24D2**
Holy I. *Eng* **54F2**
Holyhead *Wales* **53C4**
Honiara *Solomon Is.* **156E1**
Honolulu *Hawaiian Is.* **22H**
Horsham *Eng* **56G6**
Hotan *China* **110C3**
Hotan *China* **126F2**
Hoting *Sweden* **92D3**
Houghton-le-Spring *Eng* **54F3**
Houston *USA* **20D3**
Hovd *Mongolia* **111D2**
Hoy I. *Scot* **61E2**
Hradec-Králové *Czech.* **91D2**
Huainan *China* **114F3**
Huambo *Angola* **148B2**
Huancayo *Peru* **35B4**
Huangshi *China* **114F3**
Hubei Province *China* **114F3**
Hubli *India* **128F4**
Huddersfield *Eng* **55F4**
Hudiksvall *Sweden* **94D3**
Hue *Viet.* **119C2**
Huelva *Spain* **73A2**
Hughenden *Aust.* **156D3**
Humaitá *Brazil* **35C3**
Hunan Province *China* **114F4**
Hunstanton *Eng* **55H5**
Huntly *Scot* **61F3**
Huntsville *USA* **18E2**
Húsavik *Iceland* **92B1**
Hvar I. *Cro.* **77D2**
Hwange *Zim.* **148C2**
Hyderābād *India* **128F4**
Hyderābād *Pak.* **126E3**
Hythe *Eng* **56J6l**

I

Ibadan *Nig.* **145D2**
Ibiza *Spain* **75C2**
Ibiza I. *Spain* **75C2**
Ica *Peru* **35B4**
Iceland Republic *N.Atlantic O.* **14R3**
Idaho State *USA* **16B1**
Igarka *Russia* **103K3**
Igoumenítsa *Greece* **80E3**
Ikaría I. *Greece* **81F3**
Ile d'Oléron *France* **69B2**
Ile de Noirmoutier *France* **68B2**
Ile de Ré *France* **69B2**
Ilebo *Dem.Rep.of Congo* **146F5**
Iles d'Hyéres *France* **71D3**
Ilfracombe *Eng* **58C6**
Iliodhrómia I. *Greece* **81E3**
Illinois State *USA* **18E1**
Iloilo *Phil.* **120E2**
Ilorin *Nig.* **145D2**
Imperatriz *Brazil* **37E3**
Impfondo *Congo* **146E4**
Imphāl *India* **127H3**
In Salah *Alg.* **141D4**
Indiana State *USA* **18E1**
Indianapolis *USA* **18E2**
Indore *India* **128F3**
Inhambane *Mozam.* **151D3**
Inner Hebrides *Scot* **62B4**
Inner Mongolia *Province China* **112F2**
Innsbruck *Aust.* **91C3**
Inuvik *Canada* **12E3**
Inveraray *Scot* **62C4**
Invercargill *NZ* **157F5**
Inverness *Scot* **61D3**
Inverurie *Scot* **61F3**
Ioannina *Greece* **80E3**
Íos I. *Greece* **81F3**
Iowa State *USA* **18D1**
Ipoh *Malay.* **122C3**
Iquique *Chile* **35B5**
Iquitos *Peru* **35B3**
Iráklion *Greece* **81F3**
Iringa *Tanz.* **150D1**
Irkutsk *Russia* **106M4**
Irvine *Scot* **62D5**
Isafördhur *Iceland* **92A1**
Ischia I. *Italy* **79C2**
Ise *Japan* **115M9**
Ishinomaki *Japan* **115P7**
Isiro *Dem. Rep. of Congo* **146F4**
Isla Blanquilla I. *Ven.* **27G4**
Isla Coiba *Panama* **25C5**
Isla de Chilloé I. *Chile* **41B7**
Isla de la Bahia *Hondur.* **24B3**
Isla de la Juventud *Cuba* **24C2**
Isla del Rey *Panama* **25D5**
Isla Los Rogues I. *Ven.* **27F4**
Isla Margarita I. *Ven.* **27G4**
Isla Santa Inés I. *Chile* **41B7**
Islāmabād *Pak.* **126F2**
Island of Newfoundland *Canada* **15N4**
Islas Canarias *Spain* **140B4**
Islay I. *Scot* **62B5**
Isle of Man *UK* **53C3**
Isle of Wight *Eng* **57F7**
Isles of Scilly *Eng* **59A8**
Istanbul *Turk.* **130A1**
Isthmus of Kra *Thai* **118B3**
Itabuna *Brazil* **37F4**
Itaituba *Brazil* **37D3**
Iturup I. *Russia* **113J2**
Ivalo *Fin* **93F2**
Ivangrad *Yugos.* **82D2**
Ivanovo *Russia* **102F4**
Iwaki *Japan* **115P8**
Iwo Jima *Japan* **121G1**
Izhevsk *Russia* **109G4**
Izmir *Turk.* **130A2**

J

Jabalpur *India* **128F3**
Jackson *USA* **20D2**
Jacksonville *USA* **20E2**
Jacmel *Haiti* **26E3**
Jaén *Spain* **73B2**
Jaffna *Sri Lanka* **129G5**
Jaipur *India* **126F3**
Jajce *Bos.Herz.* **77D2**
Jakarta *Indon.* **123C4**
Jalgaon *India* **128F3**
Jamaica *Caribbean* **122C4**
Jambi *Indon.* **126F2**
Jammu *India* **126F2**
Jamnager *India* **128E3**
Jämsänkoski *Fin* **95F3**
Jamshedpur *India* **129G3**
Jardines de la Reina *Cuba* **24D2**
Jarvis I. *Pacific O* **162**
Jawa I. *Indon.* **123C4**

Jayapura *Indon.* 125G4
Jedburgh *Scot* 63F5
Jefferson City *USA* 18D2
Jelenia Góra *Pol.* 91D2
Jena *FRG* 91C2
Jequié *Brazil* 37E4
Jerez de la Frontera *Spain* 73A2
Jersey I. *UK* 59E8
Jerusalem *Israel* 130B2
Jhansi *India* 126F3
Ji'an *China* 114F4
Jiamusi *China* 112H2
Jiangsu Province *China* 114F3
Jiangxi Province *China* 114F4
Jiddah *S.Arabia* 132B3
Jihlava *Czech.* 91D3
Jilin *China* 112G2
Jilin Province *China* 113G2
Jima *Eth.* 147G4
Jinan *China* 112F3
Jingdezhen *China* 114F4
Jinhua *China* 114F4
Jining *China* 114F3
Jinja *Uganda* 146G4
Jinzhou *China* 112G2
Jiujiang *China* 114F4
João Pessoa *Brazil* 37F3
Jodhpur *India* 126F3
Johannesburg *S.Africa* 149C3
John O'Groats *Scot* 61E2
Johnson I. *Pacific O.* 159
Johor Baharu *Malay.* 122C3
Jokkmokk *Sweden* 93D2
Jólo I. *Phil.* 120E3
Jönköping *Sweden* 94C4
Jörn *Sweden* 93E2
Jos *Nig.* 145D2
Jotunheimen *Nor.* 94B3
Juázeiro *Brazil* 37E3
Juba *Sudan* 146G4
Jujuy State *Arg.* 40C5
Julianehåb *Greenland* 14O3
Juneau *USA* 12E4
Jura I. *Scot* 62C5
Jylland I. *Den.* 94B4
Jyväskylä *Fin* 93F3

K

Kābul *Afghan.* 126E2
Kaduna *Nig.* 145D1
Kaédi *Maur.* 140B5
Kaesŏng *N.Korea* 112G3
Kagoshima *Japan* 115H3
Kaifeng *China* 114F3
Kailua *Hawaiian Is.* 22H
Kairouan *Tunisia* 141D3
Kajaani *Fin* 93F3
Kākināda *India* 129G4
Kalabáka *Greece* 80E3
Kalajoki *Fin* 93E3
Kalámai *Greece* 80E3
Kalaupapa *Hawaiian Is.* 22H
Kalémié
Dem. Rep. of Congo 146F5
Kalgoorlie *Aust.* 155B4
Kálimnos I. *Greece* 81F3
Kaliningrad *Russia* 102D4
Kalisz *Pol.* 86D2
Kalmar *Sweden* 94D4
Kamaishi *Japan* 115P7
Kamina
Dem. Rep. of Congo 148C1
Kamloops *Canada* 13F4
Kampala *Uganda* 146G4
Kananga
Dem. Rep. of Congo 146F5
Kanazawa *Japan* 115M8
Kandahār *Afghan.* 126E2
Kandalaksha *Russia* 102E3
Kandangan *Indon.* 123D4
Kandy *Sri Lanka* 129G5
Kaneohe *Hawaiian Is* 22H
Kangaroo I. *Aust.* 155C4
Kankan *Guinea* 144B1
Kano *Nig.* 145D1
Kānpur *India* 126G3
Kansas City *USA* 18D2
Kansas State *USA* 17D2
Kao-hsiung *Taiwan* 120E1
Kaolack *Sen.* 144A1
Karāchi *Pak.* 128E3
Karaganda *Kazakhstan* 109J5
Karbalā *Iraq* 130B2
Karcag *Hung.* 88E3
Karlobag *Cro.* 77D2
Karlovac *Cro.* 77D1
Karlshamn *Sweden* 94C4
Karlskoga *Sweden* 94C4
Karlskrona *Sweden* 94D4
Karlsruhe *FRG* 90B3
Karlstad *Sweden* 94C4
Kárpathos I. *Greece* 81F3
Karshi *Uzbekistan* 109H6
Kasama *Zim.* 150D2
Kasese *Uganda* 146G4
Kashi *China* 110B3
Kásos I. *Greece* 81F3
Kassala *Sudan* 143G3
Kassel *FRG* 90B2
Kastoria *Greece* 80E2
Katerini *Greece* 80E2
Katherine *Aust.* 154C2
Kathmandu *Nepal* 127G3
Katowice *Pol.* 88D2
Katsina *Nig.* 145D1
Kauai I. *Hawaiian Is.* 22H
Kaunas *Lithuania* 95E5
Kavália *Greece* 81E2
Kawaihae *Hawaiian Is.* 22H
Kawasaki *Japan* 115N9
Kayes *Mali* 144A1
Kayseri *Turk.* 130B2
Kazan *Russia* 108F4
Kazanlük *Bulg.* 83F2
Kazan-rettó *Japan* 121G1
Kéa *Greece* 81E3
Kecskemét *Hung.* 88D3
Kediri *Indon.* 123D4
Keetmanshoop *Namibia* 149B3
Kefallnía I. *Greece* 80E3
Keflavik *Iceland* 92A2
Keighley *Eng* 55F4
Keith *Scot* 61F3
Kelang *Malay.* 122C3
Kells *Ireland* 67E3
Kemerovo *Russia* 109K4
Kemi *Fin* 93E2
Kemijarvi *Fin* 93F2
Kendal *Eng* 53E3
Kendari *Indon.* 124E4
Kengtung *Myanmar* 118B1
Kenitra *Mor.* 140C3
Kenmare *Ireland* 66B5
Kenora *Canada* 15J5
Kentucky State *USA* 18E2
Kep.Anambas I. *Indon* 123C3
Kep.Aru I. *Indon.* 124F4
Kep. Banggai *Indon.* 124E4
Kep. Kai I. *Indon.* 124F4
Kep. Leti I. *Indon.* 124E4
Kep. Mentawai, Arch.
Indon. 122B4
Kepno *Pol.* 88D2
Kep. Sangihe I. *Indon* 124E3
Kep. Sula *Indon.* 124E4
Kep. Talaud I. *Indon.* 124E3
Kep. *Tanimbar I.* 124F4
Kep. Togian *Indon.* 124E4
Kerch *Russia* 108E5
Kerguelen Is. *Indian O.* 164
Kérkira *Greece* 80D3
Kermadec Is. *Pacific O.* 165
Kermān *Iran* 131D2
Keswick *Eng* 52E3
Key West *USA* 20E3
Khabarovsk *Russia* 107P5
Khalkis *Greece* 81E3
Khaniá *Greece* 81E3
Khar'kov *Russia* 108E4
Kharagpur *India* 129G3
Khartoum *North Sudan* 142G3
Khartoum *Sudan* 142G3
Khíos I. *Greece* 81F3
Khulna *Bang.* 129G3
Kiel *FRG* 85C2
Kielce *Pol.* 88E2
Kigali *Rwanda* 146G5
Kigoma *Tanz.* 146F5
Kikladhes Is. *Greece* 81E3
Kikwit *Dem. Rep. of Congo* 146E5
Kildare *Ireland* 67E3
Kilkenny *Ireland* 67D4
Killarney *Ireland* 66B4
Kilmarnock *Scot* 62D5
Kilrush *Ireland* 66B4
Kimberley *S.Africa* 149C3
Kindia *Guinea* 144A1
Kindu *Dem. Rep. of Congo* 146F5
King I. *Aust.* 157D4
Kings Lynn *Eng* 55H5
Kingston *Jamaica* 24D3
Kingston-upon-Hull *Eng* 55G4
Kingswood *Eng* 58E6
Kingussie *Scot* 61D3
Kinnegad *Ireland* 67D3
Kintyre *Scot* 62C5
Kinvarra *Ireland* 66C3
Kiribati Is. *Pacific O.* 165
Kiritimati *Kiribati* 162
Kirkby Stephen *Eng* 53E3
Kirkcaldy *Scot* 63E4
Kirkenes *Nor.* 93G2
Kirkük *Iraq* 130C2
Kirkwall *Scot* 61F2
Kirov *Russia* 108F4
Kirovabad *Ukraine* 108F5
Kiruna *Sweden* 93E2

Kisangani
Dem. Rep. of Congo 146F4
Kiskunfélegyháza *Hung* 88D3
Kismaayo *Somalia* 147H5
Kisumu *Kenya* 147G5
Kita-Kyūshū *Japan* 113H3
Kithira I. *Greece* 81E3
Kíthnos *Greece* 81E3
Kitwe *Zambia* 148C2
Kiyev *Ukraine* 102E4
Kladno *Czech.Rep.* 91C2
Klagenfurt *Aust.* 91C3
Klaipeda *Lithuania* 102D4
Klerksdorp *S.Africa* 149C3
Knoxville *USA* 18E2
Kōbe *Japan* 115L9
København *Den.* 94C4
Køblenz *FRG* 90B2
Kochi *Japan* 113H3
Kodiak I. *USA* 22J
Kofu *Japan* 115N9
Kokkola *Fin* 93E3
Kolding *Den.* 94B4
Kolhāpur *India* 128F4
Köln *FRG* 90B2
Koloma *Russia.* 102E4
Kolwezi
Dem. Rep. of Congo 148C2
Komatsu *Japan* 115M8
Komotiní *Greece* 81F2
Kompong Cham *Camb.* 119C2
Kompong Som *Camb.* 118C2
Komsomol'sk na-Amure
Russia 107P4
Konin *Pol.* 86D2
Konjic *Bos. Herz.* 82D2
Konya *Turk.* 130B2
Kópavogur *Iceland* 92A2
Korcë *Alb.* 80E2
Korcula I. *Cro.* 77D2
Kórinthos *Greece* 80E3
Koriyama *Japan* 115P8
Kornat I. *Cro.* 77D2
Korsör *Den.* 94C4
Kós I. *Greece* 81F3
Kosice *Slovakia* 88E3
Kosovska-Mitrovica *Yugos* 82E2
Koszalin *Pol* 85D2
Kota *India* 126F3
Kota Baharu *Malay.* 122C3
Kota Kinabalu *Malay.* 123D3
Kotka *Fin* 95F3
Kotlas *Russia* 102F3
Kotor *Yugos.* 82D2
Kowloon *Hong Kong* 119D1
Kragujevac *Yugos.* 82E2
Kraków *Pol.* 88D2
Kramsfors *Sweden* 92D3
Kranj *Slovenia* 77C1
Krasnodar *Russia* 108E5
Krasnovodsk *Turkmenístan* 108G5
Krasnoyarsk *Russia* 106L4
Krefeld *FRG* 84B2
Kristiansand *Nor.* 94B4
Kristianstad *Sweden* 94C4
Krivoy Rog *Ukraine* 108E5
Krk I. *Cro.* 77C1
Kruscevac *Yugos.* 82E2
Kuala Lumpur *Malay.* 122C3
Kuala Terengganu *Malay.* 122C3
Kuching *Malay.* 123D3
Kulata *Bulg.* 82E2
Kumamoto *Japan* 115H3
Kumanovo *Macedonia.* 82E2
Kumasi *Ghana* 144B2
Kunashir I. *Russia* 113J2
Kunming *China* 117E4
Kuopio *Fin* 93F3
Kupang *Indon.* 124E5
Kuril'skye Ostrova *Russia* 107R5
Kurnool *India* 128F4
Kursk *Russia* 108E4
Kushiro *Japan* 113J2
Kwangju *S.Korea* 112G3
Kyle of Lochalsh *Scot* 60C3
Kyoto *Japan* 115L9
Kyzyl *Russia* 106L4
Kzyl Orda *Kazakhstan.* 109H5

L

Laâyoune *Mor.* 140B4
Labé *Guinea* 144A1
Lábrea *Brazil* 35C3
Labytnangi *Russia* 103H3
La Ceiba *Honduras* 25B4
La Coruña *Spain* 72A1
Lae *PNG* 125G4
La Fléche *France* 68B2
Lagos *Nig.* 145D2
Lagos *Port.* 73A2
La Habana (Havana) *Cuba* 24C2
Lahore *Pak.* 126F2
Lahti *Fin* 95F3
Lai Chau *Viet.* 118C1
Lairg *Scot* 60D2
Lajes *Brazil* 128F4
Lakshadweep Is. *India* 128F4
Lambaréné *Gabon* 145E3
Lamía *Greece* 80E3
Lampedusa I. *Italy* 79C3
Lampione I. *Italy* 78C3
Lanai I. *Hawaiian Is.* 22H
Lanark *Scot* 63E5
Lancaster *Eng* 53E3
Lang Son *Viet.* 70D2
Langres *France* 71C3
Languedoc Province *Fran* 71C3
Lansing *USA* 18E1
Lanzarote I. *Canary Is.* 140B4
Lanzhou *China* 113E3
Laoag *Phil.* 120E2
Lao Cai *Viet.* 119C1
La Palma *Canary Is.* 140B4
La Pampa State *Arg.* 40C6
La Paz *Bolivia* 35C4
La Plata *Arg.* 38E6
Laredo *USA* 23D3
Largs *Scot* 62D2
La Rioja Region *Spain* 72B1
La Rioja State *Arg.* 40C5
Lárisa *Greece* 80E3
Larne *N.Ire.* 65F2
La Rochelle *France* 69B2
La Roda *Spain* 75B2
La Romana *Dom. Republic* 26F3
La Serena *Chile* 40B5
Lashio *Myanmar* 118B1
Iasi *Rom.* 89F3
Las Palmas de Gran Canaria
Canary is. 140B4
La Spezia *Italy* 76B2
Lastovo I. *Cro.* 77D2
Las Vegas *USA* 16B2
Latina *Italy* 79C2
La Tortuga I. *Ven.* 27F4
Launceston *Tasmania* 157D5
Laurencekirk *Scot* 63F4
Lausanne *Switz.* 71D2
Laut I. *Indon.* 123D4
Laval *France* 68B2
L'Aquila *Italy* 77C2
Leeds *Eng* 55F4
Leeuwarden *Neth.* 84B2
Leeward Is. *Caribbean Sea* 26G3
Legazpi *Phil.* 120E2
Leicester *Eng* 56F5
Leipzig *FRG* 91C2
Leiria *Port.* 72A2
Le Havre *France* 68C2
Le Mans *France* 68C2
Lens *France* 70C1
León *Mexico* 23C3
León *Nic.* 25B4
León *Spain* 72A1
Lérida *Spain* 74C1
Léros I. *Greece* 81F3
Lerwick *Scot* 61J7
Les Caye *Haiti* 26E3
Leshan *China* 117E4
Leskovac *Yugos.* 82E2
Lesotho, Kingdom *S.Africa* 149C3
Lesser Antilles Is. *Carib.* 27F4
Lésvós I. *Greece* 81F3
Letterkenny *Ireland* 65D2
Levkás I. *Greece* 80E3
Lewes *Eng* 57H7
Lewis I. *Scot* 60B2
Leyte I. *Phil.* 120E2
Lhasa *China* 116D4
Lianoyang *China* 112G2
Lianyungang *China* 114F3
Liaoning Province *China* 112G3
Liaoyuan *China* 112G2
Liberec *Czech.Rep.* 91D2
Libreville *Gabon* 145D2
Lichinga *Mozam.* 150D2
Liége *Belg.* 70D1
Liepāja *Latvia* 95E4
Likasi *Dem. Rep. of Congo* 148C2
Lille *France* 70C1
Lillehammer *Nor.* 94C3
Lilongwe *Malawi* 150D2
Lima *Peru* 35B4
Limerick *Ireland* 66C4
Límnos *Greece* 81F3
Limoges *France* 69C2
Limón *Costa Rica* 25C5
Limousin Province *France* 69C2
Linares *Spain* 73B2
Lincang *China* 117E4
Lincoln *Eng* 55G4
Lincoln *USA* 17D1
Linfen *China* 114F3
Linköping *Sweden* 94D4
Linosa I. *Italy* 79C3
Linz *Aust.* 91C3
Lipari I. *Italy* 79C3

Lisbon *Port.* 73A2
Lisburn *N.Ire.* 65E2
Lisieux *France* 68C2
Little Rock *USA* 18D2
Liuzhou *China* 117E4
Livanátais *Greece* 80E3
Liverpool *Eng* 53E4
Livingston *Scot* 63E5
Livingstone *Zambia* 148C2
Livno *Bos.Herz* 77D2
Livorno *Italy* 76C2
Ljubljana *Slovenia* 77C1
Llandrindod Wells *Wales* 58D5
Lobito *Angola* 148B2
Lochboisdale *Scot* 60A3
Lochgilphead *Scot* 62C4
Lochinver *Scot* 60C2
Lochmaddy *Scot* 60A3
Locri *Italy* 79D3
Lódz *Pol.* 86D2
Logroño *Spain* 72B1
Loja *Ecuador* 35B3
Loja *Spain* 73B2
Lolland I. *Den.* 94C5
Lom *Bulg.* 82E2
Lombok I. *Indon.* 123D4
Lome *Togo* 145D2
London *Eng* 56G6
Londonderry *N.Ire.* 65D1
Long Island *The Bahamas* 26E2
Long Island I. *USA* 19F1
Longford *Ireland* 67D3
Lorca *Spain* 75B2
Lord Howe I. *Aust.* 157F4
Lorient *France* 68B2
Los Angeles *USA* 16B2
Los Mochis *Mexico* 23C3
Losinj I. *Yugos.* 63E5
Louisiana State *USA* 20D2
Louisville *USA* 18E2
Loukhi *Russia* 93G2
Louth *Eng* 55G4
Loznica *Yugos.* 82D2
Lu'an *China* 114F3
Luanda *Angola* 148B1
Luang Prabang Laos 118C2
Lubango *Angola* 148B2
Lubbock *USA* 17C2
Lübeck *FRG* 85C2
Lublin *Pol.* 88E2
Lubumbashi *Dem. Rep. of Congo* 148C2
Lucca *Italy* 76C2
Lucknow *India* 127G3
Lüda *China* 112G3
Lüderitz *Namibia* 149B3
Ludhiana *India* 126F2
Ludvika *Sweden* 94D3
Luga *Russia* 95F4
Lugo *Spain* 72A1
Luleå *Sweden* 58C6
Lundy I. *Eng* 58C6
Luohe *China* 114F3
Luoyang *China* 114F3
Lurgan *N.Ire.* 65E2
Lusaka *Zambia* 148C2
Luton *Eng* 56G6
Luxembourg *Lux.* 70D2
Luxor *Egypt* 142G2
Luzern *Switz.* 70D2
Luzhou *China* 117E4
Luzon I. *Phil.* 120E2
L'viv *Ukraine* 102D5
Lybster *Scot* 61E2
Lycksele *Sweden* 93D3
Lyon *France* 71C2

M

Maastricht *Neth* 90B2
Ma'ān *Jordan* 130B2
Macapá *Brazil* 36D2
Macau *China* 119D1
Macclesfield *Eng* 53E4
Maceió *Brazil* 37F3
Mackay *Aust.* 156D3
Macomer *Sardegna* 78B2
Mâcon *France* 71C2
Macon *USA* 20E2
Macquarie I. *NZ* 165
Madang *PNG* 125G4
Madeira I. *Atlantic O.* 140B3
Madison *USA* 18E1
Madras (Chennai) *India* 129G4
Madrid *Spain* 72B1
Madura I. *Indon.* 123D4
Madurai *India* 128F5
Mafia I. *Tanz.* 150D1
Mafikeng *S.Africa* 149C34
Magadan *Russia* 105R4
Magdeburg *FRG* 85C2
Magnitogorsk *Russia* 109G4
Mahajanga *Madag.* 150E3
Mahalapye *Botswana* 149C3
Mahón *Spain* 74C2
Maidstone *Eng* 56H6
Maiduguri *Nig.* 145E3
Maine Province *France* 68B2
Maine State *USA* 19F1
Mainland I. *Scot Orkney I.* 61J7
Mainland I. *Scot Shetland I.* 61E1
Mainz *FRG* 90E3
Maitland *Aust.* 157E4
Maizuru *Japan* 115L9
Majene *Indon.* 123D4
Majorca I. *Spain* 74C2
Makarska *Cro.* 77D2
Makhachkala *Russia* 108F5
Makkah *S.Arabia* 132B3
Makó *Hung.* 88B3
Makurdi *Nig.* 145D2
Malabo *Bioko I.* 145D2
Malaga *Spain* 73B2
Malakal *Sudan* 146G4
Malang *Indon.* 123D4
Malanje *Angola* 148B1
Malatya *Turk.* 130B2
Malden I. *Kiribati* 162
Maldives Is. *Indian O.* 128F5
Malekula I. *Vanuatu* 156F2
Mallaig *Scot* 60C3
Mallow *Ireland* 66C4
Malmö *Sweden* 94C4
Malton *Eng* 55G3
Mamou *Guinea* 144A1
Man *Cote d'Ivoire* 144B2
Mana *Hawaiian Is.* 22H
Manacor *Spain* 74C2
Manado *Indon.* 124E3
Managua *Nic.* 25B4
Manakara *Madag.* 151E3
Manaus *Brazil* 35C3
Manchester *Eng* 53E4
Mandal *Nor.* 94B4
Mandalay *Myanmar* 118B1
Manfredonia *Italy* 77D2
Mangalia *Rom.* 83F2
Mangalore *India* 128F4
Manila *Phil.* 120E2
Manitoba *State Canada* 13H4
Manizalés *Colombia* 34B2
Mannheim *FRG* 90B3
Manokwari *Indon.* 124F4
Mansfield *Eng* 55F4
Manta *Ecuador* 34A3
Mantes *France* 68C2
Manzanillo *Cuba* 24D2
Manzhouli *China* 112F2
Maoming *China* 114F4
Maputo *Mozam.* 151D3
Maracaibo *Ven.* 34B1
Maradi *Niger* 145D1
Maranhão State *Brazil* 37E3
Marbella *Spain* 73B2
Marburg *FRG* 90B2
Mardan *Pak.* 126F2
Mar del Plata *Arg.* 38E6
Margate *Eng* 56J6
Maribor *Cro.* 77D1
Marie-Galante I. *Caribbean Sea* 26G3
Mariestad *Sweden* 94C4
Marília *Brazil* 38F5
Marmaris *Turkey* 81F3
Maroua *Cameroon* 145E3
Marquises Is. *Pacific O.* 162
Marrakech *Mor.* 140C3
Marseille *France* 71D3
Marshall Is. *Pacific O.* 159
Martinique I. *Caribbean Sea* 27G4
Mary *Turkmenistan* 108H6
Maryland State *USA* 19F2
Masaya *Nic.* 25B4
Masbate I. *Phil.* 120E2
Maseru *Lesotho* 149C3
Mashhad *Iran* 131D2
Masirah I. *Oman* 133D3
Masqat *Oman* 133D3
Massa *Italy* 76C2
Massachusetts State *USA* 19F1
Matadi *Dem Rep. of Congo* 145E3
Matagalpa *Nic.* 25B4
Matamoros *Mexico* 23D3
Matanzas *Cuba* 24C2
Mataram *Indon.* 123D4
Matlock *Eng* 55F4
Mato Grosso Do Sul *State* 37D4
Mato Grosso State *Brazil* 37D4
Matsue *Japan* 113H3
Matsumoto *Japan* 115M8
Matsusaka *Japan* 115M9
Matsuyama *Japan* 113H3
Maui *Hawaiian Is.* 22H
Mauritius I. *Indian O.* 151F4
Mayaguana I. *The Bahamas* 26E2
Maybole *Scot* 62D5
Mayotte I. *Indian O.* 150E2
Mazār-e Sharif *Afghan.* 126E2

Mazatlán *Mexico* 23C3
Mbabane *Swaziland* 151D3
Mbandaka
Dem. Rep. of Congo 146E4
Mbarara *Uganda* 146G5
Mbeya *Tanz.* 150D1
Mbuji-Mayi
Dem.Rep. of Congo 146F5
Meaux *France* 70C2
Medan *Indon.* 122B3
Medellín *Colombia* 34B2
Medgidia *Rom.* 83F2
Medicine Hat *Canada* 13G4
Meerut *India* 126F3
Meiktila *Myanmar* 118B1
Meknés *Mor.* 140C3
Melaka *Malay.* 122C3
Melbourne *Aust.* 157D4
Melilla *Spain* 73B2
Melitopol' *Ukraine* 108E5
Melo *Urug.* 38E6
Melun *France* 70C2
Melvich *Scot* 61E2
Melville I. *Aust.* 154C2
Melville I. *Canada* 12G2
Melville Pen. *Canada* 14D3
Memphis *USA* 18E2
Mende *France* 71C3
Mendoza *Arg.* 40C6
Mendoza State *Arg.* 40C6
Menongue *Angola* 148C2
Menzanares *Spain* 73B2
Merauke *Indon.* 125G4
Mercedes *Arg.* 40C6
Mergui Arch. *Myanmar* 118B2
Mérida *Mexico* 20E3
Mérida *Spain* 73A2
Merthyr Tydfil *Wales* 58D6
Mesolóngian *Greece* 80E3
Messina *Italy* 79D3
Metz *France* 70D2
Mexicali *USA* 16B2
México *Mexico* 23D4
Meymaneh *Afghan.* 126E2
Miami *USA* 21E3
Mianyany *China* 117E3
Michigan State *USA* 18E1
Michurin *Bulg.* 83F2
Midway Is. *Pacific O.* 159
Mikkeli *Fin* 95F3
Mikonos I. *Greece* 81F3
Milano *Italy* 76B1
Mildura *Aust.* 155D4
Milford Haven *Wales* 58B6
Millau *France* 71C3
Mílos *Greece* 81E3
Milton Keynes *Eng* 56G5
Milwaukee *USA* 18E1
Minas Gerais State *Brazil* 37E4
Minatinán *Mexico* 20D4
Mindanao *Phil.* 120E3
Mindoro I. *Phil.* 120E2
Minna *Nig.* 145D2
Minneapolis *USA* 18D1
Minnesota State *USA* 17D1
Minorca I. *Spain* 74C2
Minsk *Belarus* 102D4
Miranda de Ebro *Spain* 72B1
Miri *Malay.* 123D3
Mirzapur *India* 127G3
Misiones State *Arg.* 38E5
Miskolc *Hung.* 88E3
Misool *Indon.* 124F4
Misrātah *Libya* 141E3
Mississippi State *USA* 20D2
Missouri State *USA* 18D2
Mito *Japan* 115P8
Mits'iwa *Eth.* 143G3
Miyako *Japan* 115P7
Miyazaki *Japan* 115H3
Mizusawa *Japan* 115P7
Mjölby *Sweden* 94D4
Mlawa *Pol.* 86E2
Mljet I. *Cro.* 82D2
M. Lampang *Thai* 118B2
M. Nakhon Sawan *Thai.* 118C2
Mo-i-Rana *Nor.* 92C2
Mobile *USA* 20E2
Moçambique *Mozam.* 150E2
Modena *Italy* 77C2
Moffat *Scot* 63E5
Mogadishu *Somalia* 147H4
Mogilev *Belurus* 102E4
Mokp'o *S.Korea* 112G3
Molde *Nor.* 92B3
Mollendo *Peru* 35B4
Molokai I. *Hawaiian Is.* 22H
Mombasa *Kenya* 147G5
Monaco *Monaco* 71D3
Monaghan *Ireland* 65E2
Mondovi *Italy* 76B2
Mongu *Zambia* 148C2
Monopoli *Italy* 79D2
Monreal del Campo *Spain* 74B1
Monrovia *Lib.* 144A2
Montana State *USA* 17B1
Montargis *France* 70C2
Montauban *France* 69C3
Montbéliard *France* 70D2
Monte Cristi *Haiti* 26E3
Montego Bay *Jamaica* 24D3
Montería *Colombia* 34B2
Monterrey *Mexico* 23C3
Montes Claros *Brazil* 37E4
Montevideo *Urug.* 38E6
Montgomery *USA* 20E2
Montluçon *France* 71C2
Montpelier *USA* 19F1
Montréal *Canada* 15L5
Montrose *Scot* 63F4
Montserrat I. *Caribbean Sea* 26G3
Monza *Italy* 76B1
Mopti *Mali* 144B1
Mora *Sweden* 94C3
Moradabad *India* 126F3
Morioka *Japan* 115P7
Moroni *Comoros* 150E2
Morotai I. *Indon.* 124E3
Morwell *Aust.* 157D4
Moshi *Tanz.* 147G5
Mosjöen *Nor.* 92C2
Moskva *Russia* 105E4
Moss *Nor.* 94C4
Mossoró *Brazil* 37F3
Mostaganem *Alg.* 141D3
Mostar *Bos.Herz..* 82D2
Motherwell *Scot* 63E5
Motril *Spain* 73B2
Moulins *France* 71C2
Moulmein *Myanmar* 118B2
Moundou *Chad* 145E4
Mount Gambier *Aust.* 155D4
Mount Isa *Aust.* 154C3
M. Phitsanulok *Thai.* 118C2
Mt. Magnet *Aust.* 155A3
Mtwara *Tanz.* 150E2
Mudanjiang *China* 112G2
Mufulira *Zambia* 148C2
Muhos *Fin* 93F3
Mulhouse *France* 70D2
Mull I. *Scot* 62C4
Mullingar *Ireland* 67D3
Multan *Pak.* 126F2
Mumbai (Bombay)*India* 124E4
Muna I. *Indon.* 124E4
München *FRG* 91C3
Mungbere
Dem. Rep. of Congo 146F4
Munster *FRG* 84B2
Muonio *Fin* 93E2
Muqhisho *Somalia* 147H4
Murcia *Spain* 75B2
Murcia Region *Spain* 75B2
Murmansk *Russia* 103E3
Musselburgh *Scot* 63E5
Mutare *Zim.* 151D2
Mwanza *Tanz.* 146F5
Mwene Ditu
Dem. Rep of Congo 146F5
My Tho *Viet.* 119C2
Myingyan *Myanmar* 118B1
Myitkyina *Myanmar* 118B1
Mymensingh *Bang.* 127H3
Mysore *India* 128F4

N

Naas *Ireland* 67E3
Naga *Phil.* 120E2
Nagano *Japan* 115N8
Nagaoka *Japan* 115N8
Nagasaki *Japan* 115G3
Nagercoil *India* 128F5
Nagoya *Japan* 115M9
Nagpur *India* 128F3
Nagykanizsa *Hung.* 91D3
Nain *Canada* 15M4
Nairn *Scot* 61E3
Nairobi *Kenya* 147G5
Nakhodka *Russia* 107P5
Nakhon Ratchasima *Thai.* 118C2
Nakhon Si Thammarat *Thai.* 118B3
Nakuru *Kenya* 147G5
Nam Dinh *Viet.* 119C1
Namangan *Uzbekistan* 109J5
Namibe *Angola* 148B2
Nampula *Mozam.* 150D2
Nanchang *China* 114F4
Nanchong *China* 117E3
Nancy *France* 70D2
Nanjing *China* 114F3
Nanning *China* 117E4
Nanping *China* 114F4
Nantes *France* 68B2
Nantong *China* 114G3
Nanyang *China* 114F3
Napoli *Italy* 79C2
Narbonne *France* 71C3

Narva *Estonia* **95F4**
Narvik *Nor.* **92D2**
Nar'yan Mar *Russia* **103G3**
Nashville *USA* **18E2**
Nassau *The Bahamas* **24D1**
Natal *Brazil* **37F3**
Natuna Besar I. *Indon.* **123C3**
Navarra Region *Spain* **74B1**
Náxos I. *Greece* **81F3**
Ndjamena *Chad* **145E3**
Ndola *Zambia* **148C2**
Neápolos *Greece* **81E3**
Near Islands *USA* **22J**
Nebraska State *USA* **17C1**
Negros *Phil.* **120E3**
Nei Mongol Zizhiqu Provin *China* **112F2**
Neiva *Colombia* **34B2**
Nellore *India* **129G4**
Nelson *Eng* **53E4**
Nelson *NZ* **157G5**
Nenagh *Ireland* **66C4**
Neubrandenburg *FRG* **85C2**
Neumünster *FRG* **85B2**
Neuquén *Arg.* **40C6**
Neuquén State *Arg.* **40C6**
Nevada State *USA* **16B2**
Nevers *France* **70C2**
Newark *USA* **19F1**
Newark-on-Trent *Eng* **55G4**
New Britain I. *Pacific O.* **125G4**
New Brunswick *Canada* **15M5**
Newcastle *Aust.* **157E4**
Newcastle-upon-Tyne *Eng* **54F3**
New Delhi *India* **126F3**
Newfoundland *Canada* **15M4**
New Georgia *Solomon Is.* **156E1**
New Hampshire State *USA* **19F1**
New Jersey State *USA* **19F1**
New Mexico State *USA* **17C2**
New Orleans *USA* **20E3**
Newport *Isle of Wight* **57F7**
Newport *Wales* **58E6**
Newquay *Eng* **59B7**
New Ross *Ireland* **67E4**
Newry *N.Ire.* **65E2**
New South Wales State *Aust.* **157D4**
Newton Aycliffe *Eng* **54F3**
Newton Stewart *Scot* **62D6**
Newtown-abbey *N.Ire.* **65F2**
New York *USA* **19F1**
New York State *USA* **18F1**
Ngaoundére *Cameroon* **145E4**
Nguru *Nig.* **145E3**
Nha Trang *Viet.* **119C2**
Niamey *Niger* **145D1**
Nias I. *Indon.* **122B4**
Nice *France* **71D3**
Nicobar I. *India* **129H5**
Nicosia *Cyprus* **130B2**
Niigata *Japan* **115N8**
Nijmegen *Neth.* **84B2**
Nikel *Russia* **93G2**
Nikolayev *Russia* **108E5**
Nîmes *France* **71C3**
Ningbo *China* **114G4**
Ningxia Province *China* **111E3**
Nioro du Sahel *Mali* **140C5**
Niort *France* **69B2**
Nis *Yugos.* **82E2**
Nitra *Slovakia.* **88D3**
Niue I. *Pacific O.* **165**
Nivernais Province *France* **70C2**
Nizamabad *India* **128F4**
Nizhny Novgorod *Russia* **108F4**
Nizhniy Tagil *Russia* **109H4**
Nkongsamba *Cameroon* **145D2**
Nong Khai *Thai.* **118C2**
Norfolk *USA* **19F2**
Norfolk I. *Aust.* **157F3**
Noril'sk *Russia* **103K3**
Normandie Province *France* **68B2**
Norrköping *Sweden* **94D4**
Norseman *Aust.* **155B4**
North Bay *Canada* **15L5**
North Carolina State *USA* **18E2**
North Dakota State *USA* **17C1**
Northern Mariana I. *Pacific O.* **121G2**
Northern Ter. State *Aust.* **154C2**
North I. *NZ* **157G4**
North Uist I. *Scot* **60A3**
Northwest Territories State *Canada* **12G3**
Norwich *Eng* **56J5**
Notodden *Nor.* **94B4**
Nottingham *Eng* **55F5**
Nouadhibou *Maur.* **140B4**
Nouakchott *Maur.* **140B5**
Nouméa *Nouvelle Calédonie* **156E1**
Nouvelle Calédonie I. *Pacific O.* **156E1**
Novara *Italy* **76B1**
Nova Scotia *Canada* **15M5**
Novaya Zemlya *Russia* **103G2**
Novi Pazar *Yugos.* **82E2**
Novi Sad *Yugos.* **82D1**
Novokuznatsk *Russia* **109K4**
Novorosslysk *Russia* **108E5**
Novosibirsk *Russia* **109K4**
Novosibirskiye Ostrova I. *Russia* **104Q2**
N. Ronaldsay I. *Scot* **61F1**
Nuku'alofa *Tonga* **165**
Nukus *Uzbekistan* **108G5**
Numazu *Japan* **115N9**
Nunivak I. *USA* **12B3**
Nürnberg *FRG* **91B3**
Nyala *Sudan* **146F3**
Nyíregyháza *Hung.* **88E3**
Nykoping *Sweden* **94D4**
Nyngan *Aust.* **157D4**
Nzérekoré *Guinea* **144B2**

O

Oahu I. *Hawaiian Is.* **22H**
Oban *Scot* **62C4**
Obi I. *Indon.* **124E4**
Odawara *Japan* **115N9**
Odda *Nor.* **94B3**
Odemira *Port.* **83A2**
Odense *Den.* **94C4**
Odessa *Ukraine* **108D5**
Odessa *USA* **23C2**
Offenbach *FRG* **90B2**
Ogaki *Japan* **115M9**
Ogasawara-Shotó *Jap.* **121G1**
Ogbomosho *Nig.* **145D2**
Ogden *USA* **17B1**
Ohrid *Macedonia* **80E2**
Okaya *Japan* **115N8**
Okayama *Japan* **113H3**
Okazaki *Japan* **115M9**
Okehampton *Eng* **59C7**
Okhotsk *Russia* **105Q4**
Okinawa I. *Japan* **113G4**
Oklahoma City *USA* **17D2**
Oklahoma State *USA* **17D2**
Öland I. *Sweden* **94D4**
Olbia *Sardegna* **78B2**
Oldenburg *FRG* **84B2**
Olomouc *Czech.Rep.* **91D3**
Olsztyn *Pol.* **86E2**
Olympia *USA* **16A1**
Omagh *N.Ire.* **65D2**
Omaha *USA* **17D1**
Omdurman *Sudan* **142G3**
Omsk *Russia* **109J4**
Onitsha *Nig.* **145D2**
Ontario State *Canada* **15J4**
Oostende *Belg.* **70C1**
Opole *Pol.* **88D2**
Oppdal *Nor.* **92B3**
Oradea *Rom.* **88E3**
Oran *Alg.* **141C3**
Orange *Aust.* **157D4**
Orange *France* **71C3**
Orbetello *Italy* **77C2**
Olréanais Province *France* **68C2**
Örebro *Sweden* **94D4**
Oregon State *USA* **16A1**
Orel *Russia* **108E4**
Orenburg *Russia* **108G4**
Orënse *Spain* **72A1**
Oristano *Sardegna* **78B3**
Orkney Is. *Scot* **61E1**
Orlando *USA* **20E3**
Orléans *France* **68C2**
Örnsköldsvik *Sweden* **93D3**
Orsk *Russia* **109G4**
Oruro *Bolivia* **35C4**
Ōsaka *Japan* **155L9**
Oshogbo *Nig.* **145D2**
Osijek *Cro.* **82D1**
Oskarshamn *Sweden* **94D4**
Oslo *Nor.* **94C4**
Osnabrück *FRG* **84B2**
Osorno *Chile* **41B7**
Östersund *Sweden* **92C3**
Ostia *Italy* **77C2**
Ostrava *Czech. Rep.* **88D3**
Ōsumi-shoto *Japan* **113H3**
Oswestry *Eng* **53D5**
Otaru *Japan* **113J2**
Ottawa *Canada* **15L5**
Ouagadougou *Burkina Faso* **144C3**
Ouahigouya *Burkina Faso* **144B1**
Ouargla *Alg.* **141D3**
Oudtshoorn *S.Africa* **149C4**
Oujda *Mor.* **141C3**
Oulu *Fin* **93F2**
Outer Hebrides *Scot* **60A3**
Oviedo *Spain* **72A1**
Oxford *Eng* **56F6**
Oyem *Gabon* **145E4**

P

Padang *Indon.* **122C4**
Paderborn *FRG* **84B2**
Pag I. *Cro..* **77D2**
Pagai Selatan I. *Indon.* **123C4**
Pagai Utara I. *Indon.* **122B4**
Pahala *Hawaiian Is.* **22H**
Pais Vasco Region *Spain* **72B1**
Paisley *Scot* **62D5**
Palan I. *Pacific O.* **158**
Palangkaraya *Indon.* **123D4**
Palau *Caroline Is.* **124F3**
Palawan I. *Phil.* **120D2**
Palembang *Indon.* **122C4**
Palencia *Spain* **72B1**
Palermo *Italy* **79C3**
Palma de Mallorca *Spain* **74C2**
Palmerston North *NZ* **157G5**
Palmi *Italy* **79D3**
Palmyra *Pacific O.* **160**
Palu *Indon.* **123D4**
Pamplona *Spain* **74B1**
Panamá *Panama* **25D5**
Panay I. *Phil.* **120E2**
Pangkalpinang *Indon.* **123D4**
Pantelleria I. *Italy* **78C3**
Papa Westray I. *Scot* **61F1**
Pará State *Brazil* **37D3**
Paracel I. *S.China Sea* **119D2**
Paracin *Yugos.* **82E2**
Paraíba State *Brazil* **37F3**
Parakou *Benin* **145D2**
Paramaribo *Suriname* **36D2**
Paraná *Arg.* **40C6**
Parana State *Brazil* **38E5**
Parepare *Indon.* **123D4**
Paris *France* **68C2**
Parkano *Fin* **95E3**
Parma *Italy* **76C2**
Parnaíba *Brazil* **37E3**
Pärnu *Estonia* **95E4**
Pasadena *USA* **16B2**
Passo Fundo *Brazil* **38E5**
Pasto *Colombia* **34B2**
Patna *India* **127G3**
Pátrai *Greece* **80E3**
Pau *France* **69B3**
Pavlodar *Kazakhstan* **109J4**
P.Dolak I. *Indon.* **125F4**
Pec *Yugos.* **82E2**
Pécs *Hung.* **88D3**
Peebles *Scot* **63E5**
Pegu *Myanmar* **118B2**
Pekanbaru *Indon.* **122C3**
Peking (Beijing) *China* **112F3**
Pello *Fin* **93E2**
Pelopónnisos I. *Greece* **80E3**
Pemba *Mozam.* **150E2**
Pemba I. *Tanz.* **147G5**
Pembroke *Wales* **58C6**
Pennsylvania State *USA* **18F1**
Penrith *Eng* **52E3**
Penza *Russia* **108F4**
Penzance *Eng* **59B7**
Pereira *Colombia* **34B2**
Périgueux *France* **69C2**
Perm *Russia* **109G4**
Pernambuco State *Brazil* **37F3**
Perpignan *France* **71C3**
Perth *Aust.* **155A4**
Perth *Scot* **62E4**
Perugia *Italy* **77C2**
Pescara *Italy* **77C2**
Peshawar *Pak.* **126F2**
Peterborough *Eng* **56G5**
Peterhead *Scot* **61G3**
Petropavlovsk *Kazakhstan* **109H4**
Petropavlovsk Kamchatskiy *Russia* **105R4**
Petrozavodsk *Russia* **102E3**
Philadelphia *USA* **19F1**
Phnom Penh *Camb.* **119C2**
Phoenix *USA* **16B2**
Phoenix Is. *Kiribati* **165**
Phuket I. *Thai.* **118B3**
Piacenza *Italy* **76B1**
Piauí State *Brazil* **37E3**
Picardie Province *France* **70C2**
Pierre *USA* **17C1**
Pietermaritzburg *S.Africa* **149D3**
Pietersburg *S.Africa* **149C3**
Pila *Pol.* **85D2**
Pílos *Greece* **80E3**
Pinar del Rio *Cuba* **24C2**
Pingliang *China* **117E3**
Piombino *Italy* **76C2**
Piraiévs *Greece* **81E3**
Pírgos *Greece* **80E3**
Pirot *Yugos.* **82E2**
Pisa *Italy* **76C2**
Pitcairn I. *Pacific O.* **162**
Piteå *Sweden* **93E2**
Pitesti *Rom.* **83E2**
Pitlochry *Scot* **62E4**
Pittsburgh *USA* **18F1**
Piura *Peru* **35A3**
Plasencia *Spain* **72A1**
Pleven *Bulg.* **83E2**
Ploiesti *Rom.* **83F2**
Plovdiv *Bulg.* **83E2**
Plymouth *Eng* **59C7**
Plzen *Czech.* **91C3**
Podgorica *Yugos.* **82D2**
Pointe-á-Pitre *Guadeloup* **26G3**
Pointe Noire *Congo* **145E3**
Poitiers *France* **69C2**
Poitou Province *France* **69B2**
Polla *Italy* **79D2**
Poltava *Ukraine* **108E5**
Ponce *Puerto Rico* **26F3**
Ponferrada *Spain* **72A1**
Pontevedra *Spain* **72A1**
Pontianak *Indon.* **123C4**
Poole *Eng* **57F7**
Pori *Fin* **95E3**
Port Augusta *Aust.* **155C4**
Port au Prince *Haiti* **26E3**
Port Elizabeth *S.Africa* **149C4**
Port Gentil *Gabon* **145D3**
Port Harcourt *Nig.* **145D2**
Port Headland *Aust.* **154A3**
Portland *USA* **16A**
Port Laoise *Ireland* **67D3**
Port Louis *Mauritius* **151F4**
Port Moresby *PNG* **125G4**
Pôrto Alegre *Brazil* **38E5**
Port of Spain *Trinidad* **27G4**
Porto Novo *Benin* **145D2**
Porto *Port.* **72A1**
Porto Torres *Sardegna* **78B2**
Porto Vecchio *Corse* **76B2**
Pôrto Velho *Brazil* **35C3**
Port Pirie *Aust.* **155C4**
Portrush *N.Ireland* **65E1**
Port Said *Egypt* **142G1**
Portsmouth *Eng* **57F7**
Port Sudan *Sudan* **143G3**
Port Talbot *Wales* **58D6**
Poso *Indon.* **124E4**
Potchefstroom *S.Africa* **149C3**
Potenza *Italy* **79D2**
Potosí *Bolivia* **35C4**
Potsdam *FRG* **85C2**
Poznan *Pol.* **85D2**
Prato *Italy* **77C2**
Preston *Eng* **53E4**
Preswick *Scot* **62D5**
Pretoria *S.Africa* **149C3**
Prince Edward I. *Can.* **15M5**
Prince George *Canada* **13F4**
Prince of Wales I. *Canada* **12H2**
Prince Rupert *Canada* **13F4**
Príncipe I. *W.Africa* **145D2**
Pristina *Czech.* **82E2**
Prokop'yevsk *Russia* **109K4**
Prome *Myanmar* **118B2**
Provence Province *France* **71D3**
Providence *USA* **19F1**
Prudhoe Bay *USA* **12D2**
Przemys'l *Pol.* **88E3**
Pskov *Russia* **102D4**
Pucàllpa *Peru* **35B3**
Puebla *Mexico* **23D4**
Puerto Armuelles *Panama* **25C5**
Puerto Ayacucho *Ven.* **34C2**
Puerto Barrios *Guatemala* **25B3**
Puerto Cabezas *Nic.* **25C4**
Puerto Cortés *Honduras* **25B4**
Puerto Juárez *Mexico* **20E3**
Puerto Montt *Chile* **41B7**
Puerto Plata *Dom. Republic* **26E3**
Puerto Rico I. *Caribbean* **26F3**
Puertollano *Spain* **73B2**
Pula *Cro.* **77C2**
Pune *India* **128F4**
Punta Arenas *Chile* **41B8**
Puntarenas *Costa Rica* **25C5**
Pusan *S.Korea* **113G3**
Puttgarden *FRG* **85C2**
Pyŏngyang *China* **112G3**

Q

Qamdo *China* **117D3**
Qazvin *Iran* **131C2**
Qena *Egypt* **142G2**
Qingdao *China* **112G3**
Qinghai Province *China* **111D3**
Qingjiang *China* **114F3**
Qinhuangdao *China* **112F2**
Qiqihar *China* **112G2**
Qom *Iran* **131D2**
Qu Xian *China* **114F4**
Quanzhou *China* **114F4**
Québec *Canada* **15L5**
Québec State *Canada* **15L4**
Queen Charlotte Is. *Can* **13E4**

Queen Elizabeth Is. *Can* 12G2
Queensland State *Aust.* 154D3
Quelimane *Mozam.* 150D2
Quetta *Pak.* 126E3
Quezaltenango *Guatemala* 25A4
Quezon City *Phil.* 120E2
Qui Nhon *Viet.* 119C2
Quilon *India* 128F5
Quimper *France* 68B2
Quito *Ecuador* 34B3

R

Raasay I. *Scot* 60B3
Rab I. *Cro.* 77C2
Raba *Indon.* 123D4
Rabat *Mor.* 140C3
Radom *Pol.* 88E2
Raipur *India* 129G3
Rajkot *India* 128F3
Raleigh *USA* 18F2
Ramsey *Isle of Man* 53C3
Rancagua *Chile* 40B6
Ranchi *India* 129G3
Randers *Den.* 94C4
Rangpur *Bang.* 127G3
Rapid City *USA* 17C1
Rasht *Iran* 131C2
Ráth Luirc *Ireland* 66C4
Rathin I. *N.Ire.* 65E1
Ratlam *India* 128F3
Rauma *Fin* 95E3
Ravenna *Italy* 77C2
Rawalpindi *Pak.* 126F2
Razgrad *Bulg.* 83F2
Reading *Eng* 56G6
Recife *Brazil* 37F3
Redon *France* 68B2
Regensburg *FRG* 91B3
Reggane *Alg.* 141D4
Reggio di Calabria *Italy* 79D3
Reggio nell'Emilia *Italy* 76C2
Regina *Canada* 13H4
Reims *France* 70C2
Renell I. *Solomon Is.* 156F2
Rennes *France* 68B2
Reno *USA* 16B2
Resistencia *Arg.* 40D5
Resolution I. *Canada* 14M3
Réunion I. *Indian O.* 151F4
Reykjavík *Iceland* 92A2
Rhode Island State *USA* 19F1
Rhodes I. *Greece* 81F3
Rhum I. *Scot* 62B4
Rhyl *Wales* 53E4
Richmond *USA* 19F2
Riga *Latvia* 102D4
Rijeka *Cro.* 77C1
Rimini *Italy* 77C2
Rîmnicu Vîlcea *Rom.* 89E3
Ringwood *Eng* 57F7
Rio Branco *Brazil* 35C3
Rio de Janeiro *Brazil* 38F5
Rio de Janeiro State *Brazil* 38F5
Río Gallegos *Arg.* 41C8
Rio Grande *Brazil* 38E5
Rio Grande do Norte State *Brazil* 37F3
Rio Grande do Sul State *Brazil* 38E5
Río Negro State *Arg.* 41C7
Ripon *Eng* 55F3
Roanne *France* 71C2
Rochdale *Eng* 53E4
Rochester *Eng* 56H6
Rochester *USA* 18D1
Rockford *USA* 18E1
Rockhampton *Aust.* 156E3
Rødbyhavn *Den.* 94C5
Ródhos *Greece* 81F3
Roman *Rom.* 89F3
Rome *Italy* 77C2
Ronda *Spain* 73A2
Rondônia State *Brazil* 35C4
Rosario *Arg.* 40C6
Roscoff *France* 88B2
Roscommon *Ireland* 66C3
Roscrea *Ireland* 67D4
Roseau *Dominica* 27G3
Rosslare *Ireland* 67E4
Rostock *FRG* 85C2
Rostov-na-Donu *Russia* 108E5
Rotherham *Eng* 55F4
Roti I. *Indon.* 124E5
Rotterdam *Neth.* 84A2
Rouen *France* 68C2
Round I. *Mauritius* 151F4
Rousay I. *Scot* 61E1
Roussillon Province *France* 69C3
Rovaniemi *Fin* 93F2
Royal Tunbridge Wells *Eng* 56H6
Ruffec *France* 69C2
Rugby *Eng* 56F5
Rugen I. *FRG* 85C2
Ruma *Yugos.* 82D1
Runcorn *Eng* 53E4
Ruoqiang *China* 110C3
Ruse *Bulg.* 83F2
Ruteng *Indon.* 124E4
Ryazan' *Russia* 108E4
Rybinsk *Rus.* 102E4
Rybnik *Pol.* 88D2
Ryūkyū Is. *Japan* 113G4
Rzeszów *Pol.* 88E2

S

Saarbrucken *FRG* 90B3
Saaremaa I. *Est.* 95E4
Sabac *Yugos.* 82D2
Sabadell *Spain* 74C1
Sabhā *Libya* 141E4
Sacramento *USA* 16A2
Sadiya *India* 127H3
Safi *Mor.* 140C3
Sagunto *Spain* 74B2
Saintes *France* 69B2
Sakai *Japan* 115L9
Sakata *Japan* 115N7
Sakhalin I. *Russia* 107Q4
Sakishima guntō *Japan* 115G4
Salālah *Oman* 133D4
Salamanca *Spain* 72A1
Salangen *Nor.* 92D2
Salayar I. *Indon.* 124E4
Salbris *France* 68C2
Salem *India* 128F4
Salem *USA* 16A1
Salerno *Italy* 79C2
Salford *Eng* 53E4
Salisbury *Eng* 56F6
Salo *Fin* 95E3
Salonta *Rom.* 82B1
Salt Lake City *USA* 17B1
Salta *Arg.* 40C5
Salta State *Arg.* 40C5
Saltillo *Mexico* 23C3
Salto *Urug.* 38E6
Salvador *Brazil* 37F4
Salzburg *Aust.* 91C3
Salzgitter-Bad *FRG* 85C2
Samar I. *Phil.* 120E2
Samara *Russia* 108G4
Samarinda *Indon.* 123D4
Samarkand *Uzbekistan* 109H6
Sámos I. *Greece* 81F3
Samothráki I. *Greece* 81F2
Samsun *Turk.* 130B1
San *Mali* 144B1
San Antonio USA 23D3
San'ā *Rep.Yemen* 132C4
San Benedetto del Tronto *Italy* 77C2
San Cristóbal *Ven.* 34B2
San Cristobal I. *Solomon Is.* 156F2
Sancti Spíritus *Cuba* 24D2
Sandakan *Malay.* 123D3
Sanday I. *Scot* 61F1
San Diego *USA* 16B2
Sandoy I. *Den.* 92A2
San Fernando *Phil.* 120E2
San Francisco USA 16A2
Sanjō *Japan* 115N8
San José *Costa Rica* 25C5
San Jose *USA* 16A2
San Juan *Arg.* 40C6
San Juan *Puerto Rico* 26F3
San Juan del Norte *Nic.* 25C4
San Juan del Sur *Nic.* 25B4
San Juan State *Arg.* 40C6
San Julián *Arg.* 41C7
San Luis Potosí *Mexico* 23C3
San Luis State *Arg.* 40C6
Sanmenxia *China* 114F3
San Marino *San Marino* 77D2
San Miguel de Tucuman *Arg.* 40C5
San Miguel El Sal. 25B4
San Pedro Sula *Honduras* 25B3
San Remo *Italy* 76B2
San Salvador El Sal. 25B4
San Salvador I. *The Bahamas* 26E1
San Sebastian *Spain* 74B1
Santa Ana *El Sal.* 25B4
Santa Catarina State *Brazil* 38E5
Santa Clara *Cuba* 24C2
Santa Cruz *Bolivia* 35C4
Santa Cruz Is. *Solomon Is.* 156F24
Santa Cruz State *Arg.* 41B7
Santa Fé *Arg.* 40C6
Santa Fe *USA* 17C2
Santa Isabel I. *Solomon Is.* 156E1
Santa Marta *Colombia* 34B1
Santander *Spain* 72B1
Santarém *Brazil* 37D3
Santarém *Port.* 73A2
Santa Rosa *Arg.* 40C6
Santa State *Arg.* 40C5
Santiago *Chile* 40B6

Santiago *Dom. Republic* **26E3**
Santiago *Panama* **25C5**
Santiago de Compostela *Spain* **72A1**
Santiago de Cuba *Cuba* **24D3**
Santiago del Estero State *Arg.* **40C5**
Santo Domingo *Dom. Republic* **26F3**
São Carlos *Brazil* **38F5**
São Luis *Brazil* **37E3**
São Paulo *Brazil* **38F5**
São Paulo State *Brazil* **38F5**
São Tomé *I.W.Africa* **145D2**
São Tomé and PríncipeRep. *W.Africa* **145D2**
Sapporo *Japan* **113J2**
Sapri *Italy* **79D2**
Sarajevo *Bos.Herz.* **82D2**
Saratov *Russia* **108F4**
Sardegna *Italy* **78B2**
Sarh *Chad* **146E4**
Sark I. *UK* **59E8**
Sarrion *Spain* **74B1**
Sasebo *Japan* **115G3**
Saskatchewan State *Canada* **13H4**
Saskatoon *Canada* **13H4**
Sassandra *Côte d'Ivoire* **144B2**
Sassari *Sardegna* **78B2**
Sassnitz *FRG* **85C2**
Satu Mare *Rom.* **88E3**
Sault Ste Marie *Canada* **15K5**
Savannah *USA* **20E2**
Savannakhet *Laos.* **119C2**
Savoie Province *France* **71D2**
Savona *Italy* **76B2**
Savonlinna *Fin* **93F3**
Saxmundham *Eng* **56J5**
Saynshand *Mongolia* **112F2**
Scarborough *Eng* **55G3**
Schwerin *FRG* **85C2**
Scourie *Scot* **60C2**
Scunthorpe *Eng* **55G4**
Seattle *USA* **16A1**
Seaward Pen. *USA* **12B3**
Sebes *Rom.* **88E3**
Ségou *Mali* **144B1**
Segovia *Spain* **72B1**
Seinajoki *Fin* **93E3**
Sekondi *Ghana* **145C4**
Selby *Eng* **55F4**
Semarang *Indon.* **123D4**
Semipalatinsk *Kazakhstan* **109K4**
Sendai *Japan* **115P7**
Senlis *France* **70C2**
Sennen *Eng* **59B7**
Sens *France* **70C2**
Seoul *S.Korea* **112G3**
Seram I. *Indon.* **124E4**
Sergino *Russia* **109H3**
Sergipe State *Brazil* **37F4**
Sérifos *Greece* **81E3**
Serov *Russia* **109H4**
Serpukhov *Russia* **102E4**
Sérrai *Greece* **81E2**
Sétif *Alg.* **141D4**
Setúbal *Port.* **73A2**
Sevastopol' *Ukraine* **108E5**
Severnaya Zemlya *Russia* **104L2**
Severodvinsk *Russia* **102E3**
Sevilla *Spain* **73A2**
Seychelles Is. *Indian* **150F1**
Seydhisfodhur *Iceland* **92C1**
Sézanne *France* **70C2**
Sfax *Tunisia* **141E3**
'S-Gravenhage *Neth.* **84A2**
Shado Shima I. *Japan* **115N7**
Shahjahanpur *India* **126G3**
Shakhty *Russia* **108F5**
Shandong Province *China* **112F3**
Shanghai *China* **114G3**
Shangrao *China* **114F4**
Shantou *China* **114F4**
Shanxi Province *China* **112F3**
Shaoguan *China* **114F4**
Shaoxing *China* **114G4**
Shaoyang *China* **114F4**
Shapinsay I. *Scot* **61F1**
Shashi *China* **114F3**
Sheffield *Eng* **55F4**
Shenyang *China* **112G2**
Shetland Is. *Scot* **61J7**
Shijiazhuang *China* **112F3**
Shillong *India* **127H3**
Shimizu *Japan* **115N9**
Shingū *Japan* **115L10**
Shirāz *Iran* **131D3**
Shizuoka *Japan* **115N9**
Shkodër *Alb.* **82D2**
Shreveport *USA* **20D2**
Shrewsbury *Eng* **58E5**
Shuangyashan *China* **113H2**
Sialkot *Pak.* **126F2**
Siauliai *Lithuania* **95E5**
Sibenik *Cro.* **77D2**
Siberut I. *Indon.* **122B4**
Sibiu *Rom.* **88E3**
Sibolga *Indon.* **122B3**
Sibu *Malay.* **123D3**
Sichuan Province *China* **117E3**
Sicila *Italy* **79C3**
Sidi Bel Abbés *Alg.* **141C3**
Siedlce *Pol.* **86E2**
Siegen *FRG* **90B2**
Siena *Italy* **77C2**
Sifnos *Greece* **81E3**
Sigüenza *Spain* **72B1**
Siguiri *Guinea* **144B1**
Sikasso *Mali* **144B1**
Sikinos *Greece* **81F3**
Simeulue I. *Indon.* **122B4**
Singkawang *Indon.* **123C3**
Sintra *Port.* **73A2**
Sioux Falls *USA* **17D1**
Siping *China* **112G2**
Sipora I. *Indon.* **122B4**
Siracusa *Italy* **79D3**
Siros *Greece* **81E3**
Sisak *Cro.* **77D1**
Sittwe *Myanmar* **118B1**
Sivas *Turk.* **130B2**
Sjaelland I. *Den.* **94C4**
Skara *Sweden* **94C4**
Skegness *Eng* **55H4**
Skellefteå *Sweden* **93E3**
Skíathos I. *Greece* **81E3**
Skien *Nor.* **94B4**
Skikda *Alg.* **141D3**
Skiros *Greece* **81E3**
Skopélos *Greece* **81E3**
Skopje *Mac.* **82E2**
Skovorodino *Russia* **106O4**
Skye I. *Scot* **60B3**
Slatina *Rom.* **83E2**
Sligo *Ireland* **64C2**
Sliven *Bulg.* **83F2**
Sobral *Brazil* **37E3**
Société, Is. de la *French Pol.* **165**
Socotra I. *Rep.Yemen* **133D4**
Sodankylä *Fin* **93F2**
Södertälje *Sweden* **94D4**
Söderhamn *Sweden* **94D3**
Sofia *Bulg.* **82E2**
Sokodé *Togo* **145D2**
Sokoto *Nig.* **145D1**
Solāpur *India* **128F4**
Sollefteå *Sweden* **92D3**
Solomon Is. *Pacific O* **156F2**
Somerset I. *Canada* **14J2**
Sondrio *Italy* **76B1**
Songkhla *Thai.* **122C3**
Sorocaba *Brazil* **38F5**
Sorong *Indon.* **124F4**
Soroti *Uganda* **146G4**
Sorrento *Italy* **79C2**
Sorsele *Sweden* **92D2**
Sosnowiec *Pol.* **88D2**
Souillac *France* **69C3**
Sŏul *S.Korea* **112G3**
Sousse *Tunisia* **141E3**
Southampton I. *Canada* **14K3**
Southampton *Eng.* **56F7**
South Aust. State *Aus* **154C3**
South Carolina State *USA* **18E2**
South Dakota State *USA* **17C1**
Southend-on-Sea *Eng* **56H6**
South Georgia I. *South Atlantic O.* **39G8**
South Island. *NZ* **157F5**
Southport *Eng* **53D4**
South Ronaldsay *Scot* **61F2**
South Shields *Eng* **54F3**
South Uist I. *Scot* **60A3**
Sovetskaya Gavan' *Russia* **107Q5**
Soweto *S.Africa* **149C3**
Spalding *Eng* **55G5**
Split *Cro.* **77D2**
Spokane *USA* **16B1**
Spratly Islands *S.China Sea* **119D2**
Springfield *USA* **18D2**
Springfield *USA* **18E2**
Springs *S.Africa* **149C3**
Srinagar *India* **126F2**
S.Ronaldsay *Scot* **61F2**
S.Severo *Italy* **77D2**
Sta.Cruz de Tenerife *Canary Is.* **140B4**
Stafford *Eng* **53E5**
St.Albans *Eng* **56G6**
St.Andrews *Scot* **63F4**
Stanley *Falkland Is.* **39D8**
Stara Zagora *Bulg.* **83F2**
Starbuck I. *Kiribati* **162**
St.Austell *Eng* **59C7**

Stavanger *Nor.* 94B4
Stavropol' *Russia* 108F5
St.Brieuc *France* 68B2
St.Croix I. *Caribbean* 26F3
St.David's *Wales* 58B6
St.Denis *Réunion* 151F4
St.Dizier *France* 70C2
Steinkjer *Nor.* 92C3
St.Etienne *France* 71C2
Stewart I. *NZ* 157F5
St.Gaudens *France* 69C3
St.George's *Grenada* 27G4
St.Helens *Eng* 53E4
St.Helier *Jersey* 59E8
Stirling *Scot* 62E4
St.Ives *Eng* 59B7
St.John *Canada* 15M5
St.John's *Antigua* 26G3
St.John's *Canada* 15N5
St.Kitts Is. *Caribbean* 26G3
St.Lawrence I. *USA* 22J
St.Louis *Sen.* 140B5
St.Louis *USA* 18D2
St.Lucia I. *Caribbean* 27G4
St.Malo *France* 68B2
St.Martin *Caribbean* 26G3
St.Mary's *Eng* 59A8
St.Nazaire *France* 68B2
St.Paul *USA* 18D1
St.Peter Port *Guernsey* 59E8
St.Petersburg *Russia* 102E4
St.Petersburg *USA* 20E3
St.Quentin *France* 70C2
Stockport *Eng* 53E4
Stoke-on-Trent *Eng* 53E4
Stonehaven *Scot* 63F4
Stören *Nor.* 92C3
Storlien *Sweden* 92C3
Stornoway *Scot* 60B2
Storuman *Sweden* 92D2
Strabane *N.Ire.* 65D2
Stralsund *FRG* 85C2
Stranraer *Scot* 62D6
Strasbourg *France* 70D2
Stratford-on-Avon *Eng* 56F5
Streymoy I. *Den.* 92A2
Strömsund *Sweden* 92D3
Stronsay I. *Scot* 61F1
Stroud *Eng* 56E6
St.Tropez *France* 71D3
Stuttgart *FRG* 90B3
St.Vincent I. *Caribbean* 27G4
Subotica *Yugos.* 82D1
Suceava *Rom.* 89F3
Sucre *Bolivia* 35C4
Suduroy I. *Den.* 92A2
Suez *Egypt* 142G2
Sukhumi *Georgia* 108F5
Sukkur *Pak.* 126E3
Sulawesi *Indon.* 124E4
Sulu Arch. *Phil.* 120E3
Sumba I. *Indon.* 123D4
Sumbawa I. *Indon.* 123D4
Sumen *Bulg.* 83F2
Sumy *Ukraine* 108E4
Sunderland *Eng* 54F3
Sundsvall *Sweden* 92D3
Suntar *Russia* 106N3
Surabaya *Indon.* 123D4
Surakarta *Indon.* 123D4
Surat *India* 128F3
Surgut *Russia* 109J3
Surtsey I. *Iceland* 92A2
Suva *Fiji* 165
Suzhou *China* 114G3
Svalbard Is. *Nor.* 103C2
Sveg *Sweden* 94C3
Sverdrup Is. *Canada* 12H2
Svetozarevo *Yugos.* 82E2
Swakopmund *S.Africa* 149B3
Swan I. *Honduras* 24C3
Swansea *Wales* 58D6
Swaziland, Kingdom *Indep.S.Africa* 151D3
Swindon *Eng* 56F6
Sydney *Aust.* 157E4
Syktyvkar *Russia* 103G3
Syracuse *USA* 18F1
Syzran' *Russia* 108F4
Szczecin *Pol.* 85C2
Szczecinek *Pol.* 85D2
Szeged *Hung.* 88E3
Székesfehérvár *Hung.* 88D3
Szekszárd *Hung.* 88D3
Szolnok *Hung.* 88E3

T

Tabora *Tanz.* 146G5
Tabriz *Iran* 131C2
Tabuaeran I. *Kiribati* 162
Tabuk *S.Arabia* 130B3
Taegu *S.Korea* 113G3
Taejon *S.Korea* 112G3
Tahiti I. *Pacific O.* 162
Tahoua *Niger* 145D1
T'ai-pei *Taiwan* 120E1
Tái-nan *Taiwan* 120E1
Taiwan,Republic *China* 120E1
Taiyuan *China* 112F3
Ta'izz *Rep.Yemen* 132C4
Takada *Japan* 115N8
Takaoka *Japan* 115M8
Takasaki *Japan* 115N8
Takoradi *Ghana* 144B2
Talavera de la Reina *Spain* 72B2
Talca *Chile* 40B6
Talcahuano *Chile* 40B6
Tallahassee *USA* 20E2
Tallinn *Estonia* 102D4
Tamale *Ghana* 144B2
Tamanrasset *Alg.* 141D4
Tambacounda *Sen.* 140B5
Tampa *USA* 20E3
Tampere *Fin* 95E3
Tampico *Mexico* 23D3
Tamworth *Aust.* 157E4
Tanga *Tanz.* 147G5
Tanger *Mor.* 140C3
Tangshan *China* 112F3
Tanna I. *Vanuatu* 156F2
Tanta *Egypt* 142G1
Taolanaro *Madag.* 151E3
Tarābulus *Libya* 141E3
Tarakan *Indon./Malay.* 123D3
Tarancón *Spain* 79B1
Taranto *Italy* 79D2
Tarbert *Ireland* 66B4
Tarbert *Scot* 60B3
Tarbert *Scot* 52B2
Tarbes *France* 69C3
Tarcoola *Aust.* 155C4
Tarfaya *Mor.* 140B4
Tarnów *Pol.* 88E2
Tarragona *Spain* 74C1
Tarrasa *Spain* 74C1
Tarutung *Indon.* 122B3
Tashkent *Uzbekistan* 109H5
Taunton *Eng* 58D6
Tavira *Port.* 73A2
Tavoy *Myanmar* 118B2
Tawau *Malay.* 123D3
Tawitawi *Phil.* 120E3
Tbilisi *Georgia* 108F5
Tecuci *Rom.* 89F3
Tegucigalpa *Honduras* 25B4
Tehrān *Iran* 131D2
Tehuantepec *Mexico* 20D4
Tel Aviv *Israel* 130B2
Telford *Eng* 58E5
Telukbetung *Indon.* 123C4
Temuco *Chile* 40B6
Tenerife *Canary Is.* 140B4
Tennant Creek *Aust.* 154C2
Tennessee State *USA* 18E2
Teófilo Otôni *Brazil* 37E4
Teresina *Brazil* 37E3
Termez *Uzbekistan* 109H6
Termoli *Italy* 77C2
Terni *Italy* 77C2
Teruel *Spain* 74B1
Tessalit *Mali* 141D4
Tete *Mozam.* 150D2
Tétouan *Mor.* 140C3
Teviothead *Scot* 63F5
Texas State *USA* 23C2
Thásos I. *Greece* 81E2
Thetford *Eng* 56H5
Thiès *Sen.* 140B5
Thimphu *Bhutan* 127G3
Thionville *France* 70D2
Thíra I. *Greece* 81F3
Thival *Greece* 81E3
Thiviers *France* 69C2
Thon Buri *Thai.* 118C2
Thule *Greenland* 14M2
Thunder Bay *Canada* 15K5
Thurles *Ireland* 67D4
Thurso *Scot* 61E2
Thurston I. *Ant.* 170
Tianjin *China* 112F3
Tianshui *China* 117E3
Tibet, Autonomous Region *China* 116C3
Tidjikdja *Maur.* 140B5
Tierp *Sweden* 94D3
Tierra del Fuego I. *Arg.* 41C8
Tierra del Fuego State *Arg* 41C8
Tijuana *USA* 16B2
Tilburg *Neth.* 84A2
Tílos *Greece* 81F3
Timbákion *Greece* 81E3
Timimoun *Alg.* 141D4
Timisoara *Rom.* 88E3
Timor *Indon.* 124E4
Tindouf *Alg.* 140C4
Tipperary *Ireland* 66C4
Tiranë *Alb.* 80D2

Tiree I. *Scot* **62B4**
Tirgu Mures *Rom.* **89E3**
Tiruchirāppalli *India* **128F4**
Titov Veles *Macedonia* **82E2**
Tlemcen *Alg.* **141C3**
Toamasina *Madag.* **150E2**
Tobago I. *Caribbean Sea* **27G4**
Tobermory *Scot* **62B4**
Tobol'sk *Russia* **109H4**
Tokelau Is. *Pacific O.* **165**
Tokushima *Japan* **113H3**
Tokyo *Japan* **115H9**
Toledo *Spain* **72B2**
Toledo *USA* **18E1**
Toliara *Madag.* **151E3**
Tombouctou *Mali* **140C5**
Tomsk *Russia* **109K4**
Tonbridge *Eng* **56H6**
Tonga Is. *Pacific O.* **165**
Tonghua *China* **112G2**
Tongling *China* **114F3**
Tongue *Scot* **60D4**
Toowoomba *Aust.* **156E3**
Topeka *USA* **17D2**
Tordesillas *Spain* **72A1**
Torino *Italy* **76B1**
Tornio *Fin* **93E2**
Toronto *Canada* **15L5**
Torquay *Eng* **59D7**
Torreón *Mexico* **23C3**
Torridon *Scot* **60C3**
Tortosa *Spain* **74C1**
Torun *Pol.* **86D2**
Tóshavn *Faroes* **92A2**
Tottori *Japan* **115L9**
Touggourt *Alg.* **141D3**
Toulon *France* **71D3**
Toulouse *France* **69C3**
Tourcoing *France* **70C1**
Tours *France* **68C2**
Tovalu Is. *Pacific O.* **165**
Townsville *Aust.* **156D2**
Toyama *Japan* **115M8**
Toyohashi *Japan* **115M9**
Tozeur *Tunisia* **141D3**
Trabzon *Turk.* **130B1**
Tralee *Ireland* **66B4**
Trangan I. *Indon.* **124F4**
Trapani *Italy* **78C3**
Trenton *USA* **19F1**
Trincomalee *Sri Lanka* **129G5**
Trinidad *Caribbean Sea* **27G4**
Tripoli *Libya* **141E3**
Tripolis *Greece* **80E3**
Tromsö *Nor.* **93D2**
Trondheim *Nor.* **92C3**
Trowbridge *Eng* **59E6**
Troyes *France* **70C2**
Trujillo *Peru* **35B3**
Truro *Eng* **59B7**
Tsetserleg *Mongolia* **111E2**
Tsuchiura *Japan* **115P8**
Tsumeb *Namibia* **149B2**
Tsuruga *Japan* **115M9**
Tsuruoka *Japan* **115N7**
Tuamotu Is. *Pacific* **162**
Tubruq *Libya* **142F1**
Tubuai Is. *Pacific O.* **162**
Tucson *USA* **23B2**
Tucuman State *Arg.* **40C5**
Tudela *Spain* **74B1**
Tula *Russia* **102E4**
Tullamore *Ireland* **67D3**
Tulsa *USA* **17D2**
Tunis *Tunisia* **141E3**
Turda *Rom.* **88E3**
Turks Is. *Caribbean Sea* **26E2**
Turku *Fin* **95E3**
Turneff Is. *Belize* **24B3**
Tuticorin *India* **128F5**
Tuvalu Is. *Pacific O.* **165**
Tuzla *Bos.Herz.* **82D2**
Tver' *Russia* **102E4**
Tyumen' *Russia* **109H4**
Tyy *Spain* **72A1**

U

Uberaba *Brazil* **37E4**
Udaipur *India* **128F3**
Uddevalla *Sweden* **94C4**
Ufa *Russia* **109G4**
Uig *Scot* **60B3**
Ujung Pandang *Indon.* **123D4**
Ukhta *Russia* **103G3**
Ul'yanovsk *Russia* **108F4**
Ulaanbaatar *Mongolia* **111E2**
Ulan Ude *Russia* **106M4**
Ullapool *Scot* **60C3**
Ulm *FRG* **90B3**
Umeå *Sweden* **93E3**
Umtata *S.Africa* **149C4**
Ungava Pen. *Canada* **15L3**
Unimark I. *USA* **22J**
Unst I. *Scot* **61K7**
Upington *S.Africa* **149C3**
Uppsala *Sweden* **94D4**
Ural'sk *Kazakhstan* **108G4**
Urgench *Uzbekistan* **108H5**
Urosevac *Yugos.* **82E2**
Ürümqi *China* **110C2**
Urziceni *Rom.* **83F2**
Üsküdar *Turk.* **130A1**
Ussuriysk *Russia* **107P5**
Ust' Kamchatsk *Russia* **105S4**
Ust' Nera *Russia* **105Q3**
Usti *Czech. Rep.* **91C2**
Utah State *USA* **17B2**
Utiel *Spain* **75B2**
Utrecht *Neth.* **84A2**
Utsjoki *Fin* **93F2**
Utsunomiya *Japan* **115N8**

V

Vaasa *Fin* **93E3**
Vadodara *India* **128F3**
Vaduz *Liech.* **70D2**
Valdepeñas *Spain* **73B2**
Valence *France* **71C3**
Valencia *Spain* **75B2**
Valencia *Ven.* **34C1**
Valencia de Alcántara *Spain* **73A2**
Valencia Region *Spain* **75B2**
Valenciennes *France* **70C1**
Valladolid *Spain* **72B1**
Valledupar *Colombia* **34B1**
Valletta *Malta* **141E3**
Valls *Spain* **74C1**
Valparaíso *Chile* **40B6**
Vancouver *Canada* **13F5**
Vancouver I. *Canada* **13F5**
Vang *Nor.* **94B3**
Vännäs *Sweden* **93D3**
Vannes *France* **68B2**
Vantaa *Fin* **95F3**
Vanuatu Is. *Pacific O.* **156F2**
Vārānasi *India* **127G3**
Varazdin *Cro.* **77D1**
Vardö *Nor.* **93G1**
Varna *Bulg.* **83F2**
Varnamo *Sweden* **94C4**
Västerås *Sweden* **94D4**
Västervik *Sweden* **94D4**
Vasto *Italy* **77C2**
Växjö *Sweden* **94C4**
Veliko Turnovo *Bul* **83F2**
Vellore *India* **129F4**
Veracruz *Mexico* **23D4**
Vereeniging *S.Africa* **149C3**
Verín *Spain* **72A1**
Vermont State *USA* **19F1**
Versailles *France* **68C2**
Vestmannaeyjar I. *Iceland* **92A2**
Viana do Castelo *Port.* **72A1**
Vibo Valentia *Italy* **79D3**
Victoria *China* **119D1**
Victoria I. *Canada* **12G2**
Victoria State *Aust.* **157D4**
Videle *Rom.* **83F2**
Vidin *Bulg.* **82E2**
Viella *Spain* **74C1**
Vienna *Aust.* **91D3**
Vientiane *Laos* **118C2**
Vierzon *France* **68C2**
Vigo *Spain* **72A1**
Vijayawada *India* **129G4**
Vila *Vanuatu* **156F2**
Vila Nova de Gaia *Por.* **72A1**
Vila Real *Port.* **72A1**
Villach *Aust.* **91C3**
Vilnius *Lithuania* **102D4**
Viña del Mar *Chile* **40B6**
Vinh *Viet.* **119C2**
Vinnitsa *Ukraine* **102D5**
Virgin Is. *Caribbean* **26G3**
Virginia State *USA* **18F2**
Vis I. *Cro.* **77D2**
Visby *Sweden* **95D4**
Vishakhapatnam *India* **129G4**
Vitebsk *Belarus* **102E4**
Viterbo *Italy* **77C2**
Vitória *Brazil* **38F5**
Vitoria *Spain* **72B1**
Vitry-le-François *Fra* **70C2**
Vladimir *Russia* **102F4**
Vladivostok *Russia* **107P5**
Vlorë *Alb.* **80D2**
Volgograd *Russia* **108F5**
Vologda *Russia* **102F4**
Vólos *Greece* **80E3**
Vorkuta *Russia* **103H3**
Voronezh *Russia* **108E4**
Voroshilovgrad *Ukraine* **108E5**
Voss *Nor.* **94B3**
Vranje *Yugos.* **82E2**
Vratsa *Bulg.* **82E2**
Vrbovsko *Cro.* **77D1**
Vrsac *Yugos.* **82E1**